GOD ON THE WESTERN FRONT

God on the Western Front
Soldiers and Religion in World War I

JOSEPH F. BYRNES

The Pennsylvania State University Press
University Park, Pennsylvania

Library of Congress Cataloging-in-Publication Data

Names: Byrnes, Joseph F., 1939– author.
Title: God on the Western Front : soldiers and religion in World War I / Joseph F. Byrnes.
Description: University Park, Pennsylvania : The Pennsylvania State University Press, [2023] | Includes bibliographical references and index.
Summary: "Explores the search for religious meaning during World War I and the wide range of spiritual responses that emerged across boundaries. Examines how religious experience and battle experience were intertwined"—Provided by publisher.
Identifiers: LCCN 2022061472 | ISBN 9780271095103 (hardback) | ISBN 9780271095110 (paper)
Subjects: LCSH: World War, 1914–1918—Religious aspects—Christianity. | World War, 1914–1918—Religious aspects—Judaism. | World War, 1914–1918—Chaplains. | World War, 1914–1918—Campaigns—Western Front.
Classification: LCC D639.R4 B97 2023 | DDC 940.4/144—dc23/eng/20230110
LC record available at https://lccn.loc.gov/2022061472

Copyright © 2023 Joseph F. Byrnes
All rights reserved
Printed in the United States of America
Published by The Pennsylvania State University Press,
University Park, PA 16802–1003

The Pennsylvania State University Press is a member of the Association of University Presses.

It is the policy of The Pennsylvania State University Press to use acid-free paper. Publications on uncoated stock satisfy the minimum requirements of American National Standard for Information Sciences—Permanence of Paper for Printed Library Material, ANSI Z39.48–1992.

*For my daughter Veronica, my son Michael,
and their families*

You should never write history until you can hear the people speak.

—ARTHUR HIBBERT

CONTENTS

List of Illustrations (x)

Prologue *(1)*
1. To the Front: Cities, Departures, and Churches *(10)*
2. The Search for Allies in Heaven *(33)*
3. God-Talk in the Armies: From Foot Soldiers to Generals *(61)*
4. Clergy at the Front *(87)*
5. Jewish Chaplains and Their Soldiers: Ministry and Preaching *(116)*
6. Day-to-Day War Experience: The Diaries *(137)*
7. Behind the Lines: Religious Traditions at War *(167)*
8. Theology Out of War Experience *(193)*

Envoi *(214)*

Acknowledgments (218)
Notes (220)
Further Reading (236)
Index (242)

ILLUSTRATIONS

All of the color illustrations for the *Missel* are available at https://www.josephfbyrnes.com/marne-color-images. The action-scene engravings are available at https://www.josephfbyrnes.com/marne-engravings.

1. Crowds in front of the Berliner Dom after the mobilization proclamation *(12)*
2. Soldier departure at the Paris Gare de l'Est *(17)*
3. The Bishop of London, Arthur Winnington-Ingram, with Admiral John Jellicoe *(29)*
4. Imaginary scene of the Angels of Mons halting the German advance *(35)*
5. A full-page (originally) color illustration in the *Missel* *(41)*
6. One of the twelve action-scene engravings in the *Missel*, showing the veneration of the relics of St. Genevieve in front of St.-Étienne-du-Mont *(43)*
7. German postcard showing the "death of a hero" (*Heldentod*) *(46)*
8. The Virgin and Child hanging perpendicular to the ground from the tower of the Basilica of Albert *(49)*
9. An English newspaper photo of the Christmas 1914 fraternizing of German and English troops *(57)*
10. Donald Hankey, soldier and Anglican deacon *(63)*
11. General Ferdinand Foch with the French Catholic churchman, Bishop Stanislas Touchet *(79)*
12. General Douglas Haig planning strategy with his leading generals *(83)*
13. The Evangelical, Jewish, and Catholic chaplains in the German army *(89)*
14. Memento card for the Jesuit novice, Lucien Chabord *(103)*

15. Sister Gabrielle, who cared for and even protected French soldiers *(105)*
16. The upstairs chapel at Talbot House *(109)*
17. The Anglican priest Oswin Creighton *(111)*
18. Jewish chaplains who served on the western front *(118)*
19. The painting by Lucien Lévy-Dhurmer of Rabbi Abraham Bloch *(125)*
20. The English rabbi, Michael Adler, with members of the 17th London Regiment *(129)*
21. German soldiers during the taking of Liège *(140)*
22. Stephan Westmann, standing by a hospital train with army officers *(147)*
23. Ferdinand Belmont, a medical doctor and a religious mystic *(155)*
24. Adolph von Harnack, preeminent German church historian *(171)*
25. William Sanday, Anglican priest-theologian and royal chaplain *(174)*
26. Covers of *La Guerre allemande* and *Deutsche Kultur* *(177)*
27. Bishop, later Cardinal, Michael von Faulhaber visiting the trenches *(188)*
28. Franz Rosenzweig at the front with others trained in ballistics *(195)*
29. Pierre Teilhard de Chardin, Jesuit and stretcher bearer, with French soldiers *(206)*
30. Geoffrey Studdert Kennedy in a formal photo *(211)*

Prologue

The long history of Judaism and of Christianity was a tale of war, often cast as the will of God. We have only to remember the whole array of divine pronouncements recorded in the Hebrew Bible, the assumption in the Epistles and Gospels that soldiers were part of normal life, and the sign in the sky given to Constantine, founding emperor of the Christian west: a cross underscored with the caption, "In this Sign thou shalt conquer." Crusader kings led their soldiers off to war to defend and extend European rule in the belief that "God wills it." The seventeenth-century wars of religion in central Europe paired dynastic goals with Catholic or Protestant religious interests. War had to be part of God's plan, according to Christian theologians from Saint Augustine through the Catholic and Protestant writers of the early twentieth century.[1] Therefore, from 1914 to 1918 religious believers and hopeful skeptics tried to find meaning and purpose behind divinely willed destruction. We have the random words of German, French, and English soldiers and the religious writings of bishops, priests, ministers, and rabbis as they tried to make sense of it all. For what collective horror could better display the mystery of a divine will than the frontline attacks and defenses across northern France, where millions of Christians and Jews on both sides of the conflict slaughtered one another for over four years?

This is a history of soldier religion and the official religion of churches and synagogues, with their clergy on and behind the front, along with the testimonies of the women who provided pastoral and medical care up by the front lines. We track experiences ranging from average men barely able to express their simplest feelings, religious or otherwise, to men fully engaged in a struggle to solve the religious quandaries within them. A few of them became philosophical and theological innovators for the twentieth century: the German Jewish philosopher Franz Rosenzweig, the German Lutheran minister Paul Tillich, the French Catholic priest Pierre Teilhard de Chardin, and the Anglican clergyman Geoffrey Studdert Kennedy. Across the book we simply let the soldiers and church people have their say about their Catholic, Protestant, or Jewish religion and have their say about being German, French, or English citizens, because what they have to *say* counts the most here. Let's call this "God-talk," expressing faith and moral choice, and let's call it "nation-talk," expressing either a simple sentiment or political, even warlike, nationalism. Of course, to narrate religious and national experiences is to narrate *anti*-religious and *anti*-national experiences also and so place in higher relief the talk about God and nation. Without evidence to the contrary, we can only believe that they are all describing their actual experiences and do our best to select, arrange, and transmit them.[2] In this history of European countries at war, the experiences of colonial troops, some of them Hindu and some of them Muslim, and American troops in the last year of the war are part of the English and French stories.

We explore, then, the "varieties of religious experience," to use the words of the American psychologist and philosopher William James, and the "varieties of national experience." At the beginning of the twentieth century, James examined the natural will-to-believe and the religious feeling at the center of each person's existence. In the middle of the century, German existentialist psychologists said that the foundations of personalities were the specific "worlds" they lived in: the natural world around them (*umwelt*), the world of fellow humans they interacted with (*mitwelt*), and the interior worlds of self-awareness and identity they constructed at the same time (*eigenwelt*). Soldiers and church leaders reported a surrounding catastrophic world, reported a chaos of interactions, and reported from within the passions of their personal existence.[3] This is the range of experiences that appears in the talk.

National sentiment and nationalism happen when populations come to interpret and concretize their collective life together, controlling regional destinies, and obtaining voting rights. Major examples of the process are the French revolutionary decade, the English parliamentary reforms of the 1800s, and the European revolutions of 1848. Broadly speaking, across the nineteenth century the greater the tensions in nation building, the greater was the utilization of religion.[4] And vice versa: the more religion was highlighted, the more was the nation given cosmic importance. Mobilized by a national government, in the uniform of its army, every person in the military was self-consciously fighting for the nation. The dramas of war and destruction were presented in apocalyptic—end of the world—language.[5] The consummate expression of apocalyptic evil was the work of the German-language author, Karl Kraus, a leading Austrian writer and journalist, who captivated listeners in Berlin with imagery that he utilized in his huge sprawling play, *The Last Days of Mankind*: a graphic portrayal of the ugliness, the futility, and the hypocrisy of the war.[6]

Religious and battle experiences in World War I interpenetrated one another, resulting in an array of emotions from despair and horror to the hope that "the Love that moves the sun and the other stars" sung by the poet Dante, could bring light out of the darkness, order out of chaos, and love out of hate. Blaise Cendrars, soldier and poet, who wrote in his autobiographical *La main coupée* (*The Severed Hand*), "God was absent from the battlefields," presumed a western front of darkness, chaos, and hate, and a God of order, light, and love.[7] Across the narratives in the following eight chapters, the men and women express their faith and moral goals on continua that go from horror to hope, from fatalism to faith, and from class or regional loyalties to full national loyalty.

1. The story of the God experience on the western front begins with the mobilization of eligible men, recruits and reservists, in Germany, France, and England, as war was declared. Focus here is on the moods expressed and behaviors recorded in Berlin and Munich, in Paris, in London, with glimpses of other cities in Germany, France, and England. The principal newspapers reported the end of diplomacy and the mobilization news in the major headlines. Reports were filled with raucous crowds, patriotic gatherings, and, more importantly, scenes of bravado and sadness at the train stations as the men left for duty, leaving wives, children, parents, and friends. Occasionally, reporters would catch a comment, focus on an embrace, and even record their own feelings. Formal German, French, and English religion-talk, duly reported in the news, came mainly from church leaders, who sent the soldiers on their way with preaching and theology that justified the grim realities of their war. In sermons and publications, the Evangelical Church authorities in Berlin, Cardinal von Bettinger of Munich, Cardinal Amette of Paris, and Bishop Winnington-Ingram of London urged their soldiers on to a triumph of arms and justice.

2. Reports of miracles fed the *imaginations* of soldiers, officers, clergy, and the general public, most of them theologically less self-conscious than the church leaders. Two military dramas that attracted serious attention were the August 1914 Battle of Mons in Belgium and the September 1914 Battle of the Marne, although it actually took years for the stories to develop into "proofs" that God was on the side of the English at Mons and on the side of the French at the Marne. The most lavishly developed presentation, out of all the publications on these dramas, was certainly the Catholic prayer book *Missel du miracle de la Marne* (Missal of the Miracle of the Marne)—published for and used by a select few, however. The average soldier on the front did not experience the Angels of Mons or the Miracle of the Marne, even though the history of the reception and belief in these heavenly interventions spanned the war years. Soldiers and civilians near the front also saw miraculous interventions in church and wayside statues that survived across the battle zones. On the front, German, French, and English devotions to Christ, Mary, the angels, and saints were most often everyday expressions of religious faith, and at times political statements. The one religious event that involved no supposed divine intervention was simply a truce, a fraternizing, and a common celebration of Christmas in 1914.

3. The soldiers of the hostile armies were a cross section of the home populations, and few of them were inclined to believe in miracles anywhere. Churchgoers, nonchurchgoers, believers, and nonbelievers were swallowed up by mobilization into a different world where they reacted with their own religion and nonreligion. Their religion was "inarticulate" or "diffusive" (as observers have described it), because the majority of the soldiers had little to say about "God" or "religion." Their conversation could reflect a simple assumption of the personal and social usefulness of religion, in fatalism and real devotion. Religious objects, such as Bibles and rosaries could be valued for their religious meaning or simply treated as charms and amulets—more and more often as the war dragged on. The letters of the soldiers, European, colonial, and American, however, regularly contained profound self-reflections, which were both traditionally religious and original in their intensity. The generals and other higher officers often expressed commitment to their religious tradition, saying less about religious feelings and more about basic faith and participation in church services. In fact, they were often seriously religious believers from youth on. Ferdinand Foch was a dedicated Catholic; Douglas Haig, an intense Anglicanized Presbyterian; the German generals, a mixture of Lutheran, Catholic, and spiritualist loyalties.

4. Of course, those soldiers who described in greatest depth and detail their religious experience in the armies were members of the clergy themselves. And here the French priests had the greatest challenge to make sense of the war, because they were the only ones obliged to become active soldiers in the killing fields. Their testimonies should be highlighted because they wrote, often passionately, about the details of the Christian belief and morality that sustained them: the centrality of Christ's crucifixion and the dilemma of killing for the sake of a national cause. As for the German, French, and English chaplains themselves, the magnitude of the physical suffering and disease depleted their energies, and they filled pages, the equivalent of books, about their experiences. German evangelical and Catholic chaplains, and English chaplains in particular, wrote about the challenges of offering comfort to men raised with little experience of Bible reading or church going. Chaplains had to find motivational language to sustain soldiers in the fight, cultivate formal faith, and sympathize with private faith. They had to make sense of the carnage and waste, for themselves as well as for their soldiers.

5. Rabbis and Jewish soldiers believed their national loyalties provided a sure way to first-class citizenship. Their history parallels the history of Christianity on and behind the front in the preceding chapters. All the Jewish chaplains, Orthodox, Conservative, or Reformed, encouraged their men to preserve Jewish solidarity and display national loyalty, which sometimes presented a dilemma for the German, French, and English Jews, because national loyalty precluded Jewish solidarity. German Jewish chaplains were able to structure a system of rabbinical pastoral care and festival celebration. They made the case that Judaism flourished in Germany and cohered perfectly with the German spirit, providing biblical references for a faith that could endure and support war. French Jewish chaplains could easily justify French Jewish rejection of the Germans, in the name of a French republicanism that guaranteed Jewish emancipation and because of perversion of Judaism into militarism in Germany. English chaplains developed a program of preaching and pastoral care to support their far-flung soldiers in prayer and in fighting Germany. Jewish soldiers' letters and diaries reveal the tenacity of community religion. German soldiers who had lived in a Berlin orphanage as boys spoke gratefully of the rigor and piety of their training. A completely secularized French Jew wrote of his wartime respect for the tradition and fidelity to the community.

6. Soldiers did not usually discuss or chat about official beliefs or moral imperatives but left all that to the clergy. In their diaries they recorded their

everyday experiences, justified their killing, and added battle stories to express both love of the fatherland and personal fears. For German soldiers, Belgian treachery was the theme; condemnation of it, the normal response, with snipers likened to Satan. They respected, engaged with, or rejected religion, their patriotism waxing and waning, as they deployed across the western front. French soldiers highlighted the butchery of war and the humanity of the men fighting on both sides. English soldiers did not hesitate to graphically describe everyday agony in the battles of each year of the war: fighting in Flanders, at the Somme, turning back the German final advance, and connecting with the French military and civilian population. But over the years, a handful of diaries, some them published only recently, set religion and irreligion in high profile. The German Stephan Westmann recorded his deep-set appreciation for religion, the Frenchman Ferdinand Belmont his personal prayer engagement, and the Englishman Arthur Graeme West his total rejection of religion.

7. Following the news and trying to understand the suffering of the fighting men, the German, French, and English clergy, bishops and priests, carried on their own war . . . of words! Spokesmen for both sides created their own theologies of right and might appropriate to the war. German and English Protestants—Anglicans in the majority—decried each other's base motives and evil actions, the English citing the bellicosity of German military men and philosophers, biblical liberalism, Kaiser-centered nationalism, and the destruction of Belgium; the Germans citing Britain's betrayal of Anglo-Saxon culture, colonial cruelties, and crass utilitarianism, mounting at the same time strong defenses of the Belgium invasion and German national sentiment. Both sides promoted the standard just-war theology common to both German and English Christians. German and French Catholic bishops and priests attacked the errors and injustices of the other side, devoting whole books of essays to the enterprise. The French accused Germans and their clergy of submission to German militarism and Protestantism, and of promoting "might makes right." When the French vaunted the Christian spirit that had developed in France since the beginnings of Christianity, the Germans responded with attacks on a Catholic France corrupted by secularism, with its newfound and specious concern for Belgian sovereignty, and its greater concern for Reims cathedral and the University of Louvain library than for human lives.

8. The old theologies of the churchmen warring *behind* the lines had none of the existential immediacy and postwar influence of four young theologians

on the front lines. Writing on postcards sent from the front, the German philosopher, Franz Rosenzweig, created a new expression of Jewish mysticism and universalism. As chaplains for the Christian soldiers of Germany, France, and England, Paul Tillich, Teilhard de Chardin, and Geoffrey Studdert Kennedy—a Lutheran, a Roman Catholic, and an Anglican—developed Christian identities and theologies to show that "God" *was* on the western front. They rejected simplistic religious interpretations of war, after much suffering and deep thinking. For Tillich, a chaplain in and out of the trenches, Luther's fundamental dictum of salvation by faith alone mutated into a twentieth-century "faith alone" conviction that could only survive if accompanied by the death of the religious imagination. Pierre Teilhard de Chardin, the Jesuit paleontologist turned stretcher-bearer, saw the killing and destruction of war as essential to evolution, leading to a cosmos ultimately transformed into the infinite Christ of faith. Geoffrey Studdert Kennedy, chaplain and poet, in order to make sense of war for himself and his soldiers, insisted that *God suffered*, not only in the passion and death of his Christ but in all human suffering, epitomized in the current war. With them, as with Franz Rosenzweig, came the blossoming of a new theological expression that developed in germ as the war progressed.

In fine, I have organized everything to explain the religious reality of this war of nations, attending to the individual psychologies, that is to say the individual experiences, of the soldiers and church leaders. This is the way it was according to the sources: a combination of classic collections of letters, diaries, and other testimonies—German, French, and English.

I do need here a formal historian's moment to point to endnotes and sources. Endnotes contain page numbers for my quotations, of course, but also provide references to helpful scholarly texts in several languages. Michael Snape and Edward Madigan for England, Annette Becker and Xavier Boniface for France, and Gerd Krumeich and Claudia Schlager for Germany deserve special mention. There are few ambiguities and even fewer disagreements among them, so I can draw from their syntheses as I present my own. The clearest breakdown of the historiography is Hanneke Takken's study of World War I chaplains. She notes the English argument on the failures and successes, dominated recently by the historians emphasizing chaplain successes; the French concentration on priest soldiers as luminaries of the *Union sacrée*, inasmuch as they reduced secular antagonism to the church; and the

German literature during the war, which criticized the chaplains' exemption from combat, on the one hand, and after the war systematically ignored their contributions, on the other. She also notes that the shape and style of chaplain and soldier religion depended on the relationship of the home churches to state, society, and nation; in other words, the government, the people, and national history of each of the belligerent nations predetermined many of the features of religion on the western front.[8]

Four major church archives served as a reality check on the data. For Protestant and Catholic Germany, I consulted the Zentralarchiv of the German Evangelical Church (Lutheranism and Reform Protestantism mainly) in Berlin and the Archiv des Erzbistums München und Freising in Munich; for primarily Catholic France, I consulted the Archives historiques de l'Archevêché de Paris; and to a lesser extent, for officially Anglican England, I consulted the online archives of Lambeth Palace, the London residence of the archbishop of Canterbury. With due appreciation of the previous fine syntheses of Xavier Boniface regarding World War I religion on all fronts and Philip Jenkins on the "holy war" elements of the conflict, I do have my own specific voice, because I have worked across the years as a historian of modern Europe and—officially only at the beginning of those years—as a priest.[9] I amass and interpret in my own way the testimonies that have come to us from that accursed western front and from those behind it on either side.

Finally, I permit myself an ego-biographical moment, because there is scarcely a book on World War I that does not begin with an image or story of the author's experience or memories of grandparents or great-grandparents who fought in the war. For me, there were the soldier uncles who went off to Europe in 1917. Decades before I was born, my mother's oldest brother, who had thought about a career in the religious life, saw action in the Argonne, and my father's oldest brother, then a young dentist, headed for Europe to spend his time crawling along his small section of the front administering morphine to wounded and dying soldiers. One uncle returned cynical about religion and the other returned cynical about Europe. Finally in 1918, my father, with his brand-new dental degree from the University of Pennsylvania, stayed in Philadelphia, hardest hit of American cities by the Spanish flu, helping out—tragically, more as an undertaker's assistant than as medical personnel. One hundred years after the November 1918 armistice *to the day*, when I was only by happenstance in Germany, I attended a Protestant-Catholic-Orthodox service in the Berliner Dom, the great church on the Unter den

Linden Boulevard: *"Frieden in Europa": Ökumenische Gottesdienst zum Ende des 1. Weltkrieges vor 100 Jahren* ("Peace in Europe": Ecumenical Worship Service for the End of World War I a Hundred Years Ago). It took a century that included a genocidal second war to get to what is even today an uneasy peace. "The last days of mankind," to use the words of Karl Kraus's play, World War I was not. But what it was, insofar as it represented the survival of the human spirit in a hellish setting, I now attempt to explain.

CHAPTER 1

To the Front
Cities, Departures, and Churches

London was, of course, the center of Anglicanism, Paris was the center of French Catholicism; Berlin, the center of the Protestant Evangelical (mainly Lutheran) church, and Munich was the capital of Catholic Bavaria. In the churches of these and other major cities, preachers were vigorous and outspoken in their support of their governments, their troops, and their people. It should be no surprise that on the streets and in the churches of London, Paris, and the two great German cities of Berlin and Munich, the days around 4 August 1914 were both somber and festive, filled with talk of right and might. It would depend on which street or square you were in, and on which church you entered. Men were off to war, off to an imagined front that would be a real line of hundreds of miles by the end of the year. Uniforms and weapons were handed out, and the railway stations resonated with the sound of soldiers tramping through the vast interiors, onto the quays and into the trains, after taking leave, stiffly or emotionally, of family and friends.[1]

Heading off to the front probably had as many personal meanings as there were soldiers, and family members they were leaving behind. The soldiers brought with them their "home religion," as they had lived or ignored it, and which in each belligerent nation had been in a state of decline between 1848 and 1914.[2] Germany, France, and England differed slightly from one another in the rates of statistical decline in church going. In England, the decline occurred mostly after 1889, affecting all regions and social classes—the small Catholic minority, less so. In France, the church going increased up to the end of the 1870s and then declined through the separation of church and state in 1905, with a slight uptick in the years before the war. Regions varied tremendously, because some never recovered from the anticlericalism of the revolutionary and prerevolutionary periods. In Protestant Germany, decline in all social classes and regions was steady in the hundred years leading to 1870. The situation stabilized for a few decades before continuing to decline (less rapidly) in the fifteen-plus years before the war. Catholics, however, about a third of the population, maintained high levels of practice. The home religion that the soldiers brought with them to the front would be conditioned by all of these variables.[3]

High-ranking church leaders encouraged and consoled. Their words, mostly heard and read by those who stayed behind, were echoed by chaplains and other frontline clergy.[4] Given the chronological order of mobilizations and declarations of war, German, French, and English war mania descended on Berlin and Munich, Paris, and London.

STREETS AND TRAIN STATIONS

On the streets, enthusiasm, agitation, and anxiety were, according to the German newspapers, palpable. Agitation and anxiety hit the German population first, because of the immediate menace of Russian mobilization. According to the *Berliner Abendpost*, though, "there was almost no sound ... one spoke softly to one's neighbor about the impending decision." In Hamburg, "most people seemed depressed, as if waiting to be beheaded on the following day," according to one report. Only when the Kaiser and his wife drove from the Brandenburg gate down the great boulevard Unter den Linden did the crowds become agitated, and finally exuberant: "The hurray-yelling crowd heated itself up to a stormy enthusiasm, it overflowed, as if the crowd wanted to show the Kaiser through their proximity how close they felt to him"; enthusiasm came alive, minus the Kaiser, in Stuttgart, Munich, and Karlsruhe. By evening, after the proclamation of a state of siege, the crowd swelled to numbers reported to be between ten thousand and forty thousand, a strangely clumsy guess in view of the detailed reports on crowd behavior. Jeffrey Verhey sums up details found in a number of newspapers, including the *Berliner Illustrierte Zeitung*. "By all accounts it was a mixed bourgeois crowd, male and female, young and old. Many *Bürger* brought along their families to watch this historic moment." Finally, at 6:30 p.m. the Kaiser appeared and gave a short speech in which he expressed his hope for peace and his willingness to defend Germany's honor. After the Kaiser's speech, in

FIG. 1 Crowds in front of the Berliner Dom after the mobilization proclamation. Photo: Chronicle / Alamy Stock Photo.

the words of a *Berliner Lokalanzeiger* journalist, "complete strangers silently shook each other's hand; there was a holy mood among the crowd, a mood worthy of the moment." Shortly thereafter, the Kaiser left the palace, once again engulfed by enthusiastic crowds. In Munich, a crowd estimated to be about twenty thousand gathered before the palace of the King of Bavaria and cheered until the king appeared before them.[5]

Similar crowds in other cities, all of this interpreted differently by the right-wing press and the Social Democratic press: on one hand, the report that "the often somewhat loud enthusiasm of the last few days was followed by a serious but elevated mood. People who had never seen each other before talked to each other like old friends, like brothers," and on the other, this detailed report from the journal *Vorwärts*: "What could have been foreseen has become a reality: the hurrah atmosphere is gone and a leaden presentiment of an approaching and nameless calamity weighs upon the great multitude of those who wait for the latest news. The sixteen year olds have completely disappeared, and the streets are dominated by adults. A massive river of people populated the Linden and in the area around the palace, however, the basic mood is serious and depressed. A few young people attempt to rouse an ovation, but it peters out sadly." In Leipzig, "nowhere was there the faintest glimmer of spontaneous enthusiasm, as one might have expected after the experiences of the last few days," in Stuttgart, "the horrible seriousness of the moment dominated all souls. No violent party atmosphere, no yells of hurrah. . . . Tears here and there," and in Essen, "one could see in the tense faces of mature men that they were fully aware of the seriousness of this decisive hour."[6]

The next day, with the proclamation of German mobilization, crowd excitement, high agitation returned. This time the number is a clearer forty thousand to fifty thousand people, with parades and patriotic songs, quiet only to try to hear the Kaiser's—later famous—words: "I see no more parties in my *Volk*. Among us there are only Germans." Yes, united Germans, but even then, as Jeffrey Verhey clearly points out, class and regional differences perdured. "All photographs of the enthusiastic crowd on 2 August 1914 show well-dressed men and women: many are wearing straw hats; no one is wearing a working-class hat; there are no workers in open shirts. . . . 'War enthusiasm' continued to be an urban phenomenon . . . the people in the countryside lacked the national sites, as well as the 'excitement and the infection of common parades of enthusiasm.'" Even in middle-class, city-center Berlin, a lawyer noted in his diary, "Under the Linden there are great crowds of people. They do not, however, provide a pleasant sight. Mostly it is young boys and their girls, who walk up and down the middle of the street—yelling and shouting. However, as soon as one comes to a side street one notices the deadening seriousness which has settled down upon the people." Equal gloom was reported in the *Münchner Neueste Nachrichten*.[7]

The Paris newspapers also reported cheering crowds, overall moods, and small incidents. Rowdyism and stealing were more obvious in reports not dealing with the soldier departures, which filled the news in the first days. Suspicious persons, mostly Germans of course, were rounded up or maltreated at work or at home by Parisians. Antoine Delécraz, who published a journal of his days in Paris at the outbreak of the war, worked his way down to the

Grand Café near the Paris Opera. Conversations were easy to overhear, because traffic was reduced: cars were surprisingly rare and buses were sent back to the depot at six o'clock. In the cafés, on the sidewalk and inside, was a mixture of young men ready to depart for the front, tourists trapped in Paris, and general spectators, and deep inside at the best tables was a fashionable crowd. Young Frenchmen, waving the flag, shouting *La Marseillaise*, encountered a group of Italians who answered with "Vive la France," all to the consternation of Delécraz, who preferred the dignified comportment of most others. In the Latin Quarter, young folk, wearing cocardes, singing patriotic songs, and doing some last-minute shopping, were driven inside by a sudden storm.[8]

A reporter for *Le Figaro* saw calmness on all faces: "They do not laugh, they do not cry." It was strangely quiet even on the great boulevards around the Madeleine and the Place de l'Opéra, with only the sound of fiacres, trams, and buses. Toward the end of the day, there were a few more patriotic songs—youths joined occasionally by passersby. At six o'clock there was some flag waving and shouts like "It's war we need right now." Stores were closed as they sold out their goods, or when owners, staff members, and clerks departed for the front. Occasional signs announced that the men therein were off to war. In the Metro there was a great crush of people toward dinnertime. Taxis were idle because the drivers had already departed or were preparing to. The reporter added an anecdote out of his own experience: the day before he had been touched by "the smiles of a taxi-driver we had managed to stop, 'Not a long ride, Okay; I'm leaving on Sunday.'"[9]

As the afternoon wore into evening, the noise level elevated somewhat, as groups gathered around the mobilization posters and sang "La Marseillaise." English tourists waved their hats, crying "*Vive la France!*" to the applause of the French crowds. Russian flags could be seen here and there as the crowds milled about, some of the people stopping outside the Italian restaurant Zucco, where they were enthusiastically encouraged by the diners. Then, nine o'clock, ten o'clock; swelling of the street crowds and the café patrons. Musicians played the national anthems of France, England, and Russia. Then came the most impressive moments for the reporter. "At ten thirty, about a thousand young people marching together arrived at the Place de la République. About a hundred of them climbed onto the lion and the base of the monument and placed their flags in the form of a huge fan. They then sang the *Marseillaise*, the onlookers joining in the chorus." Other demonstrations continued long into the night in Montmartre.[10] Only on the next day, 3 August, did *Le Figaro* report "deplorable incidents" around the Hôtel de Ville. Storefronts were smashed, those stores owned by Germans were further pillaged; enthusiasm degenerated into wholesale vandalism. Regular citizens demanded that the police reestablish order and rid the central city of this criminal element.[11]

Also on 3 August, the *Figaro* reporters wrote up church events of the day before (Sunday). In general, the curés "at one or another of their Sunday masses spoke of the war and exhorted their parishioners to do their duty." Father Imbert, the aging pastor of Notre-Dame-de-Lorette, preached to the mothers, the wives, and the sisters of the soldiers, encouraging them to a combination of "patriotism and faith," which would strengthen the courage of their men. There were tears, but the reporter believed that the sermon "would certainly have contributed to elevate the hearts of many women to the high levels of sacrifices that the fatherland demanded of them." He also reported that the archbishop of Paris would issue an instruction to the faithful for this time of war (see below). The archbishop had already organized the official chaplains, whose ministry would be extended by the many priests who had been drafted as regular soldiers. In fact, a decree was issued so that the soldier priests, who formerly would not have been allowed to minister to their fellow soldiers at the same time as they themselves were waging war could now be allowed to do so for soldiers who requested their ministry.[12]

The same page of *Le Figaro* contained general reports that had come in from across France. From the Vosges region, one government official reported that one oft-repeated phrase, "provided it is true," disappeared in the midst of great joy and enthusiasm once the mobilization postings were authenticated and the men were sure they would have a chance to fight. The countryside, however, looked desolate; with harvests unfinished and many women without resources pale and weeping. From the west of France, returning Parisians reported that order and organization, along with the attitudes of the people, could be best summed up under the heading of "calm." In the trains coming from Brittany, there was no jostling, no hesitating, and when they arrived at the Gare Montparnasse, passengers offered comforting reports. Along the way, at the Saint-Brieuc station, they could see reservists receiving their supplies, and cars and horses being sorted out on one side of the station. On one quay, the uniformed soldiers were headed for Paris, and on the other quay, the sailors headed for Brest. At Rennes and at Le Mans, where artillery was well lined up, the railway stations were organized for smooth functions. As the trains moved along, farmers were visible, heading toward the stations.[13]

A *Figaro* report from 4 August contrasted the few functioning and packed subways with their carloads of resolute uniformed men and red-eyed women, a mixture of middle class and workers . . . with the streets: stores closed, no sightseers, and the people walking straight ahead under the gray sky.[14] In and around the Gare de l'Est and the Gare du Nord, there was a mixture of railroad personnel, reservists and new recruits, and some foreign families trying to get home. Departures of mobilized soldiers for the front slowed down by evening, and Belgians who were called to service by their government had to bed down outside. The Gare de l'Est served the Verdun area, Nancy, and Belfort; the Gare du Nord, Lille, Arras, Saint-Quentin, Dunkirk, and Laon. Other stations were crowded with Parisians who were trying to get away and provincials trying to return home. Crowds of Spaniards were also fleeing, which meant that the competition for tickets was intense, with loose clothes and packages strewn about in the chaos. The Gare Montparnasse and the Gare d'Austerlitz were crowded with soldiers from the south of France, and the Gare de Lyon, soldiers from the Rhône valley and the Massif Central. From there they transferred by taxis to the Gare de l'Est and the Gare du Nord. As Bruno Cabanes put it, "In just a few days, hundreds of thousands of travelers crisscrossed these transfer points, gates of the modern city, and symbolic entrances into the war." For him the stations were determining the movements of the war, just as they had already determined the movements of city life.[15] The Gare de l'Est in particular, with its Henri Lemaire statue on the pinnacle of the West entrance, a regal seated woman representing the city of Strasbourg, presaged the retaking of Alsace-Lorraine for those who knew it well. Few could have known, however, of Plan XVII, the generals' program for an advance there. Cabanes details the movement at the grill gates in front of the train departure halls. Soldiers had to present their military identification to the Territorials (somewhat older men who had done their service earlier but remained on call) monitoring the departures and then enter through a small gate at the left of the station.[16]

A writer for the *Petit Journal* reported a combination of determination and patriotism: "It is here that the war begins. Not only determination, but separation sorrow and anxiety as the soldiers disappeared into each station, belonging no more to civil society. Wives and children strained to catch a final glimpse of the husband, the father, who was going off to war."[17]

FIG. 2 Soldier departure at the Paris Gare de l'Est. The statue symbolizing Strasbourg—and so the lost province of Alsace-Lorraine—is at the top of the façade. Photo: Photo 12 / Alamy Stock Photo.

Father Félix Klein, beginning his time as a military hospital chaplain, cast a sympathetic eye on the suffering of his fellow Parisians.

> Oh! that Saturday the 1st August, when the terrible seriousness of the situation was suddenly revealed to a people still but little anxious! That morning three whole classes, three hundred thousand men, receive individually the order for immediate departure.... The astonishing thing is that not one murmurs and many are enthusiastic; but the women and children they are leaving weep. In the streets, in the squares, in the shops to which they are already rushing for provisions, wives, mothers, sweethearts, make moan. At the stations, to which they have accompanied their men, they try, for their sake, to keep a brave front; but when they come back alone ...

Klein took the predominant attitude to be submission and dedication, believing that the soldiers were fulfilling Christ's words, *Come follow me*.[18]

When, in the middle of the afternoon, the mobilization decrees were posted all over France, Klein credits all soldiers, four million, he says, with the response, "Here we are." Across the night and into the morning of 2 August, the noise was a combination of trains, cars, even airplanes, against a background of torrents of rain in the darkness. Klein finds in the gospel of the Mass for the day, "When Jesus drew near to Jerusalem, seeing the city, he wept over it, saying, 'If thou also hadst known . . . ,'" and then comes the picture of the murders and destruction of war. The epistle for the same day was from 1 Corinthians 10, "God . . . will not suffer you to be tempted above that which you are able." He believes that God will give the tortured soldiers the strength to bear all, and he rejoices in the unity of the National Assembly on 4 August, with members voting unanimously for national defense; he likens this to the vote 125 years before to abolish all noble privileges. On 6 August, he can hardly contain his pride. "While our mobilization goes on with the most irreproachable coolness, calmness and order, Germany, who wished to take us by surprise, in the execution of her principal plan comes up against a moral and material obstacle which was the last to be expected."[19]

Inside the troop trains leaving Paris, the pressures of mobilization wore down the general earlier sangfroid, a story that contrasts notably with the observations of Father Klein. No one was in a better position to record the unpleasant details than Henri Desagneaux, a reserve lieutenant in the Railway Service. He wrote on 1 August, "From the early hours, Paris is in turmoil, people still have a glimmer of hope, but nothing suggests that matters can now be settled peacefully. The banks are besieged; one has to queue for two or three hours before getting inside. At midday the doors are closed leaving outside large numbers of people who will have to leave on the following day." We get a close look at the soldiers and families in their uncertainty and pain. "In front of the Gare de l'Est, the conscripts throng the yard ready for departure. Emotion is at its peak; relations and friends accompany those being called up individually. The women are crying, the men too. They have to say good-bye without knowing whether they will ever return." "At last at 4.15 in the afternoon . . . the order for mobilization is posted! It is every man for himself, you scarcely have the time to shake a few hands before having to go home to make preparations for departure." And so Desagneaux headed off on Sunday, 2 August. He says little about his "painful goodbyes" and much about confusion and vandalism, trivial, but it tried him as a reserve lieutenant in the Railway Transport Service. "The mobilization time table is now operative but nobody at the station has any idea when a train is due. Sad day, sad journey." There were several different trains to take that day, the last one hardly an inspiration to patriotism: "The train cars and their corridors are invaded by people from every stratum of society! ... The blinds are torn down, luggage-racks cut up, mirrors broken, and the toilets emptied of their fittings." Rowdyism, vulgarity—with or without swigs of alcohol—hardly a disciplined combination of population and soldiers. The next day, 3 August, began early, and unlike the days before, "Morale is excellent, everyone is extraordinarily quiet and calm.... French ladies have gone into action. They are handing out drinks, writing paper, and cigarettes. The general impression is the following: it is [Kaiser] Wilhelm who wanted war, it had to happen, we shall never have such a fine opportunity again." Even for Desagneaux, bravado is good. Of 4 August Desagneaux has little to say, but by August 6 the slogans and caricatures were posted: "Death to Wilhelm," "Wilhelm to the gallows," "Death to the Boches," and the sketches of pigs in German helmets. More ominously, by 6 August, convoys of wounded soldiers arrived, along with the report that "an infantry battalion has been decimated by machine-gunfire."[20]

In London, the 3 August Bank Holiday crowds reacted excitedly but not, it would appear, enthusiastically to the developing news on final discussions and deadlines for England's declaration of war. According to the evening *Globe* of 3 August—"As usual on a fine August Bank Holiday, Saint James Park and Green Park were invaded by good humoured crowds, bent on enjoying themselves to the utmost ... suddenly the sound of military music was heard from the direction of Wellington Barracks. Immediately there was a stampede. Fathers packed up their children, mothers gathered the bottles of milk, bags of cake and fruit and there was a general rush in the direction of the Palace." Newspaper estimates of crowds before Buckingham Palace varied, from six to nine thousand, in effect less than 1 percent of the metropolitan London population. Elsewhere in London, reports were that war news had ruined the holiday, which became a "dismal affair": "Many attempts were made to infuse gaiety into the proceedings, but even when these attempts were partially successful, incongruity was afforded by the harsh and discordant voices of news vendors shouting out the latest war news.... It was obvious to the observer that the idea of war was distasteful to all." In fact, interventionist popular expressions were not completely absent. In this report, "The North Londoner didn't forget all about what people call the European situation ... but remembrance of it did not weigh heavily upon him.... If anything the war lent a zest to the holiday making ... here is a scrap heard on top of a bus going from Finsbury park to Finchley. 'Pretty go this here war.'

'Bust up all round seemingly.' 'What do you reckon England will do? . . . Why stick up for her friends as soon as they're set upon—France in particular.' Quite a burst of applause greeted the speaker's conclusion."[21]

In these few days, predominantly middle-class opinion solidified as pro-interventionist, if scattered evidence is any indication. But it is certain that the principal newspapers, the London *Daily News* and the *Manchester Guardian* were editorially anti-war until August 4. After that, things changed. The *Globe* reported that "Gaily decorated motor-cars crowded inside and out, passed round and round the Victoria memorial in processional order, men and women standing on the tops of taxi-cabs and waving flags continuously. . . . There were scenes of great enthusiasm in Trafalgar Square and Piccadilly Circus when the news of the declaration of war spread. A great roar of defiance was the answer of a vast crowd in the Square of the news." Troop departures, which followed soon after, were scenes of bravado and encouragement: "The men as they were making the final preparations for leaving were in the highest of spirits. They sang their favourite melodies with vigour and shook hands cordially with friends who came to have a last word with them. . . . Umbrellas were waved in the air, handkerchiefs were waved, and all was done to make the Territorials feel that they were carrying away with them the best hope of the ancient city [Norwich]."[22]

CHURCH BLESSINGS AND SEND-OFFS

Evangelical preachers in Berlin and Cardinal Franziskus von Bettinger of Munich strongly supported the German advances; Cardinal Léon Amette in Paris and the bishops in the provinces supported the French response; Bishop Arthur Winnington-Ingram of London, with the approval of the archbishop of Canterbury, supported the English entry into the conflict.

On Berlin's Alexanderplatz, 1 August, the crowd sang not the German anthem "Deutschland über alles," but the Evangelical Church chorale "Gott, tief im Herzen."[23] This Evangelical Church, as over against a more monolithic German Catholicism, was a federation of regional churches, but it took on a somewhat proprietary religious status after the empire was established in 1871 under a Protestant Kaiser. Whatever the political and cultural power of the churches, preachers had bemoaned the moral and spiritual weaknesses; in 1914, they interpreted the war to be a painful cure for the debilitating individualism of the era. "The plague of war becomes a blessing of God," in complete contrast to the old liberal theological orientation toward "the disestablishment of the church and the unchurching of the state"—as Kurt Meier puts it. The image of the enemy, defying religion and deifying violence, perdured to the end.[24] French Catholicism, accordingly, was accused of national chauvinism—absent on the German side presumably.[25] Evangelical preachers could be well pleased by the increase in church going as well as their churches' role offering encouragement and news locally. Churches also helped with food distribution and the collection of jewelry and coins as contributions to the war effort—to which they added such metals (bronze bells and organ pipes, especially useful) as could be found in the parishes.[26]

A newspaper clipping saved on an insert dated 22 August 1914 in the Archives of the Evangelische Ober-Kirchenrat (Evangelical Senior Church Council) printed the text of the prayer ordered by the Kaiser for recitation during all church services until the end of the war. "Almighty and merciful God! Lord of Lords! We pray you in humility for your all-powerful support of our German fatherland.... Lead us to victory and give us grace, that even against our enemies we might show ourselves to be Christians. Let us attain a long-lasting civil peace to the honor and independence of Germany." Another August printout reported that the citizens were returning to church, certainly the result of God's own intervention. Songs, readings, meditations, and prayer had basic themes: patience, hope, and trust in God; turning from neglect of his word, from the search for money and pleasure, and selfish individualism. Then came the justification of the army's invasion and behavior in Belgium in the *Kriegs-Korrespondenz des Evangelischen Preßverband* (War Correspondence of the Evangelical Press Association) with the theme quote, "We are in need of [self-] defense and need knows no rules." The writer will admit of no criticism of the troops in Luxembourg and Belgium, no appeals to human rights in the face of the trials. On the contrary, Chancellor Theobald von Bethmann-Hollweg's explanation that injustice will be rectified as soon as military goals are reached is condemned. After all, Belgium was given the opportunity after the fall of Liège to renounce nefarious English support; they did not and so lost all possibility of honest self-accusation. "Church communities, remember your fallen warriors!" the writer exclaims. Weekly prayers in the churches should reflect joy in the devotion of the fallen to the fatherland and sorrow that they departed so young.[27] Preaching is never more valuable than in times of war, because war illuminates the real truths about life, "powerfully bringing together the biblical themes to [the reality of] war. The preacher himself has little to do other than make the connection, because the listeners, awakened in the depths of their souls by God's word can easily do the rest."[28]

On 2 August, during a service on the Königsplatz, Bruno Doehring, Evangelical Church preacher from the Kaiser's "cathedral," the Berliner Dom, evoked the greatness of the empire and the Prussian generals who delivered Berlin from Napoleonic occupation. "Behind us the great building of the German Reichstag speaks its own mighty language; there Bismarck, Moltke, and Roon look down upon us; from on high the Victory monument greets us, reminding us of the heroic deeds of our fathers; and from the shaded green appears—such a striking image—the old Emperor [Wilhelm I] looks down upon us." Doehring asks the assembly what they are gathered for and answers that it is certainly not to promote war or get the latest news. Putting this time of trial in the context of the Christian experience, he says to the "German brothers and sisters," that "since the day of Golgotha suffering is sanctified; since the time of Christ we know that life's greatest goods are born of suffering." Surrounded by enemies in the East and West who envy German success, the nation has no choice. It is by way of the fatherland, "the altar of the fatherland," and the words of the Kaiser that God's grace comes to the people, who respond in self-oblation. He virtually sacralizes the Kaiser on the spot, saying, "Today there is certainly no one who does not dedicate his heart's blood to him, dedicate with two and threefold eagerness, since we have come to know how much his heart was weighed down in these times, because his loyalty was repaid with disloyalty." All partisanship comes to an end, and the people rally around the one flag. "With God for king and fatherland" can be a virtual oath. Let all Germans help one another in these challenging times. "Where a young mother is weeping, where a mother needs bread for her children, where farmers have gone to war, be good friends, good neighbors." Yes, the great cry is mobilization, and Doehring ends with the best-known line from Shakespeare's *Hamlet*, "To be or not to be, that is the question" and the important New Testament quote, "Do not fear what you are about to suffer. Be faithful unto death and I will give you the crown of life" (Revelation 2:10).[29]

Two days later, Ernst Dryander preached to a congregation in the Berliner Dom itself on the occasion of the Reichstag opening: "If God is for us, who can be against us" (Romans 8:31), comparing mobilization to a winter storm that overtakes a sunny landscape. Now is the time to remember the days when the Great Elector proclaimed, "Remember that you are a German!" and such will also be the urging of the Reichstag. This is not just a Prussian military exercise or Kant's sense of duty, but also Heinrich von Treitschke's conviction that "the man who does not enthusiastically look up to his country with enthusiasm, misses out on one of the most sublime sensations in

Life." To complement the armaments brought together with mobilization, Dryander promotes the "Shield of faith and the helmet of Salvation," with a bow to Martin Luther who required each person to be ready to sacrifice life for another. Sacrifice is the absolute; relativity and softness are the evils. Dryander finally returns to the title quote, "If God is for us, who can be against us," saying that this does not guarantee victory as such, and adds the words of the poet-philosopher, Ernst Arndt, "Let us make heroism live again. Because of it alone is life worth living, and its power gives men a feeling for the eternal and unchanging so that they are ready to joyfully sacrifice themselves." He evokes then the symbol of Moses raising and lowering his arm over the battle of Israel against Amalek: arm raised, Israel dominates; arm lowered, Amalek's forces dominate. In another battle Aaron's raised arms supported his people's victory. Now the German people's prayers will effect the same domination over the enemy. The army, with the German people's prayer and selfless service behind them, will win.[30]

For the special prayer day of 5 August, the Dom preacher Ernst Vits evoked the noble figure of the Kaiser to press on to the King of Kings, from the noble German flag to the symbol of the cross, *In hoc signo vinces*. For this reason, the Kaiser himself has called the people to prayer. "I ask my people to unite together with me in prayer, and celebrate with me on August 5 a special day of prayer and repentance." Vits gives voice to the broad disappointment that the German political class felt at that moment when England joined France and Russia. Where Anglo-Saxon unity should reign, the "blood related" ["*stammverwandte*"] England had turned against Germany. He makes the case that war does not mean the end of peace, because the most important peace is inner peace, the peace of God. If Germans are at peace with God, they are truly at peace. In fact, what has been a stand-in for peace in the past, "the peace of self-righteousness and self-sufficiency, the peace of carelessness and superficiality, the peace that results from forgetting God," can now be replaced with real peace. Vits quotes Ernst Arndt, who had written in an 1813 catechism for German militias an answer to the question, "Why war?— Through misfortune and need ... we must learn to look to heaven and realize that we do not stay here below; we must, rather, search for what abides."[31]

On the first day of mobilization, the court preacher Krissinger urged support of the Kaiser, the importance of self-denial, and the renewed importance of family and society. "We find in love our true, better self, by which we give ourselves to the other in openness and truth without holding anything back; our essential destiny steps forth, the loving thoughts of our heavenly father, anchored clearly in our being; for us there is no higher duty." This duty is best explained by a comparison with the dedication and faithfulness of marriage, Krissinger here creating a long dialogue between bride and bridegroom. As if fidelity to marriage were not an even greater challenge than patriotic response to the day's mobilization decree.[32]

Cardinal Franziskus von Bettinger of Munich had just finished a brief health rest at a quiet residence of one of the religious orders of sisters in Adelholzen.[33] Immediately upon the outbreak of the war, he published an official letter, in common with the other bishops of Bavaria, in the weekly diocesan bulletin, *Amtsblatt für die Erzdiözese München und Freising* (Official Journal for the Archdiocese of Munich and Freising). "The German people and their sublime Kaiser, have not wished for, nor are they to be blamed for, this war; it has been forced upon us by our enemies." Quoting Psalm 24:1, Bettinger reminds his people that all is based on the justice of their cause: "To thee, O Lord, I lift up my soul. O my God, in thee I trust, let me not be put to shame; let not my enemies exult over me." In a broad and eloquent encouragement of sacrificial loyalty due to the king (of Bavaria) and the German fatherland, he urges his "beloved faithful people" to pray for belief and strength. "Cast your burden on the Lord, and he will sustain you" (Psalm 54:23). "Whether we live or die, we are the Lord's" (Romans 14:8). "Let not your hearts be troubled; believe in God, believe also in me" (John 14:1). Taking these teachings to heart, the faithful can have "refuge and strength, hope and trust." The faithful must care for the weakest among them and those hit hardest by the war. They must remain loyal to the king. By prayers and support they can strengthen the soldiers in *their* pain and suffering. It is a time for penance, for sacrifice, for love of neighbor, especially for those with family members in the war, those who must take in the autumn harvest. "This I command you, that you love one another" (John 15:17). There follow here final directions for prayers and services in the churches.[34]

On 5 August, Bettinger conducted a service for the departing troops and then two weeks later was off to Rome for the election of a successor to Pope Pius X. In the following months, his representative for visits to the front was Michael von Faulhaber, Bishop of Speyer, who had been in the military as a young man and succeeded Bettinger to the see of Munich-Freising at Bettinger's death in 1916.[35] Then, in the first months of 1915, Bettinger addressed himself directly to the soldiers. Lent was beginning and Easter was in view. In his thoughts were the "valiant men in the battlefields" and the "devout men suffering in the field hospitals." Months had gone by since they were called to fight by a fatherland in need. Bettinger heaps praise upon them for their "heroic battles... worthy of wonder." He encourages them in prayer, the sacraments, the spiritual life, even to the point of impressing and edifying "the enemy," and here he means the poor folk in the occupied territories. For those in the field hospitals, Lent should be a reminder of Christ's suffering, and so he pairs the suffering of the soldiers with the suffering of Christ, quoting the prayer of Christ in the Garden of Gethsemane. Meditation on Christ's suffering had already strengthened the wounded and sick in the field hospitals, wrote a chaplain whom Bettinger quotes: "Our soldiers are not only heroes in battle; they are heroes in suffering."[36]

In the next week's diocesan bulletin, Bettinger wrote that all Germans "hope and trust" that the men facing the enemy "will return victorious to the homeland." They all must face the endless misery that the war had brought to the greater part of Europe. Certainly, the German chaplains and bishops, but also church leaders everywhere, seek the gift of peace. He saw fit to insert a long and learned discourse on the history and meaning of the church—it does seem that he is more concerned about the doctrinal and social resistance to the church than about its wartime challenges—but he manages to warn his people that the anti-church governments of France and Russia would bring harm to Europe, making the defeat of these governments essential. Quoting Cyprian of Carthage, he concludes, "You cannot have God for a Father, if you do not have the church for a mother."[37]

In Paris, on 5 August, Cardinal Léon Amette called for prayer and sacrifice *and* victory. He did not indict the Germans directly but implied that the French soldiers are sacrificing for a just cause. God, "sovereign judge of the destinies of peoples," will be the final judge, he said. "Pray that our arms will be victorious as they have been so many times in the past, and find again a durable peace with honor and integrity." After a German bombing escapade in early October, he called the German violence "criminal and barbaric." It was also a "sacrilege," because Notre Dame Cathedral had been targeted, apparently by three out of twenty of the bombs dropped. He requested prayers for soldiers and scheduled for 6 November a solemn service for war victims. Saying that it is possible to hope for French soldiers to be accepted as virtual martyrs, he went into a "Holy War" mode: for a soldier who would give his life in a just war, thereby obeying God, eternal salvation might be "assumed." Perhaps a little disturbed by his own presumption, he adds a footnote, saying that while death in battle is not sufficient for justification, we can believe that those who sacrifice their lives for their country can receive the grace of perfect contrition.[38]

The *Echo de Paris* on 8 August contained a description of the Sunday service in the Church of the Madeleine where the preacher drew cheers with a "Haut les cœurs et vive la France" ("Take courage and long live France"). Then, recalling the deaths in the Franco-Prussian war in August 1870, he thundered "avenge them" from the pulpit. Cardinal Amette followed the preacher with a blessing of the people present and the soldiers, as he sent them on their way. Then facing the massed flags, he blessed them and prayed that they return "floating joyously on the road from victory under God's blue sky."[39]

Le Figaro of several days earlier summarized the pastoral letter that Cardinal Amette had just sent to the faithful of the Paris archdiocese. Amette wrote that France, after having tried so hard to maintain peace all along, right through to the end, must now endure a war. The country has come together to face a common danger. The *Figaro* reporter uses the word "proclaim" when he quotes the cardinal—appropriately, inasmuch as Amette was trying to inspire rather than describe "The value of our army, the admirable attitude of the entire nation, the support guaranteed by our alliances, permit us to envisage the struggle with confidence." Amette is duly submissive to the will of God, "who remains the sovereign judge of peoples, and awards victory according to his own will." He urges his people to pray, then, that the armies might be victorious once again—with honor and integrity, to be sure—so that they might thereby obtain a lasting peace. Amette avoids equating service with martyrdom, praying that "victims of duty" die "in the friendship of God." The reporter concludes with a list of liturgical commemorations and special devotions, including a weekly mass to be said for French soldiers and sailors for as long as the war would last. A special collection is to be taken up on 15 August for the wounded and for the families of those on the front.[40]

The bishops of Angers, Nice, and Besançon among others also highlighted in their pastoral letters the innocence of France and the unity of the people: "It is time that we come to know the joy of loving one another"; "duty has become a magic word that in a time of bloody battles, arouses everyone, breaks all selfish attachments, destroys all restraints, calms all ill-temper, and stronger than the fear of death itself, engenders heroes." The bishop of Tarbes and Lourdes on 9 August praised "this people who, well aware of the danger, face off to it and decide to confront death."[41]

The vociferously militant bishop of London, Arthur Winnington-Ingram, eclipsed the more measured utterances of the archbishop of Canterbury—who declined to compose a prayer for victory—decried the English use of poison gas in response to the Germans and visited troops to support them in their suffering, rather than cry Holy War.⁴² Winnington-Ingram's major sermons between 9 August and November, entitled *A Day of God*, were published before the year was out. Here and in all his wartime writings, Winnington-Ingram promoted war to preserve national honor.⁴³

On 9 August 1914, in Saint Paul's Cathedral, he evoked the fundamental image of Christ's suffering in the garden of Gethsemane with the text "The cup which My Father hath given Me, shall I not drink it?" Christ was human and so naturally prayed to be spared suffering and death in the garden, and so also have Christians in England for thirteen (he adds, "perhaps sixteen") centuries. Now, at the beginning of the war, it is England's turn: "What happened to Christ has happened to us. The hour has struck and the supreme test of the manhood of the English race has arrived." They are called to go unto suffering and death as did Christ, who recognized that therein lay the will of the Father. The English people must imitate the savior, overcoming also the "secondary causes," the evils of humankind. "If once we begin dwelling upon the spirit of revenge in one country, the aggressive spirit of another, the pride of another, the treachery of another, as the agencies which have brought us the trial, we lower the whole ideal. It is God Who has allowed this supreme test of our manhood and womanhood today." Drinking the cup meant death, but the people of the empire are called to this. "There is one thing at least far worse than death, and that is dishonor; and if it so happens that some dear boy, the darling of your home, passes, with unsullied honour and to uphold the nation's name into the presence of the Unseen, you will find him there waiting for you when your time comes, one of God's own children, kept most safely in His care." Few patriotic lines are better known than "*Dulce et decorum est pro patria mori*" ("A sweet and noble thing it is to die for the fatherland"), composed by the Roman poet Horace, and Winnington-Ingram commends the thought to Christian parents who lose their sons in the war. Certainly, hard times are coming, but it is good for the nation to be tried: "Has there not crept a softness over the nation, a passion for amusement, a love of luxury among the rich, and of mere physical comfort among the middle class?"⁴⁴

The cup is to be drunk calmly and "with perfect charity." He evokes the exchanged visits with German clergy and "the twenty-five German schoolboys who were singing in my garden three weeks ago, in English, are still the same boys today; they are no more responsible for the war than those in this cathedral. If Christ prayed for his enemies, so must we." This does not go against fighting courageously; in courage one imitates Christ, but there will be much to endure. "When lists of killed and wounded come in, when moments of suspense occur, when even greater sacrifices are asked, then we must pray for—and if we pray for it, we shall receive it—the courage which was shown on Calvary, undimmed and undaunted to the end."[45]

Preaching at the end of the month to five thousand soldiers at an army camp, Winnington-Ingram maintains the principle of charity, but more a background to the strong fighting that the suffering of Belgians must inspire. "I do not want to say an ill word of another nation, but we are fools if we do not see what may happen to our women and children, when we watch what the poor women and children of Belgium have had to suffer during the last few weeks." His preaching presages the strong lines of the young poet Rupert Brooke, "Now, God be thanked, Who has matched us with this hour": "There I put this to you: What a glorious chance it is for you young fellows to be alive today, to be here at this critical moment of your country's life! . . . It is your chance to be present at the second Waterloo, at which the future of the world is to be decided." Then the great *Henry V* lines from Shakespeare—Saint Crispin's day at the beginning of the Battle of Agincourt, "We few, we happy few." "The men of Agincourt—ay, and of Crecy, and Inkerman and Alma, and Waterloo, the spirits of those who died for their country on those glorious fields—are with us today to inspire us to show that we are true descendants of the men who fought there." It is all, then, "glorious." Better to fight on the other side, of course, rather than have the enemy on our own territory, though it may be that before their training is finished, the war will be won. He wants them to value the training period, to deepen their faith in God, avoiding "rowdyism" and drunkenness. "Train yourselves, get ready, and when the moment comes, in the name of God strike home."[46]

During a missionary intercession and Thanksgiving service at Saint Paul's, Winnington-Ingram, using the story of the choice of apostle to replace Judas, confronted listeners with the choice facing Europe at war, "Christ or Odin." Hardly a difficult one: the Germanic/Norse god as over against Christ. But here again, the bishop combines his evocation of the goodness of the ordinary German with the pagan government, inspired by Nietzsche, he says, and his ideological offspring. These interpretations offered in the German press, as well as the news of the soldiers' suffering on the front, are all the people know. "The German mother sends forth her son to fight for 'the Fatherland' with the same mixture of love and pride that our mothers send out theirs; that their papers are filled with stories of atrocities committed by Russians

THE BISHOP OF LONDON'S RECENT VISIT TO THE GRAND FLEET : THE BISHOP AND SIR JOHN JELLICOE ON THE QUARTER-DECK OF THE FLAG-SHIP.
On July 23 the Bishop held a special Confirmation Service on board the Grand Fleet flag-ship.—[*Photo. by Alfieri.*]

FIG. 3 The Bishop of London, Arthur Winnington-Ingram, shown in a newspaper photo on the flagship deck with Admiral John Jellicoe. Photo: Historic Collection / Alamy Stock Photo.

and Belgians as ours are of atrocities committed by Germans; and therefore that we have no right to let our firm determination to see this great contest through to the end degenerate into an un-Christian hatred of the German people." He rehearses the openness to mutual understanding and working together coming to reality: Anglicans and Catholics in France—and the Orthodox Russian leaders' developing a relationship with England. Still and all, none of this can take away the evil of the destruction of Belgium. "The God of the New Testament or the God of Battles is the choice. Christ or Odin: which is to be the master of the world?" Ultimately, it is a war for peace.[47]

"The Day of the Lord of Hosts" had come upon England, intoned Winnington-Ingram, quoting Isaiah, in a sermon some months later. In fact, he highlighted more the scene from Matthew's Gospel. "My special point now is that you have not got to wait always for the final Judgment Day. For instance, if you read the twenty-fourth chapter of Saint Matthew it is hard to see whether our Lord is speaking of the Great Day at the end of the world, or the destruction of Jerusalem which occurred in A.D. 70. The events seem completely mixed up, and you cannot tell which is which. It shows this: that the destruction of Jerusalem in A.D. 70 was a Day of the Lord—which came long before the Judgment Day." There have already been judgment days in European history and now a new judgment day is upon them. He cites the victory of Charles Martel at Tours over the Muslim forces and the victory of the English armies over Napoleon at Waterloo in proclaiming that whatever applies to the "Day of the Lord" applies to this moment. Thus, the faithfulness, moral strength, and purpose preached in Christianity as preparation for the last judgment should be operative now. Then, mercifully, and to inspire the soldiers' parents in particular, he predicts the transformation of the profound sorrows of these days into glory.

> Now, if we are in the middle of this Day of God, what manner of persons ought we to be? In all holy conversation and godliness, looking for and hastening unto the coming of this Day of God. . . . We have got to display fortitude. . . . You have lost your boys, what are they? Martyrs dying for their faith, as did the first martyr, St. Stephen. They looked up when they died in the trenches, or in the little cottage where they were carried, they looked up and saw Jesus standing on the right hand of God. And He is keeping them safe for you there when your time comes. Covered with imperishable glory they pass to deathless life. And what have we got to do? We have to go on.[48]

General faith and national loyalty were enough to get the soldiers off to the front. When the Kaiser headed up the grand boulevard, Unter den Linden, he inspired lively optimism, but in quieter settings, as the first day waned into the second, it could give way to seriousness and tears: on one hand, cavorting optimistic young people, and on the other, the pure pessimism of many working-class men and women. The newspaper columns reported the boisterous patriotism of gatherings on the Place de la République, the preoccupations of store owners, taxi drivers, and anti-German vandalism on the streets. Enthusiasm, agitation, and anxiety marked the movement of peoples. The great *va-et-vient* involved the soldiers leaving, of course, but also foreign nationals trying to get home. Farm families worried about the harvest, and for wives in the city the goal was to bring the children to wave good-bye and keep up appearances. Anger at Germany combined with plain rowdiness on the troop trains. In London, it was holiday time, so war news made the day a celebration for surface optimists and a ruined holiday for the others. Trafalgar Square and Piccadilly Circus were filled with (mostly) orderly marchers and demonstrators.

God-talk and more serious nation-talk was, in early August and the weeks following, the work of the clergy. In Berlin on the Alexanderplatz, hymns, and on the Königsplatz, the official Berliner Dom preacher Bruno Doehring evoked Germany's heroes in the same breath as he evoked the grandeur of the gospels that promised eternal reward for faithfulness and suffering. "If God is for us, who can be against us" was the rallying cry. Christians had the duty to serve and solace one another, the model being the mutual dedication of marriage. In Munich, the Catholic Cardinal von Bettinger first exalted the nobility, loyalty, and charity of his people, asking for a renewal of the virtues that would confirm the justice of Germany's—and the Kaiser's—cause. After several months he addressed the soldiers directly, asking them to be valiant, devout, and calling for them to edify the folk in the by-then-occupied territories. He encouraged religious meditation on Christ's suffering and taught basic theology as a bulwark against the religious errors of France and Russia. In Paris, Cardinal Amette did not address the French soldiers directly, but he praised the national French response to the evil German invasion; he pictured French soldiers as martyrs, saved when their self-sacrifice is accompanied by perfect contrition. The Anglican bishop of London, Winnington-Ingram, combined devotional reflections on English Christianity and its centuries-long commitment to goodness and justice, with devotional, really mystical, reflections on the suffering and death of Christ. He wanted to inspire a repeat of the English soldier heroism displayed in the great battles of history, from Agincourt to Waterloo, with a renewed self-sacrifice that would show forth forgiveness of the enemy and the glories of martyrdom. As did Cardinal Amette, Bishop Winnington-Ingram would have sorrowing families rejoice in having soldier saints in heaven.

Church leaders gave the soldiers no reason to believe that there was any real conflict between their religion and war. The voices of minority Christian groups such as the Mennonites in Germany and Quakers in England—which must be mentioned here—were drowned out by the voices of the great national churches. Soldiers were left to believe that religion legitimized war and that they were called to sacrificial heroism. Reconciling themselves to this, they salvaged what they could of faith in an all-good God, the angels, and the saints. On an earth in tumult, they sought allies in heaven or worked out their own substitutes thereof, and in their letters and diaries they narrated these experiences as best they could.

CHAPTER 2

The Search for Allies in Heaven

Soldiers arriving at the front imagined heavenly allies that could offer some release from the mass death and suffering. From 4 August to 25 December is just short of five months, and yet by some rough estimates there were a million and a half casualties by the end of 1914. Even 1916, the year of those renowned battles of the Somme and Verdun, did not produce worse. There were miracle stories of major battles in 1914, indeed, and they had a long afterlife. The survival of a church tower here, a wayside crucifix there, and the random preservation of religious images at the center of scenes of destruction provided the raw material for interpretations of divine intervention. Of course, the principal faith-image for Christian soldiers on all sides was the suffering Christ, with the image of the Sacred Heart (the divine-human heart as the symbol of Christ's love) promoted for Catholics in particular. For Catholics and some Anglicans, the mother of Christ could be a consoling thought or devotion. Favored saints were Michael, the warrior archangel, George, the dragon slayer, and the patron saints associated with the military activity of the belligerent nations. And nothing received more attention than the series of minor truces on the front for Christmas 1914: the result of shared human suffering and religious sentiment and the simple need for respite.

So then, heavenly personalities inhabited the imaginations of the men in the form of assumed visions or simple faith in signs and miracles, and in the form of mental pictures to go with religious devotion—all of which the French get into one word, the *imaginaire*. The label "Allies in Heaven" comes from the testimony and experience of Joan of Arc, the saint who led the French in battle five centuries before World War I and was beatified by the Catholic Church five years before the war (then canonized in 1921). Father Stéphen Coubé, whose preface to the *Missel du Miracle de la Marne* (The Missal of the Miracle of the Marne) is an official interpretation of the "miracle," wrote that the title of his book, *Nos alliés du ciel* (Our Allies in Heaven), was inspired by the mission of Joan, whose visions of the archangel Michael and her favorite saints determined both her spiritual and military behavior.[1]

Beginning with the dramas of heavenly visions, across devotional images, down to the simplest Christmas nostalgia, we record the religious experiences of allies in heaven. To display these experiences, illustrations from the World War I era are essential: for Mons, artists' evocations of the angels; for the Marne, images from the *Missel*; for angels and saints, representative postcards from the huge and unique collection housed in the museum at Bad Windsheim, Germany; for the Christmas truce, photos from English newspapers.

THE "MIRACLES" OF MONS AND THE MARNE

In reality, the miracle stories were later (1915–16) creations, but the raw material for them was the confusion, the exhaustion, and often enough the semi-hallucinations of many soldiers in August–September 1914. False perceptions of troop movements, imaginary cavalries, and scores of other images out of the chaotic fighting were, so to speak, real. The miraculous and graphic features of the sightings became the angels and other heavenly personalities that appeared at Mons in Belgium, August 22–24, near the French border. The British Expeditionary Force joined a large, unexpected, and confusing battle against the German soldiers (here the Second Army of von Bülow) making the wide sweep toward Paris. Then, weeks later, some French officers and soldiers were convinced that the battle won along the Marne River, a fifty-mile front from Paris to the river Ourq, was effected by a heavenly team of Notre Dame and the great French saints. Here appearance stories were at a minimum, however. The "miracle of the Marne" stopped the German advance and saved France, though it did not bring about a quick end to the war.

In Belgium, the French army facing the German advances was falling back, and the recently arrived English forces were forced to face the invading Germans at Mons, just over the border from France. They were soon forced to retreat to the French town of Le Cateau but managed to keep their army intact. Afterward, stories began to circulate in England that the troops had supernatural help. Some men presumably had visions of Saint George, angels, and spirits of the battle of Agincourt. These took place over four days, beginning on 22 August, and for those who believed in the visions, the protection of these heavenly spirits explained how a presumably small English contingent could hold and save itself from a presumably much-larger German contingent. In fact, the experiences of wounds, exhaustion, terror, and confusion, unquestionably widespread, were later consolidated around stories concocted back in England.

According to the story, on 23 August, part of the English forces seemed surrounded, when "angels descended from heaven dressed as archers stopping the Germans in their tracks. The English, under their protection, were able to retreat in the darkness, thereby saving the brigade from annihilation." London reports of mysterious cavalry men in the sky appeared almost a year later in September 1915, and reports of angels above in April and October of the same year. The stories then proliferated: visions of lights, imaginary archers, castles, persons known to individual soldiers, dark and menacing thunderclouds. In his *Angel of Mons*, David Clarke writes, "These stories suggest that among the thousands of English soldiers trapped in the path of

FIG. 4 Imaginary scene of the Angels of Mons halting the German advance. Photo: Chronicle / Alamy Stock Photo.

the advancing Germans there were a few individuals who came to believe they had been saved by a miracle." By 26 August, the English had to take a stand at Le Cateau, where, according to a lieutenant colonel cited in that September 1915 issue of the London *Evening News*, many squadrons of cavalry men were seen riding alongside the English forces.[2]

The key to understanding the miracle is the writing of the English author, Arthur Machen. And for *his* story we go back a year to September 1914 when all this drama is supposed to have taken place. He published a brief personal story in the *Evening News* of 29 September 1914, the Anglican calendar feast day of Saint Michael and All the Angels. Story it was, and fiction he proclaimed it to be, derived in no way from contemporary reports from the front.

> The English see that the position is hopeless.... They know that they are doomed to death beyond all hope or help.... Then [a soldier] remembers the motto... *Adsit Anglis Sanctus Georgius*—May St. George be a present help to the English. He utters this prayer mechanically; and falls instantly into a waking vision. He hears a voice, mighty as a thunder-peal, crying, "Array, array, array!" and the spirits of the old English bowmen obey the command of their patron and ours. The soldier hears their war-cries: "Harrow, harrow! St. George be quick to help us." "Dear saint, succor us!" He sees the flight of their arrows darkening the air.[3]

By the end of the story, ten thousand Germans lie dead without any visible wounds on their bodies, deaths attributed (in much smaller numbers) by the Germans to poison gas but attributed by Machen's English readers to Saint George and the bowmen of Agincourt. Until the end of the war, and even for the rest of his life, Machen tried to convince the public that he wrote fiction and not news from the front. But the narrative served as an inspiration for tale tellers, who imaged and interpreted their own experiences. An English nurse, Phyllis Campbell, reported that a number of soldiers in her care had seen these visions, and an army officer, Brigadier General John Charteris, wrote about the visions in a February 1915 letter to his wife.[4] At the end of his study of the Angel of Mons, David Clarke writes, "Unfortunately the most important source of first-hand evidence—private correspondence between soldiers and their families—has not yielded a single account of supernatural phenomena at the battle of Mons."[5]

There may have been as many thoughts, emotions, and hallucinations in hundreds of other World War I battles, but this was the first month of the war and a pattern was set. Even if we dispense with the religious imaginings, there remains the numbers game of the official military reports. Terence Zuber's *The Mons Myth* contains nothing, nary a word, about the rumors of angels. He offers a logistically detailed set of reports and interpretations to show that proportionately English losses were far higher than German losses at Mons, and that Le Cateau, far from being a quasi-English victory with 15,000–30,000 German deaths, was an English defeat, with 2,900 German casualties and twice as many casualties for the English.[6] On one hand, the Mons story had been reworked with a heavenly cast, and on the other hand, with statistical wishful thinking.

After Mons and Le Cateau, pushing back the English and French units before them, the armies of Alexander von Kluck and Karl von Bülow raced toward Paris. The French supreme commander, Joseph Joffre, with an aplomb and originality that barely made up for previous miscalculations, repositioned his armies, sacking the retreating General Charles Lanrezac and bringing up the determined General Ferdinand Foch. The two German armies, really victims of their own earlier success, did not have the strength or supplies to take Paris and had to turn away from the city, separating and exposing the First Army flank as they moved southwest along the Marne. Between 6 September and 12 September, the two German enemies were separated and pushed back to the river Aisne. German hopes for winning Paris, crucial for winning the war quickly and to Germany's advantage, were totally destroyed. For Joffre it was pure military strategy, and for Foch it was determination and heavenly help.

One of the few unabashed heavenly intervention stories about the Marne victory trickled down to the local *Courrier de Saint-Lô* for 8 January 1917. In this story, a captured German priest, before dying in a French army hospital with religious sisters in attendance, said that his unit was clearly winning when they all saw the Virgin Mary, clad in the white garment with blue sash of the Notre Dame de Lourdes apparition to Bernadette Soubirous. The Virgin turned away from them, seeming to push them back. Two officers, wounded captives along with the priest, when they saw a Lourdes statue (white with blue sash) said, "Ah, the Virgin of the Marne." A third soldier story, supposedly recounted by a German chaplain to French priests and witnessed by a sister, reported a similar appearance, adding that one hundred thousand

German soldiers had seen it and were sworn to silence under pain of death by their superior officers—a fantastic narration found only in a private collection.[7]

These accounts of heavenly intervention stand in total contrast to a standardized, ecclesiastically approved interpretation of the miracle of the Marne in the beautiful *Missel du Miracle de la Marne*, bound in leather (15.5 × 9 × 2 cm) with gold details on each small image, which was a prayer book containing liturgical prayers and other devotions for use during Mass or for private use. The preface, a Catholic theology of the meaning of miracles, was written by the abbé Stéphen Coubé. Joseph Girard produced the four color illustrations, and the sixteen engraving designs, which were then realized in the engraving studio of Victor Dutertre. It was published by the Limoges house of P. Mellottée and officially approved by the bishop of Limoges, Hector Raphaël Quillet. Annette Becker, a prominent French historian of World War I, highlighted this missal, not because it was widely used, but because it was a veritable compendium of clerical and folk religion. She writes that Girard "gives a resumé of Catholic thought on the miracle of the Marne, resituated in the full context of the war since mobilization."[8]

In his preface to the *Missel*, Stéphen Coube cited the simple distinction made the year before by Bishop Charles Gibier of Versailles. There were "absolute" miracles such as the resurrection of the dead, instantaneous cures, or events involving the suspension of natural law. In the case of "relative" miracles, God directs or focuses natural forces, and so secondary causes, to produce unexpected results. At the Marne, God enhanced generals' decisions, soldiers' determination, and the disorientation with subsequent panic of the enemy troops. A review of the developments across early September would be enough to prove it all. After the retreats from Belgium and northern France, the enemy was practically at the gates of Paris (Chantilly and Luzarches). But on 3 September, Coubé writes, the name of Joan of Arc permeated the soldiers' ranks, and on 5 September, the three days of prayer to Saint Geneviève began in Paris. The retreat from the Marne tributary of the Ourq toward the Marne itself began the day before the 8 September closing of the triduum with the veneration of the reliquary of Saint Geneviève at Saint-Étienne-du-Mont, the very day also of the celebration of the feast of the Nativity of Mary. Finally, the Germans began their major retreat on 12 September, the feast of the Holy Name of Mary.[9]

To emphasize the magnitude of the victory, Coubé dramatizes the strength of the German armies and ignores the major problems they were facing. How could victorious German armies so fail? And how could the French army, "poorly equipped, defeated, decimated, pursued for three weeks get back on its feet, trembling [with anticipation] and splendid, effect a prodigious recovery, and drive back two million men armed with formidable canons"? Certainly, Kluck's judgment failed. Coubé seems to telescope the action, saying that the split occurred between Kluck's army and the army of the "crown prince" (Wilhelm of Prussia), and that General Foch drove a wedge between the two. It was really the British Expeditionary Force that cut between the First Army of Kluck and the Second Army of Bülow. Foch's attack driving back German forces was against the Third army of Max von Hausen.[10]

Those "secondary causes" of the cleverness of the French generals, the bravery of the troops and the "sublime order" handed down by General Joffre (no mention of how he had gotten so much wrong before his last-minute brilliance) effected the French victory. Coubé omits the story of the exhaustion of the German armies after their race across northern France, the problems of supplying the two armies and maintaining coordination between the two, the problem of communication with the German high command, with both General Helmuth von Moltke and the Kaiser in fact, and the disagreements among other German generals and high officers. No, for Coubé the victory was of a piece with the other great French victories of history: over the Alemanni at Tolbiac, the English at Bouvines, Orléans, and Patay—the last two under the leadership of Joan of Arc. Recognizing that everything that happens is somehow the will of God, Coubé teaches that these victories, and now the Marne, are an expression of God's special favor: "When this combination [of circumstances] has the quality of a favor, of a mark of love, it honors in a special way the nation that receives it. Such a nation should be proud of it."[11]

The color illustrations and black-and-white engravings in the *Missel* are a visual summary of French patriotic Catholicism, theologically introduced by Courbé in his preface, but also stand as interpretations of the soldiers' way of seeing Christ, not literally but with the eyes of faith. They display the following scenes (and can be viewed at http://www.josephfbyrnes.com/world-war-I).

1. Christ in loincloth and crown of thorns hanging on the cross, topped with the plaque marked INRI, and emanating rays of light from his body. At the foot of the cross on a patch of grass are three French soldiers in uniform, one lying down, apparently dead, and the other two perhaps wounded. The one on the right rears back to view the vision. The terrain behind the cross is war-torn with a faint image in the distance of a half figure rising with face and one arm uplifted.

2. Joan of Arc, holding a sword looks up to a vision above of the Pietà with only the foot of the cross visible and Christ's crown of thorns falls from his head to the ground. A shield leans against her on which is embossed a map of France and a French Adrian helmet with its chin strap over the visor sits on laurel leaves below. She gestures to a field of burial crosses behind her, those graves closest are heaped with recent soil and one marking cross is topped by a helmet, while the other's helmet has fallen to the ground.

3. A long, full line of French infantry march along a dirt road with destruction suggested by an abandoned wagon with a broken wheel and a small pile of equipment to their right. Poplars line a ridge behind them on their left. Red light in the low sky gives evidence of ongoing battle in the far background. Overhead appears an image of Christ and his disciples in a boat with a flapping sail depicting the story of Christ calming the waters in a stormy sea (Matthew 8:23–27; Mark 4:35–41, and Luke 8:22–25). One soldier looks up to see the vision.

4. A full processional march of officers in dress uniforms on horseback, with two dense columns of infantry men on either side of them, passes through a stylized Arc de Triomphe decorated with the French tricolor flags and garlands of leaves. Three flags are single colors; a blue flag (the color associated with Saint Martin) and two red flags (the color associated with Saint Denis). Other tricolors fly from poles in front of the arch and along from poles along the route. The procession comes toward us from left to right. Above them hovers an angel, and, higher in the sky, Christ appears in a red cloak as the Sacred heart (image of a burning heart under a cross surrounded by the crown of thorns on his breast) with the cross-nimbus and arms raised in blessing. He is surrounded by figures, of which one kneels and another appears with the crusader cross on his tunic or breastplate. The point figure in the line, the officer who appears first, looks up to see the vision and has lowered his sword with an open right arm. He is the only figure who seems to see it.

The series of small black-and-white engravings is repeated across the volume, which makes for an illustration at the top of every single page, no matter what the prayer text on the page. The first six images are purely geographical and human (the military operations and prayer gatherings.

1. *Mobilisation, 2 août 1914* (Mobilization, 2 August 1914). A central figure, not yet in uniform, waves a farewell with his cap. On the left side of the image, a mother and child in front of a mounted officer and other soldiers. On the right, further good-byes, seemingly between parents and son and a spouse to a uniformed soldier. In the near background, a soldier on horseback, and

THE SEARCH FOR ALLIES IN HEAVEN 41

FIG. 5 A full-page (originally) color illustration in the *Missel*: the fourth and most elaborately worked-out scene. From *Missel du Miracle de la Marne* (Limoges: P. Mellottée, 1916).

several officers carrying their rifle, and in the broad background, industrial buildings, electrical or phone high wires before them, and a huge crane behind them: leaving modern life for a modern war.

2. *En contact, août 1914* (Contact, August 1914). The contact scene for August pictures French soldiers in the background on two sides of a dirt lane. One fully equipped soldier leaves a group on the right to run across a road to a larger group of soldiers while another, wounded or dead, lies on the ground and two remain in place. Village structure and a church are in the background behind a split-rail fence. Further back, one can discern the spiked helmets of German soldiers.

3. *En retraite* (Retreat). The retreat across the countryside appears orderly; some soldiers march along a road while others rest under a sheltering tree to the side. Their guns and backpacks rest on the grass beside them. Their postures suggest dejection; the foremost figure rests his head in his hands, while the others look down at the ground. A long train of wagons, each pulled by horses, begins midpicture and curves around behind to the far, tree-marked background.

4. *L'ennemi en vue de Paris* (The enemy within sight of Paris). In the foreground, three men with spiked helmets have dismounted under a signpost marked "Paris" from a group of mounted soldiers grouped on the left. Two hold papers; one appears to consult a map while the central man has his back to the viewer, appearing to look through binoculars at the city skyline in the distance. We can distinguish the shapes of the dome of Sacré Cœur, the Eifel Tower, and the western towers of the Cathedral of Notre-Dame silhouetted against the light clouds.

5. *Adoration au S.-C. 4 sept. 1914* (Adoration of the Blessed Sacrament, 4 September 1914). With the German armies closing in on Paris, a service of benediction and adoration of the Blessed Sacrament was held with an accompanying sermon. In the lower half of the scene, set in the nave of a church, a dense congregation, mainly of women, faces the preacher. Three women kneel in the foreground, below the pulpit that is against one pier on the left side, with a man and a boy behind them and two more men in a row of kneelers to their right. In the upper left, the altar is apparent with a half-visible monstrance and mounted candles. A priest in a surplice bends forward from the pulpit, extending his hands over the congregation. The walls are adorned with French flags; both hanging chandeliers and a large stand against a pier have more lit candles to illuminate the space.

6. *Triduum—6.7.8. sept. 1914* (Triduum—6, 7, 8 September 1914). Three days of special prayers were held in September 1914. We see an image of a large crowd gathered in the Place Sainte-Geneviève before the church of Saint-Étienne-du-Mont in Paris's fifth arrondissement. In the center of the steps of the main entrance the great reliquary (*châsse*) of Saint-Geneviève has been set within flying French flags to the left while a priest raises both arms in oration on the right. The German armies began their long pull back from the Marne to the Aisne on 9 September, the day after these prayers ended, as if in heavenly response.

FIG. 6 One of the twelve action-scene engravings in the *Missel*, showing the veneration of the relics of Sainte Geneviève in front of Saint-Étienne-du-Mont, which took place across the three days before the Germans began their retreat from the Marne. From *Missel du Miracle de la Marne* (Limoges: P. Mellottée, 1916).

The next four images present earthly religious action in a war setting and figures in heaven, but the two dimensions do not interact.

7/8. *Absolution* (Absolution) and *Immolation* (Immolation). Two images portray soldiers before and after a battle. In the first, a priest in cassock and stole raises his hand in absolution over a small group of fully equipped kneeling and standing soldiers, presumably after a general confession (a common prayer instead of individually enumerated sins) just before battle. They stand inside a small grove of protective bushes with a larger tree on the left pointing one bare branch toward the sky where a large filmy white cross against a gray circle is centered. At its crossbar is Christ's pierced hand raised in absolution. In the second image, standing soldiers behind a tree on the left look over a small vignette of destruction in the foreground, where a few dead and dying are grouped on the ground. Centered in the sky above hovers the head of Christ crowned with thorns, within a gray cross-nimbus and another faintly yellow aureole. One figure before the tree on the ground has fallen on his back and stretches his right arm up toward this vision. On the right, a farmhouse stands with high sloping roof and partially visible chimney.

9. *Reims, la cathédrale martyre* (Reims, the Martyr Cathedral). Major bombardment of the cathedral itself began on 19 September. The damage was extensive, so "martyred" may not be too strong a label. In this most dramatic of the small engraved scenes, the cathedral fills the center left background with flames and smoke rising into a sky filled with white-haloed saints, three of them mitered (suggesting they are bishops). Many of these figures appear in an attitude of supplication toward an unseen higher locus. In the foreground, facing the cathedral, stand citizens and French soldiers, their shadows cast long toward the viewer by the light of the burning cathedral. Buildings are sketched on the right, and in front of a low wall a barrel is perched on top of a pile of debris—whether for a liquid or gunpowder is unclear.

10. *La bataille de la Marne* (The Battle of the Marne). This scene also appears in two tiers. In the lower scene, earthly soldiers feed a canon from an upturned shell wagon in the right foreground, while massed troops advance toward a church and village on the left. Explosions and battle-scarred trees are on the horizon. Above in the sky, a shadowy battle is shown with cavalry carrying banners, axes, and lances, followed by foot soldiers shouldering guns.

With the last four images, we are back to earthly liturgies at the front and in Paris or Rome.

11. *La messe aux tranchées* (Mass in the trenches). A group of soldiers appears gathered around the cutaway of a large, reinforced trench where a

small table has been set up as an altar with a cloth sewn with a cross draped over the wall. A priest is turned away from the standing and kneeling men, inclining toward the altar with its lit candle and covered chalice. A shovel and pick lay abandoned on the grass in the foreground.

12. *Les tombes militaires* (Military tombs). A priest in cassock, surplus, and stole holds an indecipherable object (probably for sprinkling holy water) over three freshly closed graves marked with Celtic crosses. Behind him stand two other clergymen and an officer, followed by a group of other soldiers, all with their caps removed. Facing the graves on the right, an honor guard of four fully uniformed soldiers hold their rifles at attention in a line leading back from the foreground. In the background on the left, an irregular mass of five more small crosses suggests further graves.

13/14. *La France au Montmartre* (France on Montmartre) and *La France au Vatican* (France in the Vatican). Two images of monumental churches are used in the series: the Sacré Cœur Basilica up in Montmartre, behind its double staircase, and Saint Peter's Basilica in Rome, within Bernini's enclosing piazza with its ancient Egyptian obelisk. Sacré Cœur is fronted by a huge statue below in the esplanade of a soldier holding a shield and flags. Crowds appear to mount toward the Sacré Cœur esplanade carrying banners. On either side of the church, buildings are shown, Saint-Pierre de Montmartre, on the left, and modern Montmartre buildings on the right. In the aerial scene of Saint Peters, we also see crowds processing with banners. Other groups of people, some in carriages, move through the piazza and cluster on the steps around, and on, the level above the columns. A few buildings appear behind the colonnade.

Together, all of these engravings offer a condensed visual overview of military and religious events between 2 August and 12 September—the end of the Marne battle—when German troops withdrew back to the Aisne River.

On the German side, there were no physically intervening heavenly allies. Battle successes and failures could be militarily explained, and so recourse to angels and saints belong to everyday faith and devotion. But soldiers had their angels, and illustrators produced not a unified volume like the *Missel* but random postcards. Two German postcards dramatically portray these beliefs.

1. The hero's death (*Heldentod*): against a purple, battle-scarred land and a darkening skyscape flecked with the pale red of a late sunset, a luminous angel cradles the head of a dying soldier, before bearing his soul to heaven.

FIG. 7 German postcard showing the "death of a hero" [*Heldentod*] in the arms of an angel. From Heidrun Alzheimer, ed., *Glaubenssache Krieg: Religiöse Motive auf Bildpostkarten des Ersten Weltkriegs* (Bad Windsheim: Fränkisches Freilandmuseum, 2009).

2. Against a forest background a German soldier stands warily in a clearing. The center of the card is filled with a winged angel who stands between the soldier and an enemy soldier firing his rifle from the edge of the forest. Angels as guardians and protectors belonged to a popular Christian tradition, originating in biblical passages such as "Because you have made the Lord your refuge, the Most High your habitation, no evil shall befall you, no scourge come near your tent. For he will give his angels charge of you to guard you in all your ways. On their hands they will bear you up, lest you dash your foot against a stone," words of Psalm 91:9–11, quoted in the gospels of Matthew (4:6) and Luke (4:10–11)[12]

Michael the archangel was a national warrior image for German Protestants. The theologian Otto Scheel believed that the most famous of all German reformers, Martin Luther, in his self-discipline and religious daring had been led by Saint Michael to the throne of God, the Judge. The historian Thomas Fliege believes that German Catholic leaders sought to emphasize more the consoling function of Michael as one who protects, comforts, and defends, a counter-idea to this national, essentially Protestant, martial tone. There was only infrequent reference to Michael in Catholic writing and preaching in the first half of the war; later, references were more frequent. The development of the "nail figure" practice by 1915 gave a number of cities and communities a Saint Michael image (among other nail figures, the most famous of which was General Paul von Hindenburg). A statue would be erected in such a way that participants could come alongside and pound nails into it until the statue became a nail figure. Such Michaels were set up in Hamburg, Breslau, Krefeld, and Osnabrück. Many thousands could participate, making the practice an expression of national religion or simply of nationalism. In a major sermon preached by Paul Kaiser in Leipzig in the second year of the war, Michael was the symbol and guarantee of "God with us." Toward the end of the war, the massive and final German offensive was named "Michael," after consideration of several other names, including "Archangel."[13]

THE WAYSIDE WONDERS IN BATTLE ZONES

Bizarre survivals of statues belonged to the category of signs and wonders in the *imaginaire* of soldiers and church people. But here the images themselves were ready-made, involving neither altered human perceptions nor theological insights but simple prayerful attributions. In Saarebourg, a crucifixion monument on the outskirts (Bühl) was partly destroyed on 20 August during the battle that crossed the terrain. The armies of the French generals Paul Pau, Auguste Dubail, and Noël de Castelnau had pushed into the area before being thrown back by the German forces under Josias von Heeringen. The dramatic detail for the German soldiers who came upon it after the battles was that the corpus of Christ remained after the cross had been destroyed. This wonder of the upright body of Christ, surviving alone on the pedestal impressed the soldiers and local inhabitants more than it did the hierarchy. When Cardinal von Bettinger of Munich visited Saarebourg in 1916, no mention was made, or at least nothing was recorded, about the wonder cross. But the image made its way into the postcard repertoire, as recorded by the writer Josef Jurinek, who believed that there were several hundred thousand of these distributed.[14]

Other postcard types, of which three are described here, could be more elaborate. The first gives the scene after the battle: on the left of the vertically arranged scene is the upright corpus upon a pedestal in high relief showing both an image of the Virgin Mary and below her the skull of Adam, which was often imaged at the foot of the cross in Christian iconography; roses grow up around the monument, which is surrounded by a small metal fence. The right side of the card image opens up to a combination of the idyllic and the tragic, showing grass, fields, and a tree in bloom, along with destroyed engines of war, several French dead, and a burning home in the distance. Underneath the title, "Das Crucifix auf dem Schlachtfelde bei Saarburg" (Crucifix on the Battlefield near Saarebourg), is a short poem evoking Christ's suffering for the sake of peace. In the second postcard type, a broad color display of the battle in progress has the Christ image in the center, high on its pedestal and dwarfing the thousands of troops charging along the surrounding plain. The cross fragments are flying into the air, surrounded by explosions looking like giant flower blooms; in the background huge fires rage and the sky just above is darkened by the smoke. At the top of the card: "Schlacht bei Saarburg am 20 Aug. 1914" (Battle near Saarebourg); just underneath, a longer description divided into two parts on either side of the Christ figure: "The battlefield cross on the country road to Bühl. The cross was shot away, but the statue of the savior wondrously remained in place." On the back of the card is a prayer poem by the Strasbourg author Franz Winter, celebrating the victory but begging for peace in the homeland and in foreign lands. The last type features a poem with a clear and graphic image of the Christ corpus to the left of the scene. And at the bottom lies level barren fields with several buildings on the low horizon; all is in black and white with the darkened field and the bright open sky. In every case, viewers are invited to picture and ponder.[15]

A very different visual experience was the Virgin and Child atop the tower of the Basilica of Notre-Dame de Brebières at Albert in Picardy, although the figures came to be interpreted in ways similar to those other shrines and statues and were seen by far more people. The literary historian Paul Fussell recorded the attempts to find meaning in the Virgin and Child dangling from the tower, parallel to the ground.

Fussell writes, "The war would end, the rumor went, when the statue finally fell to the streets. Germans and English shared this belief, and both tried to knock the statue down with artillery." When this proved harder than it looked, the Germans promulgated the belief that the side that shot down the Virgin would lose the war. After the town was captured by the Germans, the English both trained artillery on and send bombing planes over the town and its basilica, which was reputed to be a look-out post. Private Frank Richards recorded events this way: "Every morning our bombing planes were

FIG. 8 The Virgin and Child hanging perpendicular to the ground from the tower of the Basilica of Albert. Photo: Historical Images Archive / Alamy Stock Photo.

going over and bombing the town and our artillery were constantly shelling it, but the statue seemed to be bearing a charmed existence. We were watching the statue one morning. Our heavy shells were bursting around the church tower, and when the smoke cleared away after the explosion of one big shell the statue was missing." Then he adds that the English newspapers, with some awareness of the destroy-statue-lose-the-war story, reported "that the Germans had wantonly destroyed it, which I expect was believed by the people that read them at the time." There is no necessity to restrict thoughts, religious or otherwise, to the win-lose interpretation, writes Fussell, because the statue was "an emblem of pathos, of the effect of war on the innocent, on women and children especially." He quotes Paul Maze, a French liaison officer: "The statue of the Virgin Mary, in spite of many hits, still held on top of the spire as if by a miracle. The precarious angle at which she now leaned forward gave her a despairing gesture, as though she were throwing the child into the battle." This interpretation was seconded, according to Fussell, by Philip Gibbs who saw in the statue a child-offering gesture, and so a "peace-offering to this world at war." S. S. Horsley, a soldier whose diary and notebook are preserved in the Imperial War Museum, wrote, "Marched through Albert where we saw the famous church with the statue of Madonna and Child hanging from the top of the steeple, at an angle of about 40 degrees as if the Madonna was leaning down to catch the child which had fallen." Max Plowman, author of *A Subaltern on the Somme*, believed the Virgin to be "bowed as by the last extremity of grief." The eminent poet Edmund Blunden, a veteran of that area of the front, thirty years after the war wrote "When the Statue Fell." In the poem, an old soldier responds to his grandchild's question, "What was the strangest sight you ever saw?" by telling the story of Albert, its Basilica, the statue, its curious suspension, and its final fall, which he makes coincide with the end of the war.[16]

EVERYDAY DEVOTIONS FOR WARTIME

The Sacred Heart, the Virgin Mother Mary, and the angels and saints belonged to the everyday *imaginaire* of soldiers and church people, varying according to the devotional dedication of the believer. In modern French and German Catholicism, the image of Jesus Christ as Savior, heart on fire with love of humankind, has been preached, promoted, and probably appreciated more than any other. The heart, sometimes set against the image of a clothed Christ and sometimes as an isolated symbol, could be found in churches and in homes and even on flags, this last placement popular during the French Revolution and during World War I, and had been an essential element of French piety and religious nationalism from the time of King Louis XIV. There was pious precedent for this imagery when Marguerite-Marie Alacoque, a cloistered nun at the monastery of Paray-le-Monial in Burgundy, revealed her apparition experiences of Christ in whose breast she saw a fiery heart. Great upheavals in French society and political life propelled these stories throughout the land. At the height of the 1789–99 Revolution, the conservative Catholic militias opposing the Republic marched under banners bearing the symbol of the Sacred Heart, and after the massacre of participants in the Paris Commune, money was raised with the support of the official government to build the basilica of Sacré Cœur on Montmartre, center of the Commune rebellion, as an act of reparation. For explanation of the Sacred Heart as a personal devotion and as an instrument of religious nationalism, we look to the preaching and publications of the French and German clergy directly or indirectly involved in the war effort, and to the testimonies of a few of the more religiously expressive soldiers. By World War I, a person would not have to be an especially devout Catholic to see Christ as the Sacred Heart. Across the war years, there were consecrations of dioceses and dedications of images in France, beginning with ceremonies in the basilica itself. Catholic extremists were inspired by the story of a young visionary named Claire Ferchaud, who wanted President Raymond Poincaré to have the Sacred Heart superimposed on the French flag, and rallied behind her request.[17]

Both German and French Catholic religious publications during the war propagated the Sacred Heart devotion; the channel for these pages was the preaching of the chaplains, and in the French case, the priest soldiers. Claudia Schlager has compared the German and French versions in a model comprehensive study. The archdiocese of Munich, followed by the diocese of Speyer, prepared a Sacred Heart scapular medal specifically for soldiers in the field. Naturally, the Catholic religious publications in both countries were dedicated to war themes; journals specifically for preachers offered sample sermons for use at the front. The German Jesuit publication *Chrysologus* preached that hope for victory based upon Christ's intervention would not be disappointed, and that the army and navy would have brilliant victories. The Christmas pastoral letters of the German bishops cited in evidence insisted on prayer as the only way of guaranteeing God's favor even so. There was a German version of Claire Ferchaud in the person of Barbara Weigand. Medals and emblems concretized the Sacred Heart experience for French and German Catholic soldiers, often simply as talismans rather than as religious inspiration. As usual, the religious postcards illustrating field altars, shrines, and reliquaries provided dramatic imagery for soldiers and families at home. Of course, on Sacred Heart themes, the French had the advantage because they originated there: the *Pèlerin de Paray-le-Monial* was published at the site of the apparitions. More like than unlike, German and French Catholics each had to make a case to their respective nations: Germans to a Protestant empire and French to a secular republic.[18]

The image of Mary as mother and queen, the Notre Dame of the cathedrals, was central to church ministry and soldier devotion on the western front. Annette Becker, presenting highlights of soldier devotion as an extension of mainline French Catholic devotional tradition, begins with the drama of the poet Charles Péguy, who lived the last hours before his death as an "immense pilgrimage at the end of which he would meet the virgin." The simple faith of other soldiers could be equally passionate, as in the note written with personal eloquence and grammatical innocence (observable in the original French): "Our Lady of Lourdes I address you so you will give me the grace to return one day to my little home with my good little family, which I am so distant from. Preserve me from the misfortune that I risk each day, and I beg you to stop as quickly as possible this terrible Carnage that makes so many corpses. Please lift up your arm to stop all of that, and I will be so grateful to you for the rest of my life." Similar sentiments are found on thanksgiving plaques put in place in a number of churches after the war. Prayers and pious acts received mention in notes written to publications at Marian shrines, as in the message from a mother to the *Annales de Notre-Dame de la Salette* (Annals of Our Lady of La Salette), who said her son was protected many times, because he wore a medal of the Virgin and carried an image of the Sacred Heart.[19] For German Catholics and English Anglicans also, devotion to the Blessed Virgin was part of a pious upbringing.

French soldier invocations of the saints highlighted Joan of Arc and Thérèse of Lisieux, both of them actually canonized as saints *after* the war. To give one example, Becker cites a church in Artois, partially destroyed and being used for a military hospital, where three images were placed on the altar, the Virgin Mary, Joan of Arc, and Thérèse. Numerous letters were collected by the Carmelites of Thérèse's home monastery of Lisieux during the war, with a view to canonization. Soldier letters date in particular from the year of Verdun and the Somme with lots of stories of bullets warded off by relics, medals, images, and even brochures having to do with Thérèse. One long tale of salvation and protection is presented by Becker.

> I had distanced myself from the church after my first communion. However, I accepted a relic and an image of our little Sister, and every time that I found myself in combat danger, I instinctively called for her help, seeing that each time she protected me.... There was one difficult moment, with the artilleries thundering. I thought with great sadness of my little family and I said to [her]: "Sister Thérèse, I beg you to get me back to my wife and my children, and I promise to go [pray at] your tomb...." I had scarcely said this prayer, when I saw a cloud open and the face of the saint again the blue sky. I believed that I was hallucinating. I rubbed my eyes several times, but I could no

longer doubt, for her face became more clear and resplendent. . . . From that time on, I never felt alone. And I also had firm hope of seeing my family, and the unshakeable resolve to return to the God of my youth.[20]

And on the German side, Protestant and Catholic, other saints were honored in addition to Michael the archangel, including Saint George, Saint Joseph, and, on a smaller scale, Saint Barbara, Saint Moritz, and Saint Hubert. In one image from 1914, Saint George, in armor and riding a white horse, plunges his spear into the gaping and flaming mouth of a dragon. The armor evokes the Germanic Middle Ages broadly, and the action vaguely evokes Siegfried, the hero of Germanic folklore. That he is the patron of cavalry is clearly shown in the high color of another image where the figure on the horse is a German soldier. The Saint Joseph imagery includes his usual robes, carpenter's tools, and the white lily (a purity symbol, developed out of Joseph legends). This, combined with a background of soldiers constructing trench fortifications, symbolizes Joseph's role as protector, builder, and guarantor of purity, dedication, and faithfulness. His general patronage of all handworkers channeled into patronage of the German soldiers who create defense works for their comrades. The bizarre Saint Barbara story has a long and complex history that includes her imprisonment after conversion to Christianity, martyrdom at the hands of her pagan father, and the subsequent death by lightning of her father. At first, she escaped her prison tower through a ground crevice, but a betrayal led to her martyrdom. She became patroness of miners because of the crevice escape, and of artillerymen because of the lightning strike. She could be heroically pictured with sword and crown, carrying a model of the escape tower, with soldiers on horseback pulling up artillery in the background. Saint Moritz was the patron saint of the infantry; Saint Hubert, the patron saint of riflemen. The role of Saint Moritz dates in particular from Bavaria in the eighteenth century and took on no new identity specific to World War I. And as legend Saint Hubert's personality was a mixture of an existing bishop of Liège (of all places: the first great siege after the German invasion of Belgium!) and a hunter on pilgrimage who befriended a deer with a cross appearing between his antlers—later retiring to a hermit's life. The good bishops, the saintly hunter and marksman, and the self-providing hermit inspired knightly orders and brotherhoods and, finally the riflemen of war. As the years of war ground on, patron sainthood could be accepted with a touch of satire, witnessed to by an image of "St. Barbara in front of

Verdun" makes clear. Here, a smiling soldier is holding an umbrella over a Barbara, crowned and holding a bouquet and wearing high heels, who has elevated the lower portion of her dress to save it from the rain, as she marches across a makeshift walkway. All is worth a laugh, if not a prayer.[21]

THE CHRISTMAS TRUCE

We return to the end of 1914, with those million and a half German, French, and English, casualties. In spite of these numbers, at Christmas, the eve, the day, and sometimes for a day or two afterward, the celebration of the holiday on each side changed into a common celebration in numerous places along the front. We have the newspaper reports, the letters home, the army records, and the commentaries of churchmen on the front and at home. From all of this we can surmise that the story and celebration of the birth of Christmas was part of the ordinary wish to stop fighting, if only for a brief time.

Soldiers had fraternized before on the front, according to an erratic "live and let live" policy between major attacks. Some had written home questioning atrocity reports, expressing respect for soldiers in the enemy trenches. In fact, there was a surprising openness in the newspaper reports about this fraternizing, which could, of course, degenerate into lack of effort and fighting spirit. Citing the *Manchester Guardian* in particular, Terri Blom Crocker writes that the newspaper editors and authors "had no qualms about admitting that English soldiers did not hate the dreaded Hun of newspaper clichés, but rather felt respect for and even a certain kinship with the enemy." And beyond the *Guardian*, "there were newspapers, and therefore members of the public, who were able to view the war in a more balanced way." Soldier letters, certainly the English letters in the early part of the war, did not omit the blood, the mud, and the atrocious suffering.[22]

There was not one Christmas truce. There were a number of truces along the English and German front line, and we can name the English army units that were involved. Between the French and German troops, also, there were pauses in the fight at Christmas. Christmas trees on the trench parapets and the Christmas carols in the background were regularly the start-ups in the fraternizing, but some cease-fires were worked out more formally, and burying and praying over the dead were essential parts of these days, perhaps even the primary motivation. At times large numbers of soldiers came out of the trenches, and when this happened there was exchange of food, drink, cigars, and souvenirs of all kinds. There were even a few cobbled-together soccer games, which for all their rarity (where to get soccer balls or usable substitutes for same?!!) made for great stories.

Just climbing out of those trenches was in every case a wager. According to Wilbert Spencer, of the 2nd Wiltshires, "On Christmas Day we heard the words 'Happy Christmas!' being called out, wherefore we wrote up on a board 'Gluckliches Werhnnachten!' [For 'Gluckliche Weinachten']. There was no firing, so by degrees each side began gradually showing more of themselves, and then two of their men came halfway over and called for an officer."[23] Lieutenant Alfred Chater wrote home, "I was peeping over the parapet when I saw a German, waving his arms, and presently two of them got out of their trenches and came towards ours—we were just going to fire on them when we saw they have no rifles, so one of our men went out to meet them." Spontaneous exchanges of gifts followed, a natural result after the soldiers had received Christmas presents from their own governments. Private E. H. Squire wrote, "Germans came out of theirs [the trenches] and we met halfway and talked and exchanged souvenirs our own bullets for theirs and they also gave some of our fellows cigars of which they said they had plenty and we gave them tins of bully beef as they said they had very little food." Officer Frank Black wrote, "Crowds of Germans came out and more of my men, till we formed a group of about 100, all shaking hands, and trying to make each other understood and exchanging souvenirs." Reporting on one of the real soccer games, Sergeant H. D. Bryan with the 1st Scots Guards, said that his side won "easily by 4–1," without adding anything about organization or play of the game.[24]

Naturally, it was a priority for both sides to decently bury the dead, and with a Christmas truce common funeral prayers were possible. D. Lloyd-Burch, with an ambulance corps, wrote that he "went to the East Lancer trenches and found the German and English troops burying the dead between the trenches[;] cigarettes and cigars were exchanged." A soldier named Pelham-Burn (no information about full name, rank, or unit) described a joint burial service, "read first in English by our own Padre and then in German by a boy who was studying for the ministry. It was an extraordinary most wonderful sight. The Germans formed up on one side the English on the other the officers standing in front, every head bared." Arthur Pelham-Burn, of the 6th Gordon Highlanders, also said that the collection of the dead bodies for the burial service was "too awful to describe so I won't attempt it." Whether at prayer or at play, soldiers remained aware of a possible breakdown in the quasi-truce. Frank Black, of the 1st Royal Warwicks, noted that the Germans far outnumbered his comrades and was happy to have his commanding officer order the troops back into their trenches. Another reported that he was ordered to stay awake all night. Middle ground was essential, because the officers and soldiers did not want the other side to get a close look at their own trenches. Most, though not all, of the official war diaries of the individual brigades of the English army corps also recorded these truces, which were notably absent from the corps commanded by General Douglas Haig and General Horace Smith-Dorrien. In some cases, the mention was very brief, and in others, defensive or apologetic—for example, the first advances were made by unarmed men from the German side. Serious consequences, threatened by the higher commands, did not occur, however. Crocker writes, "Of the leaders of the four army corps whose battalions were involved in the armistice, only General Smith-Dorrien of the II Corps threatened the officers of those battalions with any punishment for allowing the truce—and he backed down within forty-eight hours of receiving those officers' reports."[25]

The English newspapers provided extended coverage of the Christmas truces without extensive commentary. Crocker writes that "the press dealt with the 1914 armistice . . . in the same way as it handled accurate information about the conditions at the front and the attitudes of the English frontline troops." She quotes reports from the *Daily Telegraph, Manchester Guardian, Morning Post,* the *Times,* and the *Daily Mail* that appeared from 31 December 1914 up to 20 January 1915, with the sources generally characterized as letters home. In the *Telegraph*: a "merry Christmas together" with "sort of 'matey' conversation with the enemy," exchanges of cigarettes, and disappointment that a soccer game could not be brought off. The *Telegraph* printed other letters from soldiers who reported handshakes, and exchanges of buttons and hats after the carol singing and tree lighting. To the soldiers' surprise, there were Germans who spoke English and in some units "a great number of them had come from London. One man said he had lived in London for ten years, and he was going back." More details in the *Manchester Guardian*: a sort of soccer game with an empty beef can and a haircut by an enemy barber. The *Morning Post* quoted an army captain who described the Christmas carol scene and ended his account with the gracious remark, "Here the English soldiers and their adversaries mutually respect each other. And our officers certainly admire the Germans for putting up such a great fight, and this is quite the common opinion." The *Times* printed letters that clarified the detailed cease-fire arrangements behind the fraternizing, an indication that for some of the truces at least, both sides, especially the officers, wanted to take no chances

FIG. 9 An English newspaper photo of the Christmas 1914 fraternizing of German and English troops. Photo: Chronicle / Alamy Stock Photo.

on losing men or territory. The *Daily Mail* featured both anti-German editorials and touching soldiers' reports on mutual respect that characterized both the silly and the serious, as when a rabbit appeared and the soldiers quickly turned the moment into a match to catch the thing, even at the same time as the English chaplain and the German commander were trying to arrange burials. After this, "a sudden friendship had been struck up, the truce of God had been called, and for the rest of Christmas Day not a shot was fired along our section."[26]

The "truce of God" expression could cover a wide range of soldier thoughts about the day, from a sincere belief in the power of love as expressed in the Christmas gospels through the basic need for exhausted soldiers to have a little respite. This Christmas experience was given meaning by beliefs and memories of home. Malcolm Brown, in "The Christmas Truce 1914: the English Story," quotes one especially full letter, from Major Arthur Bates to his sister, evoking the Christmas Eves at home and appreciating the carols at the front: "In the ordinary way of things, my father would be making Rum Punch from an old family recipe, which had been written out by his grandfather, as was kept, of all places, in the Family Bible! Earlier, after the evening meal, we would have decorated the living rooms and hall with the traditional greenery, and would now be looking forward to wishing one another a 'Happy Christmas.'" But there he was in a muddy trench on the front looking out at a ruined landscape. "Then suddenly lights began to appear along the German parapet, which were evidently makeshift Christmas trees, adorned with lighted candles, which burnt steadily in the still, frosty air! Other sentries had, of course, seen the same thing, and quickly awoke those on duty, asleep in the shelters, to 'come and see this thing, which had come to pass.'"

With this reference in quotes to what has to be the story of the shepherds being convoked to Bethlehem, he begins his description of the carols.

> Then our opponents began to sing "*Stille Nacht, Heilige Nacht.*" . . . They finished their carol and we thought that we ought to retaliate in some way, so we sang "the First Nowell," and when we finished that they all began clapping; and then they struck up another favourite of theirs, "*O Tannenbaum.*" And so it went on. First the Germans would sing one of their carols and then we would sing one of ours, until when we started up "O Come All Ye Faithful," the Germans immediately joined in singing the same hymn to the Latin words "*Adeste Fideles.*" And I thought, well, this was really a most extraordinary thing—two nations both singing the same carol in the middle of the war.[27]

The French also fraternized with the Germans opposite, though there are not nearly as many reports. There, too, Christmas songs moved some of the soldiers to think of common humanity. The Frenchman Eugène Lemercier wrote: "What an outstanding night / a night beyond compare, where beauty triumphed, where despite its bloodstained failings, humanity showed the reality of its conscience. . . . Hymns, hymns everywhere. It was the everlasting search for humanity, the unquenchable springing of order in beauty and harmony." There were talented singers' voices out there, and the great carols, according to Eugène Pic: "At midnight, a few fine voices chanted the '*Minuit chrétien.*' They responded over there and a choir rang out in marvelous harmony with '*Stille Nacht! Heilige Nacht*'!"[28]

The experience of physically visible heavenly allies could have come out of everything from existential fear through shell shock, and they were experienced by a small number of soldiers. When the French and English were driven back toward Paris, narrow escapes at Mons (Belgium) and Le Cateau (France) engendered stories of angels and saints protecting the English forces. And when the French successfully held off the German armies at the Marne, outside of Paris and further along the river as far as Reims, stories of the visible intervention of Notre Dame and evocations of the Joan of Arc paralleled the ardent devotions back in Paris in public and private prayers. Some of this enthusiasm was tempered by church-approved interpretations such as the *Missel du Miracle de la Marne*. The *Missel* was a gather-all of vision-experience, Catholic devotion, and certainties of God's blessing, although it was available for and used by a miniscule group of French Catholics. Color images of soldiers marching and dying, their eyes trained heavenward as they went, and engravings of key events, both military (e.g., confronting the enemy) and religious (e.g., veneration of Saint Geneviève's relics at the church of Saint-Étienne du Mont), accompanied the earnest theology of "ordinary" miracles, written by Joan-of-Arc scholar, the abbé Stéphen Coubé. German trust in Saint Michael the archangel and the other angels also involved the eyes of faith but clearly came out of an ingrained national culture ("Nail figures" of Michael paired with nail figures of earthly heroes) and required popular participation. Stories of physically visible miraculous intervention on behalf of the French at the Marne and on behalf of the English at Mons in Belgium were both more sensational and more quirky. No real historical confirmation or theological justification of them has been possible.

As religious experiences, wayside wonders, so interpreted, are halfway between the visions and hallucinations, and the everyday devotions—which arose out of the spiritual imagination. Witnesses actually saw these shrine remnants and damaged churches; they did not have to evoke any miraculous appearances. But the unlikely survival of shrines and crucifixes in battle zones provided raw material for imaginary intervention stories; German picture postcards of these religious objects were as dramatic as the French missal engravings. For some English soldiers, nothing was more salient than the Virgin and child atop the basilica in the town of Albert, because shelling had knocked the statue perpendicular, causing both religious and human (a mother and child, after all) sympathy, and the fanciful notion that when the statue fell the war would end. What came of these sightings finally was the visionless realization that across the war participants had allies in heaven.

More generally, for soldier believers the pantheon of the Sacred Heart of Jesus, the Virgin Mary, and the patron saints proper to France and to Germany, were objects of pious and fanciful thoughts. This traditional religious devotion was, of course, war specific, infused as it was with hope for consolation and strength amid suffering and death.

But the simplest level of soldiers' religious experience involved mental pictures of home religion during a brief pause after five months of war for the feast of Christmas, famous for holiday trees and soccer games, and involving a bizarre range of soldier experiences. The truce was inspired by nostalgia, homesickness, war weariness, and awareness that the enemy soldiers were suffering the same horrors. It was also inspired by awareness of the peace message of the old Christian and European Feast of Christmas.

CHAPTER 3

God-Talk in the Armies
From Foot Soldiers to Generals

How could soldiers think faith, fatalism, or anything in the chaos of battle? The historian and novelist, Gerard Jaeger compares a 1915 Paris sermon about God's help in mortal danger with the haunted reflections of a soldier under machine-gun fire at Verdun to dramatize the difference between the home-front religious experience in time of war and the battle experience. A preacher could exude confidence, but "on the battle ground, under the bombs and in the slime, men trapped in front of the great mowing machine found in prayer only a comfort for their panic attacks . . . they were no more than kids who had seen phantoms." Here the soldiers have "phantasms, chimeras" that "crush them in the bestiary of their own fears." Such were the *imaginaires*. The instinctual, ferocious striving to survive, the rage in seeing companions torn up and destroyed, and seeing fields of bodies clouded men's minds. There were very few times when savagery was not, so to speak, obligatory, the most notable being in the air war, involving encounters that could have the quality of the joust—almost sportsmanlike. Otherwise, savage weapons, invented by scientists at home, were gratefully activated by soldiers to destroy the enemy, and worst of all was the gas, destroying bodies totally or almost totally. Soldiers had also to endure the absence of love of wife or girlfriends on a daily basis, so that all the complexities of sex that are central to human life added to the hell of a soldier's experience. If the marriage was a loving one and both partners could be sure of fidelity, the separation was all pain. If the soldier was promiscuous on the front or in nearby towns, and the spouse was meeting new partners at home, feelings of suspicion and betrayal ruined every reverie. Fear of pain and fear for life itself were attended by a host of other fears. It is remarkable that any God-talk could have emerged from all of this.[1]

"INARTICULATE" AND "DIFFUSIVE" CHRISTIANITY

Writing about the religion of the soldiers, a young English officer, Donald Hankey, reached a wide audience during the war. After some years of theological studies and even missionary work, he had declined ordination to the Anglican priesthood, and, at the beginning of the war, commission as an officer. For Hankey, the majority of the soldiers were naturally good men, and religious only in *that* sense, because they did not talk God. "It was when we had got out to Flanders, and were on the eve of our first visit to the trenches, that I heard the first definite attempt to discuss religion, and then it was only two or three who took part. Before falling asleep, a few of the men began to mock some of the stories and miracles of the Old and New Testaments." Hankey believed he could see real Christianity behind the façade of artificial religious indifference. "Here were men who believed absolutely in the Christian virtues of unselfishness, generosity, charity, and humility, without ever connecting them in their minds with Christ; and at the same time what they did associate with Christianity was just on a par with the formalism and smug self-righteousness which Christ spent His whole life trying to destroy." The chaplains of his experience had it wrong, Hankey says. "They saw the inarticulateness, and assumed a lack of any religion. They remonstrated with their hearers for not saying their prayers, and not coming to Communion, and not being afraid to die without making their peace with God." He concludes, "As a matter of fact, I believe that in a vague way lots of men do regard Christ as on their side. They have a dim sort of idea that He is misrepresented by Christianity, and that when it comes to the test He will not judge them so hardly as the chaplains do."[2]

By 1916 and the battle of the Somme, Hankey found it every bit as much of a challenge to make religious sense of the war for himself, as to make religious sense of the war for his soldiers. "Day and night we have done nothing but bring in the wounded and the dead. When one sees the dead, their limbs crushed and mangled, their features distorted and blackened, one can only have repulsion (revulsion) for war. It is easy to talk of glory and heroism when one is away from it, when memory has softened the gruesome details. But here, in the presence of the mutilated dead, one can only feel the horror and the wickedness of war." Hankey saw it all: pride, arrogance, lust for power,

FIG. 10 Donald Hankey, soldier and Anglican deacon, who praised the inarticulate but genuine Christianity of the men around him. Photo: Lebrecht Music & Arts / Alamy Stock Photo.

nothing but horror and pain—all these his labels—and hope. Introducing the theme of forgiveness of and suffering for sins, Hankey does not ask if human sins could have been so terrible as to merit this punishment. He compared soldiers' deaths to martyrdom in the early church, though his soldiers had "little of the fanatical exaltation of faith that the early Christians had to help them." No, Hankey is realistic, one might say, when he tries to portray these men as mostly quiet souls, loving their wives and children and the little comforts of home most of all, little stirred by great emotion or passions. Their virtues were undramatic—Hankey did not say "small"—in that "they had some love for liberty, some faith in God—not high flaming passion, but quiet insistent conviction." In fact, it was precisely because of their lack of (religious?) imagination that they suffered their way through it all: "It was enough to send them out to face martyrdom, though their lack of imagination left them mercifully ignorant of the extremity of its terror. It was enough, when they saw their danger in its true perspective, to keep them steadfast and tenacious."[3]

Such Christianity was a diffusive Christianity, a lowest common denominator of God and religion talk. In Hankey's England, "diffusive Christianity" was the expression that English churchmen were using at the beginning of the twentieth century to label a Christianity that comprised good neighborliness, friendliness to the church, and, on the part of the middle and upper classes, an appreciation of Anglicanism as a support of English identity. Apparently, the working classes appreciated most religion as a guide and moral code.[4] Two reports from the war years, an official *Army and Religion* report and the impressionistic *Catholic Soldiers* of Father Charles Plater, found evidence of a general and diffuse religious faith among the soldiers. A main ingredient of this faith was a fatalism that ran the gamut from a clearly religious submission to the "will of God" to the simple notion that you are wounded or die "when it's your time," religious belief in the broadest sense. One of the reporting clergy wrote, "The fatalist expression, 'My name may be on it,' was very common, and thoroughly accepted as true, but the men had only a vague notion of what it meant really, and if you pressed them, you found that their fatalism was, after all, Divine and Providential."[5] Indeed, the occasional but rare attempts to report the denominational adherence as "Fatalist" had no real success, because the label could mean anything. "Our correspondents differ a good deal on their interpretation of this sudden apparition of an ancient creed. Some associate with it the remarkable popularity of Omar Khayyam among the better educated men. Several are struck by its resemblance to the fighting creed of Islam, and one Scottish Presbyterian chaplain thinks it due to a re-awakening of the Calvinism which has been the hereditary creed of Scotland."[6]

Belief in amulets and visions (one's own or other soldiers') were everyday versions of standard religion, according to English chaplains and soldiers. The Bible itself, or objects such as pictures and prayer beads could be used as good luck charms in place of or alongside an orthodox religious use. Arthur Smith, an English staff officer on the front through much of the war, certainly not admitting that the Bible was a good luck charm, believed that it had saved his life on one occasion. "Presented to him by his father and bearing on its flyleaf a text from the 91st Psalm ('Because thou hast made the Lord thy refuge. There shall no evil befall thee. For he shall give his angels charge over thee to keep thee in all thy ways'), Smith had been hit by a piece of shrapnel that had 'cut right through the Bible until that page in the Psalms from which the text was taken.' According to Smith, 'that to me was a very significant thing and encouraged my faith.'" The opposite could happen and apparently did. For example, a Methodist chaplain reported that a soldier had been killed by a bullet that "had gone straight through the Greek Testament in the boy's breast-pocket." Catholic rosaries and image-bearing medals in particular lent themselves to good-luck use and were even sought by non-Catholic soldiers. In the field, battles occasionally overran shrines and statues (some of them on churches, of course), and these, too, took on the quality of amulets—community amulets, in a sense.[7]

German chaplains recorded a gradual makeover of religious life as the war went on. The young men had to discover a religious meaning in violence if they were to preserve the high spirits in place at their departure, and of course it was their home religious upbringing they were processing in all that. Heroism and trust in God were expressed in Christian devotion that tended to evolve into a combination of fatalism and superstition. Crises at home destroyed earlier illusions.[8]

Even if the majority of the soldiers were inarticulate, there were still vast numbers of them who could express their beliefs and moral views, although there is no way to do complete justice to "the complex mental worlds of soldiers on the western front."[9]

LETTER-WRITING SOLDIERS

According to one very rough estimate, French soldiers alone wrote about four million letters a day for every day of the war. Six billion, two hundred and forty million letters! And perhaps just as many came back from the home front. Rough estimates also give us an idea of the letters exchanged on a daily basis between soldiers and the people at home: for Germany, seven million, and for England, one to two million—counting from and to the front for both countries.[10]

The letters contained only limited news about the soldier's military action. In the French case, the reasons are clear, principally the censure of letters from and to the front. Martyn Lyons worked over the correspondence at the French Army archives, finding little spontaneity or originality. The men could do little more than repeat political, religious, and personal clichés because of postal censorship and the trying circumstances of the front. Soldiers didn't want authorities to know what they were thinking, nor their loved ones to know the horrors of life on the front. Lyons says that "Soldiers' writing leaves us with an overwhelming sense of banality." He quotes the French soldier novelist, Maurice Genevoix, who complained that it was impossible to write much more than "good health," "lots of hope," and he quotes the French scholar, Annick Cochet to this effect: "The soldiers made many sacrifices, including the sacrifice of their own sincerity. What they reported to civilians was the civilians' war: their own war was a secret." Lyons and others were looking for details about the battles and personal suffering, discounting expressions of love and religious feeling, both placed in relief by Martha Hanna in her praise of the letters as excellent sources of soldiers' personal expression.[11]

This leaves us with millions of letters that were in some way "articulate" about faith and morals. During the war and in the decade and a half after it, several collections—German, French, and English—were published, each of them considered by the editor of the volume to represent typical responses to the basic frontline war experiences. Gerd Krumeich revisited the question of letter anthologies and how editors represented more interesting personalities and more patriotic expression, praising Philipp Witkop for choosing the theme of "fallen students," who represented a variety of vocations and social classes. But he notes that "today we can no longer determine the criteria according to which Witkop chose which letters to publish, and whether he really published them in precisely their original form."[12]

Witkop's collection of German soldier letters appeared in Germany in 1916, 1918, and again in 1928; the English translation came a year later in 1929. He chose them from about twenty thousand letters that were made available to him by the German Ministry of Education. The English translation was reprinted in 2002, with a necessary reorientation by Jay Winter, who clarifies Witkop's role as "a patriot and liberal intellectual," focusing on the wisdom and generosity of the letter writers. The soldiers were students in law, architecture, theology, and philosophy, and so, of course, hardly "inarticulate."[13]

Franz Blumenfeld, the law student, joined the army without enthusiasm, not really believing that things would get any further than mobilization. He told his mother that some home defense might be necessary and that refusal to help here would only be cowardice. On the train through Belgium, he wrote, "Even yet one can't realize the war in earnest, and I keep catching myself simply enjoying all the novel impressions," the most rewarding of which was the earlier experience in Lorraine: a chaotic soldier-gathering in a peasant living room, with two old women ladling out soup and serving coffee. He thought war was an "evil thing," but was ready to sacrifice for the fatherland. In fact, he thought that readiness to sacrifice was more important than the object, or goal, of the sacrifice. War was "inhuman, mad, obsolete, and in every way depraving," and somehow he had to help ensure that it would never take place again. Blumenfeld saw the death and destruction and lived through the awful weather, the lack of food, and the gross living conditions at the front but professed to be inured to all that. What he really feared was his own loss of humanity, asking, "What is the good of escaping all the bullets and shells, if my soul is injured?" and labeling his underlying sentiment "spiritual loneliness."[14]

Herbert Weisser, a technical school student in architecture, was more convinced than Blumenfeld of the righteousness of the German cause and the greatness of the German character, with its discipline, dedication to the general good, sense of justice, and culture. "Other nations can tear down and destroy in war, but we understand, better than any other, how to build up, and of this I have been certain only since the beginning of the war." This he holds to, whether or not Germany wins the war. Furthermore, he has nothing against individual Frenchmen and regrets all loss of life. He thought that fear or death and belief in the afterlife had been worked out by his fellow soldiers, and he hoped to survive at least in what he "had created" and "in the influence . . . exercised on the younger generation." He cannot feel particular sympathy for the fathers of families, because they have been loved by their wives and have transmitted their heritage to the children. Traditional views of the heroism in war covered up the "bloodthirstiness and unjust hatred which a nation's political views spread among its members." Nonheroic also were the vices: drunkenness, brutality, spiritual and physical laziness, unfaithfulness; he was haunted by memories of the flaming villages.[15]

A theology student, Alfons Ankenbrand combined a take-down of war as heroic with his own religious consciousness. As did many others, he was angered at the newspaper reports that praised the gains but said nothing of the blood that was shed and the "cries of agony that never cease." The newspaper readers do not see how their heroes are often buried in the trenches they die in. His religion was based on faith and commitment—hardly fatalism. He wrote, "I have commended my soul to the Lord God. It bears His seal and is altogether His. Now I am free to dare anything. My future life belongs to God, my present one to the Fatherland, and I myself still possess happiness and strength."[16]

A philosophy student, Kurt Peterson, raged against the evil of war, even as he raced into battle. "Away with this vile abortion brought forth by human wickedness!" His anger is reserved in the letter for those who cause this thing where "human-beings are slaughtering thousands of other human-beings, whom they neither know, nor hate, nor love." "Cursed be those who . . . bring it to pass! May they all be utterly destroyed, for they are brutes and beasts of prey!" The next day's sun and the possibility to once again commune with nature made him a human-being again, resolved to rebuild human culture at the end of the war, "if the Almighty grants me a safe and happy return." And he inserts a prayer to the "Guide of the Universe" before he concludes the letter to his parents with an "Adieu."[17]

Johannes Haas, a divinity student, wondered as the war began whether he should become a clergyman, feeling forced to decide for or against God. But the war itself brought only doubt and irresolution. He rejected the easy ethical solutions of the preachers back home, and he could barely trust his own conscience because he believed it to be clouded by the self-preservation instinct. "One looks with astonishment and horror at the more and more cunningly elaborate means devised for destroying the enemy." The dilemma lay in the opposed obligations: to the fatherland and to the sacred law to murder not. While militarism is an evil, devotion to duty is not. Germans have more of a sense of duty than others, "and so we stick to this ghastly war."[18]

There was no lack of ethical and devotional reflections in other letters. Christmas with its message of love can, in spite of war, produce more love than ever (of God and one's own people). One soldier felt that he was safe in the hands of God and destined for resurrection and life, because he acknowledged Christ as savior. Before Christmas, another soldier used his entire brief letter to evoke the Christ child . . . "on this Holy Eve." The sharing of goods reminded another of the "Early Christian community . . . which ordains the sharing of everything as one of the highest virtues." One aviator was so sure of his death that to his mother he quoted the Bible passage "Be thou faithful unto death and I will give thee a crown of life." Resignation to God's will could be a profound faith experience, all the more joyfully experienced after having coming through a battle safely. When all self-regard is gone, said one soldier, one achieves contemplation of "the region in which God lives." If these testimonies are to be believed, a soldier can get beyond ethics and devotion and into contemplation.[19]

In 1922, a committee headed by Marshal Foch published the collection entitled *La dernière lettre écrite par des soldats français tombés au champ d'honneur 1914–1918* (The Last Letter Written by French Soldiers Fallen on the Field of Honor 1914–1918), a recent edition of which appeared in 2014. Letters were submitted by families who wanted to share their sons' last words, and so making this a highly selective collection, emphasizing the faith and culture of the family. Letters detailed the soldiers' reception of the sacraments, confession and communion in particular. A sublieutenant at Douaumont reported an evening mass "for the living and dead," where the curé knew exactly what to say to the men, then asked all who wished for absolution (normally after individual confession) to kneel. All the men in the partially destroyed cathedral knelt and then went to communion. With the artillery in the background, the priest assigned a penance, "Go and fight." Leaving the service, the soldier heard in his heart, "Happy are those who believe," and wrote, "I have seen impressive masses, I have seen such difficult things, but never have I been as moved." A soldier wrote his mother shortly before the battle of the Marne that he just went to confession to a local curé, who gave him a religious medal he was happy to have. A pilot on the western front, obviously a grateful Catholic, wrote that when his plane is shot down, he will be filled with peace and sing "Gloria in excelsis Deo." At the end, suffering and death, but for him it will be "a full 'Magnificat' ['(My soul) magnifies (the Lord)']: the praise of adoration to the one God, great and merciful, a prayer of thanksgiving for all that has been given to me with such generosity from every direction, a prayer of expiation for all that I have omitted and all that I have done; and then a supplication that cannot go unheard, asking for eternal life, strength, and consolation for those I leave behind."[20]

Expressions of strong faith included devotional details. "I live in continual communion with God," wrote one soldier to his wife, before he was killed in the third week of the war. He told her, too, of a pilgrimage promise he had made to the Blessed Virgin, when the family would be reunited. For a soldier, writing to his parents, death for France would be "beautiful" because it has been "the kingdom of the Blessed Virgin"; he is certain that he will be "with God" and so undeserving of their tears. More often, expressions of devotion and faith included some element of resignation, often from soldiers who had been wounded or were about to begin a major attack. One lieutenant wrote his mother that they would be reunited in heaven, in eternal happiness. This resignation was expressed as reliance on divine providence and not as unadorned fatalism. "I am the child of God and nothing will happen to me that is not in conformity with his will," wrote a soldier who labeled himself as "serene" to his sister. Another soldier used the expression "in the heart of God" to explain that he was completely dependent upon divine providence. He hoped the family would not mourn; with submission to the will of God, they would all be reunited in heaven. One lad who had volunteered at age seventeen wrote to his girlfriend that God's will must be done and not theirs: "God will decide my fate." The men with strong faith often thanked their parents for it at the same time. For example: "I ask your pardon for all the hurt I may have caused you, and I thank you with all my heart because you have raised me in our religion, and I pray to God to bless you for that."[21]

Still and all, the evil of the enemy must not be left unpunished. From his parents, one soldier learned that duty comes first, although the sentiment ultimately came from God, "whom you taught me to see as the source of the destiny of peoples and of families." Learning that his brother had died on the front, a soldier wrote his parents that God, "in his mercy," would unite them all again. If God lets him live, however, he will avenge his brother. More than vengeance, hatred was sometimes called for. The soldier who recognized the will of God in the descent into chaos and rejected all opposition to his will as he wrote to his parents also told them to "hate the Germans, source of so many crimes and misfortunes," though they should not lament his own death but should work instead for the greater glory of France.[22]

Corresponding to the Witkop-edited *German Students' War Letters*, the soldier correspondence edited by Laurence Housman, brother of the poet, in *War Letters of Fallen Englishmen* show the men to be pragmatic and equally serious. Jay Winter also sets this collection in context, emphasizing especially Housman's "search for the sacred": "[He] looked for spirituality, for a sense of beauty and for a kind of courtesy and kindness that embodied what he took to be the best of the men who had gone to war in 1914."[23] The aristocratic Julian Grenfell wrote "[War] is like a big picnic without the objectlessness of a picnic," although he pitied the misery of the local families (and their animals). His were sporting thoughts: "One loves one's fellow man much more when one is bent on killing him." Accordingly, he admired a captured German officer who returned his scowls and curses with a dignified salute. Admitting to frayed nerves after many hours of shelling, he reported on a successful sniper expedition when he caught a German in his sights, laughing and talking so that he could see the teeth glistening. It was a success he was clearly happy to report. The down to earth Melville Hastings lamented the death of a young German officer whom he found hanging by one leg from the ceiling of the trench. "Get the harrowing details out of the mind; remember only the faithful service," he said, and he advised forgetting hatred, forgetting their "nastiness" and remembering "our own" instead. The hatred within one's self provides the real hell. Clearly his inspiration here is Christ and Christianity: "All the world over a boy is a boy and a mother is a mother. One there was Who after thirty years of thinking appealed to *all* mankind, and not in vain." Think of the poor young German, think of his poor mother—Hastings was even happy to be reconciled to the little dog from the German line who, in no-man's land, ran over to lick his face. He cannot forget how many Germans and English knew one another, worked with one another—settling in each other's countries—before the war. He tells stories of Germans on the front who declined to shoot, who even liberated himself and later one of his friends, the first German soldier calling out with a laugh—"Hallo Johnny Bull"—and the second revealing that he was an Oxford graduate who had begged not to be posted to the English front.[24]

Soldiers who did not renounce religion themselves were aware that religious expression was a turn-off for their companions. The officer Christian Carver wrote to his brother about the "semi-aversion" to religion, saying, "I find, in this sort of job, that I have to pray." He looked up to "a God of Hope, and the Kingdom." In fact, he worked to picture heaven as he ran through the mud amid explosions and corpses. Clearly high church, officer John Engall wrote to his parents three days before he died that he had taken communion the day before, "and never have I attended a more impressive service. I placed my soul and body in God's keeping." And, looking to the future, the Irishman Thomas Kettle wrote his wife that, if he survived, he would "accept it as a special mission to preach love and peace for the rest of my life. . . . writing and working to drive out of civilization this foul thing called war." Deep devotion combined with patriotism in the words of a private Roger Livingston writing to his mother: "The very principles for which Christ gave His life are identically those principles for which Britain is today giving her life-blood." Somehow, he took this nationalism-inspired selflessness to be Christ's own— as "first martyr to the cause." It was the old laying down one's life for one's friends that made the comparison possible. Edward Tennant, two days before his death, assured his mother that he took Holy Communion and was carrying his medal of the Blessed Virgin. Nevertheless, it was easy to lose faith, given the destruction of human bodies by artillery and bombing. What could it mean? "I don't believe even God knows." And Peter Layard was torn between the mystery of why God could let those artillery shells explode and why he himself survived explosions that killed others near him.[25]

Sergeant Ernest Boughton, a stockbroker's clerk in civilian life, presented an elaborate literary evocation of a soldier who experienced the beauty of the fields, the chaos in the trenches, the cemeteries, and finally a beautiful church and a glorious service within. One wonders if he is describing his own experience—the evocation is written in the third person—or a synthesis of experiences. In the church scene he wanders free after the battle, entering a town where the church tower was visible in the distance. It is a saint's day, the French congregation is singing a "litany," the choral music is inspiring, the altar is brightly lit, the priest's voice is solemn, and light floods through the stained-glass windows. The scenario includes the singing of an "intermezzo" and a finale of an organ sonata at the end. Such a contrast, then, between "the soft world of artistic susceptibility and the present life of the armed camp." The soldier passes the sentries and the noisy village tavern as he finishes his reveries. In one case—one wonders how typical—thoughts of his lady love give John Rapoport faith and assurance. He writes her that the two of them have such faith that God will see them through: "I feel sure God would never have let us love each other as we do if he was going to get rid of me." All his letters here are filled with love phrases, flowing and sweet. A small, personalized compendium of Christian theology, political and personal, was divided across several letters the officer Eric Lubbock sent his mother. The Christianity that is proposed for private life must be proposed for public life, and the war is ensuring that Christianity will be so applied. "We should feel proud that we are suffering for that step and sweating blood to help the world, as One once sweated blood before to save it." Death—and he does not want his mother to grieve—has to be the beginning of something better or life, with all its unfairness and evil, could make no sense. To say that death is a perfect sleep and the end of all cares is not enough: "If this imperfect world with all its passions, sorrows and griefs" is all that there is, "then the great Giver of Life is but a torturer." The human desire and striving for good is the sign that God is good, and that this life is preparation for another. He urges his mother, "Let your love for me conquer pain and bless the chance that brings me to Eternal Joy."[26]

Hell-talk existed alongside God-talk, although it found little place in the classical letter collections. Edward Madigan, in his *Faith Under Fire*, quotes English soldiers who found preached religion worse than ineffectual for themselves and for their companions. Private J. Bowles rejected the chaplain's idea that war made people serious and pushed them toward the comforts of religion. On the contrary, men would fight and die, yelling and cursing, and surely with little or no thought of religion. For Bowles, "in war there is no place for a God of Love" and no likelihood of worrying about future punishment when their lives at the front were hell already ("that the devil himself would be proud to reign over.") Similar thoughts, eloquently expressed, from Major C. E. Lyne during the third battle of Ypres; for him, it was beyond anything that Dante had imagined: "a half formed horror of a childish nightmare. . . . Surely the God of Battles has deserted a spot where only devils can reign." "Days are terrible; nights are terrible; weeks are without end; shells, rain, mud, and gas together make the "inferno."[27]

In general, French army soldiers from Arab North Africa and sub-Saharan Africa were Muslim, and English army soldiers from India were either Muslim or Hindu. Each of these colonial armies, French and English, has received serious attention from Richard S. Fogarty and David Omissi, showing that colonial soldiers could express their loyalty-relationship to France and England, and acknowledge the sustaining power of their religious identity in ways similar to the Christians and Jews from the mainland. Political and military authorities, for their part, worked to accommodate the soldiers' political or ethnic sentiments and their religious sentiments. German authorities never contemplated the use of troops from their own colonies and were critical of both France and England for doing so.

From letter collections of colonial soldiers in the French and English armies, and American soldiers fighting beside the French, we can catch a glimpse of religious experiences. In the French army there were two overlapping types of Islam: Arab Islam, with its aura or originality and authenticity, and the more recently converted ethnic groups from West and Central Africa. Fogarty writes that this led French authorities to simple and not particularly useful distinctions. "The stark contrast between this stereotype of relaxed West Africans practicing a relatively benign 'Islam *noir*' and that of 'fanatical' North African Muslims was decisive in shaping French military attitudes and policies."[28] The presumably more orthodox North Africans might take seriously the role of the Turkish sultan as the guarantor of Muslim orthodoxy and so be tempted to disloyalty—to the point of crossing over to the enemy when confronting the German ally, Turkey. North Africans were also most accustomed to a system of clergy, Imams, whose services were unavailable to the troops, at least on the front lines. Notable, however, was the figure of Lieutenant Si Brahim, of a prominent Muslim Algerian family, who promoted total loyalty to France and also served as a prayer leader for burials and a spiritual counselor.[29] Muslim dietary laws preoccupied both French army officials and the Algerian soldiers. Some, certainly, drank wine and were more interested in eating than in a religiously correct diet. Sincerely loyal Muslims, however, gave the matter serious thought, as did an Algerian soldier quoted at length by Gilbert Meynier.

> I can't even find the Qibla [direction of the Kaaba in Mecca].... I still say my prayers, cleansing myself with sand because I cannot take off my clothes or do my ablutions completely.... The meat is served to us in platters, but we do not know if it is lawful or unlawful, and this

is a source of torment for me: I think about it night and day, and you must tell me what my current situation is with regard to Allah. Know, my dear brother, that I shall never abandon my faith even if I were assailed with more terrible misfortunes than I find myself in at present. I am not boasting by telling you this, I am inspired by Allah. I ask him to help me remain faithful and to bring me through.[30]

Muslim soldiers were in the main loyal to Islam and to France, with the exception of a few men captured by the Germans and subject to German pro-Turkish propaganda at their internment camp.[31]

Indian troops joined the English forces in France in the first months of the war, building to 28,500 across the winter, and by the end of the war had contributed 827,000 combatants. Regarding their religion, Omissi writes, "For the most part, the soldiers' consciously stated religious beliefs were fairly orthodox: several Hindus, for example, suggest that defeat in battle would release them from the cycle of death and rebirth, rewarding them with immediate Paradise."[32] He adds that war did cause them to moderate the rigidity of some beliefs (e.g., diet) and the regularity of some practices (e.g., daily observance). In the Omissi edition of Indian soldier letters, Hindu, Muslim, and Sikh soldiers speak of similar concerns. The Hindu Garhwali Subedar wrote in February of 1915, "It is a noble fate for us to be allowed to sacrifice our bodies for our King. If our ancestors help us and God shows us favour, if we die on the battlefield in the service of our King, this is equal to entering heaven."[33] And Sonu Gaekwar wrote in August of 1915, "Even if my life should be lost, . . . such an opportunity to die is never likely to recur. Such a death is a true liberation from future birth."[34] Indian soldiers of the Sikh faith (a little over 20 percent) received as much attention from military officials as the Muslims. Omissi writes, "When English military censors noted complaints in Sikh soldiers' letters about the shortage of Sikh religious artefacts, for example, the Indian Soldiers' Fund commissioned a cutlery firm in Sheffield to make steel daggers, bracelets and combs for Sikhs to an approved pattern." And Indian authorities sent religious objects and prayer books from home.[35]

Christian troops from the colonies, such as Catholics from Vietnam, Protestants from Madagascar, and Anglicans from India, were less of a challenge. They could benefit from the ministries of the regular French and English chaplains, although the ethnic differences introduced misunderstandings that Europeans did not experience.

As for the Americans fighting beside the French troops, Jonathan Ebel argues that the soldiers "believed in the communal and personal value of their errand, believed that in answering the call of arms, they were answering the call of their faith. Experiences of the Great War altered but did not undermine their beliefs."[36] Letters, but also some diaries and memoirs, are the sources here. Ebel highlights the value of the army publication *Stars and Stripes*, as well as a collection of published and unpublished sources in the New York Public Library. For some Americans it was a war to guarantee the fulfillment of God's will for the whole world as well as for the United States. For others, such as the Massachusetts native Elmer Harden, "a soldier's life is a series of miraculous escapes, or else we must believe in fatality."[37] Luck, fatality: it was all the same thing. Imitation of Christ's suffering and the Christian tradition of martyrdom were held in balance with the imperative to fight and kill for the sake of justice. Formation in the Protestant or Catholic traditions came across clearly, as in the view of heaven of the Irish American soldier, Joyce Kilmer, who highlighted the archangel Michael and the Irish saints Patrick, Bridget, and Columbkill.[38] A positive but enigmatic—and certainly not traditionally religious—sentiment was expressed by Quincy Mills to his mother. "For yourself, I would have you bear in mind the immortal philosophy placed by Maeterlinck in the mouths of Mytyl and Tytyl [happiness-seeking brother and sister in *L'Oiseau bleu*]: 'Where are the dead? There are no dead.' In my brief experience in the army no truth has been driven home to me so forcibly as this. Live by it."[39] The varieties of the Spiritualist movements that were current in Europe inspired some American soldiers and their families: everything from the immortality that human memory gives to the departed through the conviction that communication between the dead and the living would be possible.

Jewish soldiers, nearly 250,000 of them, served in the American army. As with the European Jews, preservation of Jewish identity while attaining first-class citizenship was a cultural goal. Rabbi Stephen S. Wise wrote in the *New York Times* that their military service "mark[ed] the burial, without hope of resurrection, of hyphenism [Jewish-American], and will token the birth of a united and indivisible country." Julius Kahn, chairman of the House Military Affairs Committee during the war, said, "I desire to congratulate my co-religionists on the splendid showing they are making in the matter of serving our country in this war." Soldier testimonies, randomly gathered, are still, at the centennial of the war, only minimally accessible.[40] Also still to be mined is a collection of surveys filled out by African American soldiers during the war and now digitized by the University of Virginia. But the history of the African American experiences in the decades after the war is a separate study, already initiated by Richard Slotkin for the racist treatment of the men in America and Jennifer Boittin for their postwar reception in France.[41]

THE GENERALS: IDENTITY OF NATIONAL AND PERSONAL RELIGION

Supreme commanders of the first war years, in the main, took religion quite seriously. Their faith does not appear to be closely related to fear of their own deaths, as it did with the frontline soldiers, but belonged, rather, to their self-image, a combination of early family experience and cultural loyalty. Helmuth von Moltke, who began the war as the German chief of staff, was a cultural Protestant who was attracted also to Spiritualism. Paul von Hindenburg was a loyal Lutheran whose family could make the case that they were descended from Martin Luther. Crown Prince Rupprecht of Bavaria was rigorously schooled in the Catholicism that had marked the Wittelsbach dynasty since the Reformation, although he scandalized family and tutors by his skepticism.[42] Ferdinand Foch, supreme commander of the French and Allied forces the last year of the war was so noted for his traditional Catholicism that even the anticlerical premier Georges Clemenceau would not disturb him at worship. There were other generals, de Castelnau in particular, who were members of the aristocratic Catholic families that found a place for their young men in the French army across the secularizing years of the Third Republic governments.[43] Douglas Haig, the English supreme commander for the greater part of the war and arguably more responsible for more deaths than any other, was a dedicated Calvinist with a high appreciation of Anglicanism, having attended Anglican services across the greater part of his life. The ranking Anglican chaplain for the western front, Bishop Llewellyn Henry Gwynne, was pleased with the religious seriousness of other principal generals, including Herbert Plumer (Second Army), Julian Byng (Third Army), Hubert Gough (First Army) and Henry Horne (First Army).[44]

Helmuth von Moltke, successor to his uncle, the von Moltke of the Franco-Prussian War, and Alfred von Schlieffen himself, was appointed chief of the general staff in 1906. Negative comments, in the press at least, outnumbered the positive, criticizing in particular his philosophical and cultural preoccupations. He read the German historians, Treitschke and Theodore Mommsen, as well as Thomas Carlyle and, bizarrely, the racist Houston Stewart Chamberlain. His recent biographer, Annika Mombauer, adds that "his letters attest to his anti-Semitic, xenophobic, nationalistic and monarchist views and demonstrate clearly his bellicose designs from the 1880s onwards." His religious interests were not nationalistic, in that he was taken with Spiritualism and the occult, to the chagrin of the Kaiser's brother-in-law, who fumed about "that wretched faith-healing, this first-class nonsense that the Moltke family practices with a vigour worthy of better things." Moltke's wife was a dirigée of Rudolf Steiner, founder of the quasi-Spiritualist system Anthroposophy, and he himself was also under Steiner's influence. The chief of the military cabinet was reported to have said that "he [Moltke] was a religious dreamer, [who] believed in guardian angels, faith-healing, and similar nonsense." Moltke began contact with Steiner a few years before appointment of chief of general staff and remained in contact until his own death in 1916. From Moltke himself, we have the testimony that he once explained Anthroposophy and Theosophy while on the royal yacht: "Because I was the only one who knew something about these matters I had to lead the conversation. At first some laughed, then they became more and more serious and in the end they listened to me as to the priest in church." The Kaiser himself, despite a reputed interest in Spiritualism, told Moltke to stop "dabbling" in Spiritualism on becoming chief of the general staff. For Moltke, Anthroposophy was the faith, described by Robert Galbreath in *Spiritual Science* as a fusion of scientific and religious postures, concern with inherent meaning, emphasis placed on spiritual wholeness in an age of fragmentation, and positive attitude to the nonrational facets of man. The part of Spiritualism that emphasized contacts with other worlds put off Moltke, but he respected his wife's preoccupation with it. He wrote her, after the beginning of the war and after a brief meeting with Steiner, "If I do not accompany you on all your journeys then this is because I have a very real profession and have to remain with both feet firmly on the ground, as long as I want to do justice to that profession."[45]

Ferdinand Foch was born into a very devout Catholic family in Tarbes, not that far from Lourdes, in fact. He received Jesuit schooling along with his younger brother, who went on to be a Jesuit priest. After the baccalaureate, he did more months at the Jesuit college Saint Clément at Metz, noted for successfully preparing students for entrance into the École Polytechnique. A successful student, he suffered from the climate, so different from his Tarbes in the Pyrénées.

After the victory on the Marne, upon entering Châlons, he countered the praise of the bishop of Châlons with the Latin, "*Non nobis, Domine, non nobis, sed nomini tuo da gloriam*" ("Not to us, O Lord, not to us, but to your name give glory"). That this was more than just avoiding hubris, became clear when he learned of the 22 August battle deaths of his son and son-in-law, both of them in the army of General Maurice Sarrail. Foch trembled, it was reported, and then asked his staff to leave him alone for a short while. Readmitted, they tried to console him, but he insisted that they all immediately get back to work. A week later he wrote to his old mentor General Millet:

> Bécourt and my son were killed on the twenty-second of August near Yprecourt, on the Belgian frontier. I heard of it on the thirteenth and I have discreetly broken the news to my wife, who is still at Ploujean. One ought to disregard everything, and yet I quake as I think of the disturbance which is bound to occur there, to the grief of my poor womenfolk. For my part I am steeling myself on this subject so as not to fail in my duty. The cruel sacrifice we are making ought not to remain sterile. I am working to this end with all the energy of which I am capable, absolutely full of confidence in the issue of the fight, with the help of God.[46]

During the last German offensive, he had to deal with English anxieties over his counter-offensive plans for his (and their) troops. At his headquarters, all was order and punctuality, with "the austere simplicity and regularity of life in a cloister," Liddell Hart was at pains to point out. He would rise at six in the morning and walk to the village church for morning prayers, High Mass on Sundays, "following in his book the prayers of the Mass . . . and when the tinkle of the bell announced the beautiful invocation, 'Holy, holy, holy, Lord God of hosts,' humbly kneeling and so remaining until the end of the oblation of the divine sacrifice." When an urgent message came from Clemenceau, Foch was in church. To the messengers he said, "You see, when I have some free moments—and that does not often happen—I spend them in this abode. Nevertheless, I'm a bad Christian, for frequently, instead of praying, I allow myself to slip into meditation on profane matters, on operations I'm preparing, but the Lord, I'm sure, will not be angry with me. For always, when I leave his temple, I feel stronger and above all less uncertain— it's there very often that I've taken the most grave decisions on the war." Then, after the armistice, as the French army moved back into the lost territories of Alsace and Lorraine, Foch wanted in particular to go with them to Metz, where he had once been a student. He was entranced. "To see French

FIG. 11 General Ferdinand Foch with the French Catholic churchman, Bishop Stanislas Touchet, not long after the war. Photo: The History Collection / Alamy Stock Photo.

troops marching past on the Place de l'Hôtel de Ville at Metz was the reward for all my efforts," and at the end of the ceremony he said, "Now I am going to thank the Lord of Hosts for having granted me the victory." Of this visit to the cathedral, he wrote, "I always used to tell myself, in the old days, that I should not like to die till I could hang up my sword, as a votive offering, on the wall of Metz Cathedral. Oh, I shall do it! I have promised!" There was a certain closure to his mission when, the day after the 14 July 1919 victory celebration in London, he stole off to go to High Mass in Westminster Cathedral: passing before the statue of Joan of Arc, behind which hung the French and English flags, he stopped, paused, and made a profound genuflection. Ferdinand Foch, as he lived out his profoundly ingrained Catholic life, had said, "Once my motto was Knowledge and Faith. I still keep it, but now say, rather, Faith and Knowledge. Yes, Faith first. . . . for that is what matters more."[47]

Douglas Haig's strong Presbyterian background provided the ideal religious fatalism for his military mission. Other key English generals relied in the main on a reverent Anglicanism that appears more devotional than doctrinal. Michael Snape notes that among the upper- and upper-middle-class families of the officers, regular church going, basic Bible knowledge, and prayers at home were taken for granted. Haig, then, "developed a habit of prayer, a sense of divine oversight and a great familiarity with scripture at an early age, being required to send [his mother] commentaries on selected biblical passages every week while at school." His sister encouraged his prewar interest in Spiritualism, an auxiliary confirmation (Napoleon was flourishing in the spirit world) of his convinced Christianity. By the time he became commander-in-chief, he could write to his wife, "All seem to expect success as the result of my arrival, and somehow give me the idea that I am 'meant to win' by some Superior Power."[48]

Haig acquired a Presbyterian personal chaplain, George S. Duncan, whose theology of providence and dramatic preaching to the soldiers he admired, and by the end of the war he was allowing Duncan access to his personal diary, a combination of daily record and religious thoughts. To his wife, as the battle of the Somme was about to begin, Haig sent this message, "You must know that *I feel* that every step in my plan has been taken with the Divine help and I ask daily for aid, not merely in making the place, but in carrying it out, and this I hope I shall continue to do until the end of all things which concern me on earth. I think it is the Divine help which gives me tranquility of mind and enables me to carry on without feeling the strain of responsibility to be too excessive." The next day, of course, he lost twenty thousand men and suffered another forty thousand casualties, ever so many more than the biblical version of Israel's God suffered King Jehoshaphat to lose while battling the Moabites and Ammonites (2 Chronicles 20:15), a biblical passage that consoled him two years later when repulsing the 1918 German offensive. In his diary he also compared the fate of Germany and the fate of ancient Assyria. This spiritual self-confidence was defended as a virtue by Duncan, who wrote that "Haig was no fanatic. There was about him a mental balance which was associated not a little with his stern sense of duty.... He takes his place with those heroic figures (like Moses and Joshua in the Scripture records, or like Cromwell and Lincoln in the story of the nations)." But General John Charteris (who figured curiously in our story of the Angels of Mons tradition) feared the "fatalistic" qualities of Haig's religion, because, as Snape puts it, "the will of a providence as to the outcome of the war was far from clear" and "the same sermons that Haig found so inspiring could quite easily have given heart to Hindenburg."[49]

Duncan reported in *Douglas Haig as I Knew Him* that Haig would write brief comments on Sunday sermons: usually the theme and biblical passage highlighted. In his chapter entitled "The Man of Faith," Duncan purports to distinguish the real Haig from the stereotypes: religious, sincere, and solid, without fanaticism or presumption. According to Duncan, Haig never invoked special divine help or protection in addressing his troops, or any others—not even in private conversation. Only in replying to his wife's injunction to seek divine help before the battle of the Somme did he admit to such invocations. Once Duncan did press him for a general reaction to the battles of Mons and Ypres, and he answered, "This is what you once read to us from Second Chronicles: 'Be not afraid nor dismayed by reason of this great multitude; for the battle is not yours, but God's' [2 Chronicles 20:15]." He was a little more forthcoming in response to a personal note that Duncan sent in the middle of the dark days of Germany's all-out attack of 1918.

> My dear Duncan,
> One line to thank you most truly for your letter. I am very grateful for your thinking of me at this time, and I know I am sustained in my efforts by that Great Unseen Power, otherwise I could not be standing the strain as I am doing
> Yours most truly, D. Haig
> I missed my Sunday morning greatly. But it could not be helped.

Duncan felt compelled to interpret further, however, with a scriptural aside to highlight Haig's combination of "realism" and "*élan vital.*" Duncan added a short list of scripture quotes that Haig sent him after the war: (1) "Fear thou not, for I am with thee; be not dismayed" etc. . . . as far as "with the right hand of my righteousness," (2) "They shall renew their strength, they shall mount up with wings" etc. as far as "they shall walk and not faint," (3) "Only be thou strong and very courageous." Most of all, Duncan wanted to refute the accusation that Haig considered himself divinely appointed to lead in battle and win the war. "Never during the whole time I was with him did I hear language of that kind from his lips." Better, then, to compare Haig to Abraham Lincoln's trust to Providence, rather than to Oliver Cromwell's image of himself as divine agent.[50]

Duncan cites several postwar letters as sure evidence of Haig's religious spirit during the war. After Duncan had sent him a photo of a church hut in the village of Montreuil, Haig wrote, "What memories the sight of the interior of your little hut will conjure up for me, and what a spirit of peace combined with high resolve came into one on entering it." "Peace" and "high resolve" especially pleased Duncan. And to Duncan's thanks for permission to read his "Memorandum on the War," Haig answered that what helped him to maintain his resolve all along was the opportunity to have things "put into proper perspective on Sundays." Haig appreciated both the Church of England and his Scottish Presbyterian heritage, attending Anglican services across the earlier years of his military career in the Anglican Church, but renewing his appreciation of the Scottish church of his youth in the latter part of his career. More importantly, he wanted a reconciliation of the two for the sake of the nation, recognizing the Scottish contribution to his youthful and later years. He promoted Anglican precedence at a national commemoration at the same time as he served as a Presbyterian elder in the little Scottish village of Bemersyde.[51]

A student of Duncan's writing has more recently written that "Haig's religious faith did occasionally obscure the real war. If intelligence from the front conflicted with his vision of the war, he often either ignored and subconsciously misinterpreted it." And subsequent historians, Basil Liddell Hart and Denis Winter believed that Haig's religion interfered in no small way with his generalship.[52]

Herbert Plumer, a kindly man of unprepossessing appearance who gained a reputation for his special concern to spare the lives of his men as much as possible, was a man of sincere Anglican piety, and during the war he attended church twice on Sundays. His chief of staff reported that as the battle of Messines ridge was beginning, Plumer "was kneeling by his bedside praying for those gallant officers and men who were at that moment attacking." A Canadian staff officer wrote that religion "seemed to be just a part of himself. He was a devout Christian gentleman and it seemed to form a very important part of his personality, his perspective and his background." Bishop Gwynne reported that Julian Byng told him that "even this great material force (his Third Army) was an expression of the spiritual power behind the material and thought that all the big men here were called out by God for this work; that God gave him his present job." Hubert Gough, though dismissed as First Army commander in 1918 after failing to stop the initial German offensive,

FIG. 12 General Douglas Haig planning strategy with his leading generals. Left to right are Hubert Gough, Henry Rawlinson, Henry Horne (seated), and Herbert Plumer. Photo: Archive Images / Alamy Stock Photo.

was convinced (in 1916) that "Our success in this great struggle depends entirely on whether God is on our side. He certainly will not be unless we are his servants." In his preface to a chaplain's pamphlet, *The God of Battles*, he wrote, "A Real Faith in God and His justice and His Power in the end, whatever happens, to make Right conquer, is a great support to courage; in fact I might say without exaggeration it is an absolute necessity for the maintenance of our courage." Gough was both as sparing of lives as he could and less convinced of a divine mandate; convinced, rather, that God would *not* be on the English side if faith and morality were lacking. Henry Sinclair Horne, who also attended church twice on Sundays, was quite pragmatic about prayer and religion. "I am convinced that prayer puts the finishing touch to our sense of duty.... History tells us how men fight for a cause which concerns their religion." During the Third Battle of Ypres, as infamous for wanton soldier destruction as the first days of the Somme, Horne said, according to a report of a chaplains' conference, "Every blow at the Germans is a blow for the Kingdom of Christ."[53]

Concrete God-talk and nation-talk brought to expression the complex *imaginaires* of the men. To begin with, the soldiers' alternating hatred and respect for the enemy, accompanied by their own physical suffering and mental agony, virtually displaced any such talk when fighting was underway. Off- hours before and after combat left the men time to articulate the feelings of the moment. The Anglican deacon and plain soldier Donald Hankey, observed everything from general good will and fraught fatalism through a gracious willingness for self-sacrifice. Secondly, inarticulate or diffusive verbal expression of religion can hardly be called God-*talk*, but the soldiers embraced the simple family virtues of loyalty and generalized Christian faith, sometimes counting on the magicalized protection attributed to religious objects (medals and pocket New Testaments). Although letters could be self-sanitized reports about success and hope, many articulate soldiers felt psychologically and intellectually compelled to evoke the horrors of war and the vision of a world finally purged of absurdity, hate, and indifference. Even the hell-talk resulted from ideals that had not been realized and belief in a God who seemed absent.

Only a minuscule percentage of the billions of letters sent between the front and home have become available, but we do have a considerable number of them. Some of the most sensitive soldiers teetered between atheism and a sincere prayerfulness born of moving worship services or states of contemplation. God was certainly more incomprehensible in wartime than in peacetime, but the human love of spouses and children could serve as symbols of divine love. There was a pattern of deep questioning, traditional faith, and personal devotion. Doubts and hate, if often rejected, could be justified. To find solutions to their quandaries, some men were planning on a life of dedication to truth should they survive, or, if not, a life of glory in heaven. German soldiers highlighted sacrifice and mortal danger, spiritual as well as physical. Some of the men expressed Christmas devotion, desire for mystical union with God (contemplation of "the region in which God lives") and hatred of war. French soldiers based their devotional expression on their Catholic liturgical experiences, some even innocently unaware that their devotional talk attained mystical expression. Beyond this, there were those for whom the intense sentiments were love of family and hatred of the enemy and all who caused the war. English soldiers wore their nationalism lightly, some of them happily surprised by their chance run-ins with English speaking, even anglophile Germans, who were trying in a sporting way to renounce hatred. Religious experience could be beautiful liturgies or prayerful resignation to the will of God.

In the letters of Muslim and Hindu soldiers fighting in the English and French armies, we see the struggle to understand how their vital religious beliefs and moral values could justify their own and their families' sacrifices on behalf of the continental European power. The American soldiers fighting alongside the French brought high levels of American Catholic and Protestant loyalty to a fight for what is right, rather than a fight for French territory. Jewish troops had the added motivation to show loyalty to a homeland that offered the possibility of first-class citizenship; African American troops, the motivation to claim their first-class citizenship.

High-ranking officers and generals found support in the religious traditions they were educated into. The salient German generals looked to Lutheran, Catholic, or spiritualist teachings. Paul Hindenburg came from a loyal Lutheran noble dynasty, and Rupprecht of Bavaria was a nominal Catholic. Helmuth von Moltke exhibited a mysticism that was almost secular—we would say "new age" today—in form. The French generals looked to Catholic teachings and practice, if they were religious at all. Ferdinand Foch was extremely pious, always revivified by his private devotions and church going. The English generals looked to the biblical and liturgical foundations of the Anglican and Presbyterian churches. Douglas Haig's excellent biblical education gave him a larger repertoire of stories and verses to strengthen his resolve. Writing to intimates he said that this gave him the feeling that his ways were right. Presbyterian in formation, he had a profound appreciation of the Anglican liturgies. Herbert Plumer, who had the best reputation for preserving his men as best he could, was often on his knees before an attack. For all of them, religious loyalties paralleled national loyalties, both loyalties heartfelt and loyalties necessary, if they were to carry on.

Of course, there were few soldiers more challenged to understand the will of God than the members of the clergy who served as chaplains for the belligerent forces, and especially those who were drafted into the army as actual combatants—as was the case with the French priests. During the years of seminary formation and as youthful priests and pastors, they could scarcely avoid meditating the will of heaven and the dangers of hell. At the front they were in a sort of hell trying to safeguard their visions of heaven. Their stories must also be told.

CHAPTER 4

Clergy at the Front

With priests, ministers, and rabbis close to or in the trenches, the churches and the synagogue were on the front. Chaplains were the official representatives of the home religions, but more important for the *presence* of organized religion in the trenches were the priests and those few other chaplains who were side by side with the soldiers. The French Catholic priests were the most engaged participants of them all and the best chroniclers of those trench years, for one basic reason: so many of them were ordinary, gun-toting soldiers, because the secular government of France allowed for no military exemptions to priests who were ordained after the separation of church and state in 1905.[1] Germany and England had no such requirement: chaplains were chaplains, and even when they were at the front or in the trenches, did not officially do any of the actual fighting.[2] So then, with the French priests (and seminarians) we get the most articulate of soldiers telling of their own experience of religion and war, and reporting the experiences of their fellow soldiers. French nuns, when close to the front, also had to combine spirituality and national service. The German, French, and English Christian clergy went about their tasks as best they could and reported their ministerial and faith experiences while fulfilling the roles assigned to them by their armies and their churches. The war made them all reexamine the role of the government, the role of the church, and their own spiritual deficiencies.

Jewish chaplains reinforced their soldiers' will to fight, but with more hesitation than the Christian clergy, because the killing of fellow Jews who had the same anti-Semitism to face in their home countries was a dark prospect. Individual piety depended so much on specifically Jewish solidarity, that rabbis and their soldiers together are a separate story, told in the next chapter.

GERMAN CHAPLAINS: MINISTERING TO SOLDIERS AND OCCUPIED PEOPLES

German ministers and priests left for the front with their armies, almost all of them remaining behind the lines but close enough to minister to the men before and after battle. In spite of the high virtue promoted at home in Berlin and Munich as the war broke out, sermons to soldiers in the field could be unabashedly down to earth, sympathizing with the basic pain of separation from families and the daily pain of bodily suffering as the soldier experienced it or witnessed it. Field division Pastor Fischer on 19 September preached to the men, "Under the thunder of guns, we remembered our homeland and our lives there." He evokes a return home, the soldiers crowned with glory and with weapons gleaming. He imagines a world gazing in total wonder at the heroism of the soldiers, and a world learning a master lesson from them at the same time. "Then will the whole world not only take notice of German heroic bravery and German military deeds, but also, wide-eyed before truth and reality, will have to respect the solid power and the worthy culture of the German people." Behold then, the German soldier, sword in hand, defending an eminently just cause at the front, heroic and suffering. Indeed, the heart is weighed down and the eyes are moist when the soldiers must bury their comrades dying so young and far from the homeland. All on the battlefront and on the home front suffer, knowing that "with the message of a hero's death to an old father, the tears run down his grey beard, while the mother mourns for her fallen son." Fischer has seen enough to know that fear for life itself is the ultimate concern of his men, an insight that puts him well beyond the preachers back at the Berliner Dom. "And then the question raises itself—Will I ever see them again on earth, or will the next grenade sweep me away also?" Of course, the remedy Fischer counsels is faith and virtue. "Christ has overcome death and he shows us the eternal house of the Father.... If we are certain of the living gracious God, we fear men no more, and if we go on our way trusting, brave, unshaken, then we go along it with God."[3]

Evangelical church authorities expected their chaplains to serve also as intermediaries between the soldiers at the front and the families at home. They thought it better that news of wounds and death should be delivered

FIG. 13 The Evangelical, Jewish, and Catholic chaplains (left to right) in the German army responded to the spiritual and emotional needs of their soldiers. Photo: Lebrecht Music & Arts / Alamy Stock Photo.

with the church's prayers and consolation by the pastors at home than by a bare government notification. Accordingly, they suggested that local churches could coordinate with the war postal system so that a "dead" or "fallen" notice could be delivered to the family by a pastor.[4] With or without sad news, chaplains at the front could help the wounded soldiers maintain contact with their families. Ministry to the field hospitals was, therefore, essential, even to the point of arranging family visits where possible. In light of the family connection, present and future, a primary concern of the church authorities was the spread of venereal disease, of which there were a number of cases in the field hospitals. This was not so much a problem in a war of movement, but the disease spread rapidly with the occupation of Belgium and Northern France.[5] Pamphlets were distributed to the troops about sexual temptations, described as all the more potent by alcohol. The pages of the Evangelical archives for July–September 1915 contain the pamphlet, *Ein Laufender Feind hinter der Front* (A Day-to-Day Enemy Behind the Lines). The author compliments the soldiers, acknowledges their sufferings, and admits that this disease was a danger for all armies of the past. The problem now is that the longer the war lasts, the more does the disease danger increase. Even with this danger and all the others, a chaplain was able to write back to the home church authorities that it was a "'brilliant time' for our Evangelical Church, and perhaps even more, 'the crucial hour.'"[6]

At the front, and so in conquered territory, pastors Siegfried Eggebrecht and Wilhelm Stählin kept diaries that, more fully than the others that have come down to us, reveal the German chaplain experience.

Siegfried Eggebrecht, Wilhelm Stählin, and Other Evangelical Chaplains

Eggebrecht was a Protestant theologian, who headed for the front as chaplain in December 1914 and was later assigned to Verdun before being transferred to the eastern front. The Artois offensive, north of Soissons began in the middle of December, but Eggebrecht was in Cologne, away from the field and close to the cathedral. As soon as he returned to the field in France, he entered into his diary on 19 December a frank criticism of German militarism. "People in the homeland idealize the German soldier too much. They attribute to him virtue that he does not have and cannot have. The field grey [uniform] is an idealized figure for Germans." The next day he was preoccupied by the liturgical celebrations leading up to Christmas, trying to meet the challenges of the setting, which was a field hospital in a partially destroyed church. Then came the feast itself, with its brief and uneven cease-fire actions and fraternizing—already studied—that became the great religious story to close 1914. On the last day of the year, Eggebrecht meditated on the happiness of his marriage and his confidence that the new year would certainly be better than the old.[7]

One week into 1915, Eggebrecht was preoccupied with burials and the destruction all around. A crucifix was still standing in the bombarded church, but the cemetery itself was unusable. His 18 January entry was a pages-long description of the town, Trosly-Loire, and the destruction there. He was particularly stressed by the grenade destruction that he saw in the captured French trenches, encumbered as they were with bodies and trash. By February he had to admit that some sort of "hatred," along with thoughts of the fatherland would be necessary in order to effectively carry out an attack at the enemy, though the next month he was telling himself that he was not in France "to destroy, but rather to service the peace." He added, "I do not believe in a new religion as they announce it from out of the battle stations, above all, not in a religion with a German God." Field hospital service was the setting for Eggebrecht's ministry of consolation and prayer, even as he pondered what a call to penance could possibly mean for soldiers in this war. On the feast of the Ascension, he looked at the *Kultur* around him, which, of course, was making no progress in spirituality or rationality. The challenges of a chaplain became more and more difficult as the war of attrition ground on. The sounds of war drowned out words of encouragement and clouded thoughts of homeland and home life. Even so, when the dead comrades are buried, he wondered what the men could make of a pious hymnody of God's will, "What God does, is well done." How can they not rebel against this?[8]

When the Battle of Verdun began in February 1916, Eggebrecht was close by. He preached at a burial of German officers (and one French soldier), which gripped him more than any that had gone before, and he found it ironic that in the middle way between the French and German lines stood a crucifix with one arm pointing toward the German graves and one arm pointing toward the French, as if to say, "I die for you both; find yourselves in me." Still near Verdun but farther away from the destruction, he could briefly enjoy nature, the bright sun and the trees beginning to bloom (by this time it was April). But there was still the poison gas danger and the burials, this time with thoughts on Psalm 68, "Blessed be the Lord, who daily bears us up; God is our salvation. Our God is a God of salvation; and to God, the Lord, belongs escape from death." In June, Eggebrecht's last month on the western front, he struggled to cope with the death of his brother Erich, filling his diary with details of Erich's suffering and his own attempts to get to see him. A fellow chaplain asked him, "by the way," if he had heard that his brother had been wounded, adding the assurance that the wound was light. But following a complex operation, his brother slowly slipped away. After the funeral service, with the hymn "We live, so let us live for the Lord," he left carrying Erich's things with him, headed for home, and thence to the eastern front.[9]

Wilhelm Stählin's experience of the war as an evangelical chaplain is the most complete individual witness published thus far, and in its present edition it includes almost nine hundred pages of his reports and thoughts on religious services, morality, Catholic colleagues and local pastors, and the dogmatic themes of preaching. He also covers soldiers' reactions to the sermons, describes wounds both light and tragic, and rebelliousness and its penalties. And for him it was also normal to describe museum visits and concerts well behind the front.

Crossing through Belgium, Stählin was struck by the hunger of the populations and did not hesitate to describe German destructiveness. His sympathies lay with the wives and children of both the German and Belgian soldiers. Facing the resistance of the Catholic priests of Belgium and France to his use of their churches, he would conduct his services from the altar rail, instead of from the altar itself. His relationships with some of the Bavarian Catholic chaplains were excellent, but he did think that the Protestant combination of Bible reading and sermon was best for wartime dangers and settings. Stählin consoled the wounded and dying soldiers in the field hospitals, not hiding his surprise at just how mangled were some of the bodies. As he approached Christmas—that first Christmas on the front—he marked off the liturgical calendar each day. He witnessed the caroling on the front lines across the brief truce and wrote that the English were good at it but that Christmas celebrating was a German specialty.[10]

The Christmas joy was mixed with other concerns. The soldier who told him about his wife's infidelity at home was hardly an exceptional case, and Stählin too, along with doctors and higher officers, was deeply concerned by the high incidence of syphilis; the doctors had even formed a committee to consider and deal with the problem. There were areas of the front where a truce never took hold or, if brief, seemed to be an occasion for the English to study the German frontline set-up. Afterward, apart from the arrival of the King of Bavaria and the parade in his honor, there was no distraction from Stählin's sad task of tending the mortally wounded and the trials of the nighttime marches.[11]

Then came Neuve Chapelle and Second Ypres, bringing Stählin to a nervous breakdown of sorts in March. He wrote less about that and more about church matters, such as the quality of singing in the cathedral and the usual problems that Catholic authorities had with a Protestant use of the building. The fading away before his eyes of the severely wounded formed a strange conjuncture with the arrival of Holy Week, Palm Sunday through Good Friday to Easter, and celebrations in the "Christophkirche," a Catholic parish in Tourcoing. Stählin was also present for the visit of the head chaplain of the Bavarian army corps, Bishop (later Cardinal) Michael von Faulhaber. Thereafter, he detailed the wounds of the soldiers and the medical people there to care for them. He helped write letters as usual, pausing to hold the hands of the agonizing, but reporting the good humor and comradery of the soldiers who were still capable of it. He avidly followed the stories and the rumors of the progress of the war.[12]

Stählin's moral sensitivity permeated his meditations on the justice of war. "This new phase of the war lies heavy upon the souls. Is there to be no end? And is it true that the whole world has gone crazy. Are we right? It is fearfully difficult to maintain this self-consciousness." He regularly went over in his mind the destruction of part of Belgium, rejoicing in the preservation of the churches and the other fine architecture of Ghent and Bruges, and anxious for Belgians who welcomed or worked with the Germans in any way, because they would be executed by the French. With a fellow chaplain he discussed whether or not it was necessary to annex Belgium. "The population is not friendly. There are few reflective types. Even Brussels up until now, despite all efforts to spare the population, has remained hostile." Also it would seem that in the annexation of Belgium, there lurked the danger of a wider war and struggles among Germans themselves. The Belgians would be more amenable if, instead of Prussians, the Bavarians came along. Through their Queen [originally from Bavaria] they have some kind sympathy for the Bavarians. Naturally, he strongly disapproved punishment of Belgians who criticized the German occupation. Two hundred and fifty citizens, including the pastors of all eleven parishes, were to be deported to Germany for forced labor. Children see their fathers led away. "Within myself I am on the side of the French and I see in this whole incident an indication of how splendidly we Germans, when we are trying to be 'upright,' understand how to make ourselves hated." A priest had even been condemned to death for saying in church that Alsace and Lorraine belonged to France while a German officer was present. Stählin wanted him pardoned. Cognizant of all this, Stählin was still hurt that people hated Germany in general and hated him in particular, citing the moment when he saw small children playing around the entrance to their house being shooed inside by their mother when she saw him coming.[13]

These kaleidoscope experiences of Eggebrecht and Stählin stand in contrast to the single-issue accounts of Martin Schian, general superintendent of the Silesian province of the Evangelische Kirche, and Hans Lehmann—both of them published by the Evangelical Union Press—and the two books by the nonchaplain pastor Heinrich Niemöller, father of the renowned U-boat captain in World War I and Hitler opponent in World War II, pastor Martin Niemöller. Schian, Lehmann, and Niemöller concerned themselves mainly with the religious fidelity of the German soldiers.[14]

Schian stands out because of his field hospital preoccupation. In *Gedanken im Lazarett* (Thoughts in a Field Hospital), he said that there is no joy in hospitals for those who would much prefer to be in the field, but as for himself hospital confinement was preferable to being killed! There are prayers and psalms on the battlefield, yes, but such is not for everyone, even though more pray there than in ordinary time, and the men seem more reverent before a field altar than before an altar in church. There are also more communions than at home. In a second volume, evoking the length of the war, Schian asks, "Who knows what the future will bring?" and highlights a story of how one soldier "stayed on track," by simply continuing his old job when home on leave.[15]

Lehmann in his *Erinnerungen eines Feldpredigers* (Memoirs of a Chaplain), waxes eloquent and at length on the glory of the Kaiser and the celebration of the *Kaisertag* in a church behind the lines: an hour of celebration of the fatherland brought the soldiers into the candlelit village church. In his last chapter, "True Comradeship," he poetically reflects on a sunny spring Sabbath service in a village near the front and his return to the front; then he ruefully describes the fighting, the wounded, and their suffering. At a graveside, he praises the bright day, the vineyards, and the little French villages where he and the soldiers are billeted, but the ever-returning memories of his brother, who died the year before, stay with him at the new burial. He concludes with a rebuttal of the old theme, "German barbarians." Recognizing that "war is as horrible as plagues from heaven," he names the divisions he has visited in battle camps and under fire: Bavarians, Prussians, Rhinelanders, men from Lower Saxony. "Barbarians? No, I found no barbarians. I found rather the German heart, German humility in all its varieties from joking through suffering [*vom Scherz zum Schmerz*]."[16]

Heinrich Niemöller, pastor at Ebenfeld, in his *Sieben Bitten an das deutsch-evangelische Christenvolk in schwerer Kriegzeit* (Seven Requests to German-Evangelical Christians in a More Difficult Time of War), listed virtues imperative in wartime, clearly to promote church engagement, for nothing could be more loveable—even family and fatherland—than "our Evangelical Church." "She is the possessor of all grace and gifts, which are our only consolation in life and in death. She is the giver of numberless joys which in the brilliance of Christmas and the sun of Easter, the sounds of organ and the ringing of bells. In word, song, and prayer she has led us from the cradle to this difficult hour. Her banner is the cross; her Magna Carta is the Word of God."[17] In his *Friedenziele über die gesprochen werden darf und muss* (Peace Goals That Must Be Spoken Of), he exalts spiritual life over everything. "We look out for a peace that not only brings us a victorious, strong, and indestructible fatherland, but also what is of much greater value, a new German Empire in which hearts, families, individual peoples, and the churches are ruled and sanctified by God's Spirit. We hope that it will become so, in spite of all our insufficiencies. . . . We cannot believe that our God would cast [the church] into the crucible of this war without it emerging reformed, purified, and sanctified."[18]

Ludwig Berg and Bernhard Kreutz

The priests Berg and Kreutz shared the church-first views of the evangelical churchmen. They were Catholic chaplains in the predominantly Protestant Prussian divisions and so were a mirror image of Stählin, the Protestant chaplain who served in the predominately Catholic Bavarian divisions. Their chaplaincies were marked by a good relationship with those Protestant military authorities, from regional heads of the chaplains' corps right up to the Kaiser himself (in the case of Ludwig Berg)! In fact, there were very few personal spiritual reflections, despite the many pages of reports on pastoral care, religious services, and church politics. The German historian, Gerd Krumeich points out that the German Catholic chaplains could see how the first experiences of mobilization and chaplain organization gave them the chance to bring Catholicism into mainline life and into the consciousness of higher echelons of the Empire, just as the French Catholic church could try to win over the respect and attention of the secular French Republic through whole-hearted patriotic engagement in the war. Krumeich puts at 1,441 the number of Catholic chaplains in the Prussian army and believes that there was little difference between Catholic and Protestant pastoral care and theologies of war.[19]

For his pastoral duties, Berg celebrated the liturgical services, prayed at burials, and, in particular, visited, supported, and consoled wounded and dying soldiers. In the field hospitals he told them to urge their spouses to raise their children Catholic, obviously not considering this to be an unfair use of spiritual authority. On the western front, Berg was part of the winter campaign in the Champagne region and then saw the devastation on the Somme. He heard the confessions of the men when they got away from the front lines and tried to somehow encourage them when they had to return. Back in Charleville, after a stint on the eastern front, he became the garrison chaplain. He accompanied a French spy to execution, accompanied also French civilians who for other reasons were sent to execution by the occupying forces. Ironically, he was also called upon to work with the soldiers forced to do the executing! Berg's talks to soldier groups underline the morality and decency required for a Christian life, but he also lectured on Islam, and on the political and religious history of France.[20]

Ludwig Berg eventually met and talked to the highest German authorities. He helped with the visit to the western front of the archbishop of Cologne—and so the ranking Catholic prelate in Prussia—Cardinal Felix von Hartmann. At the pontifical High Mass celebrated by Hartmann, even the Kaiser was in attendance. In dealings with the Protestant head chaplain, he managed to be invited to a soirée with Hindenburg and there took the opportunity to suggest to Hindenburg that field hospital soldiers should have the chance to journey closer to home when able. This would increase the soldiers' desire, he thought, to fight more intensely for the fatherland. Hindenburg promised his support and arranged for discounted, sometimes free, travel, and several hundred soldiers were able to profit from Berg's efforts. Berg was traveling to Aachen on an inspection tour with one of the Kaiser's aids, when the Kaiser asked the priest to sit beside him to discuss his difficulties with the Belgian clergy, his fear that the Catholic ally Austria would start negotiating with France, and the unwillingness of the Holy See to appoint two German curia cardinals. Later Berg suggested to the Kaiser that Cardinal von Hartmann and Archbishop von Faulhaber write pastoral letters in support of fidelity to the monarchy.[21]

The Kreutz diary is a very simple record of church service and military action, his short sentences giving only the bare essentials. His ministry closely paralleled the ministry of Berg, but we know all that from letters and other documents included in the published edition, more than from the diaries themselves. For him, battles were "fearful" or "life endangering," and in the midst of this the chaplain should carry on, and make a record of, his sacramental ministry. He reported his Berg-like willingness to teach and lecture on government generosity and German greatness as a motivation for the soldiers. He wrote, "To maintain a good spirit among our troops, and to take away as many cares as possible, which they might have stemming from ignorance of the government's welfare laws for soldiers, I am ready to give talks during peace intervals, in barracks and other places on the topic, 'How a thankful fatherland cares for the families of the men taking part in the war, as well as for those hurt by war and remaining behind.' Perhaps it would be good to suggest this occasionally in division-day instructions." Other topics were more academic: Lord Herbert Kitchener, General Paul von Hindenberg, Prince Otto von Bismarck, the English fleet, and French Catholicism.[22]

SOLDIER PRIESTS AND NURSING SISTERS OF FRANCE:
SUFFERING FOR THE SALVATION OF THE *PATRIE*

According to one reliable estimate, more than 32,500 members of the French clergy, including major seminarians, were mobilized.[23] Those ordained before the 1905 Law of Separation of Church and State were allowed to serve as stretcher-bearers and medics, making it difficult to calculate the exact percentage of priests who were true combatants. Joseph Brugerette thinks that about twelve thousand were on the front with guns in their hands, with an equal number of stretcher-bearers and medics.[24]

This makes their experiences strikingly different from the officially appointed German, English—and French—chaplains, who were noncombatants. In any case, the majority did provide priestly services to their fellow soldiers, whatever military function they fulfilled. *La Preuve du sang* (Blood Proof), a laudatory commemoration volume or *Livre d'Or* (Golden Book), is an invaluable source of fundamental information about the types of priests in military service and the specifically military activities that gained them recognition in the army. In his introduction, Henry Bordeaux summarizes the exploits of the priest combatants who are presented in brief encyclopedic entries across the two volumes.[25] And he lavishly praised some priests for capturing enemy positions, bombing German-held cities and towns, and encouraging soldiers to the attack. The abbés Amiot of Angers and Mirabail of the Collège de Saint-Caprais figure among Bordeaux's striking examples. Amiot had "forced his way across the Aisne under enemy fire and penetrated into the village of Balhan, where he played a large part in the capture of the whole garrison." Mirabail was an aviator who "shot down Fokkers [and] bombed Metz-les-Sablons and Karlsruhe. When he was returning from this last exposure [to danger] . . . engine trouble forced him to land, and he had the presence of mind, before his descent, to jettison his machine gun and destroy his card and papers."[26] These were certainly warrior priests: one led the attack, and the other dropped bombs.

Prêtre aux armées (Priest in the Armies), one of several reviews published for priests in the armed services, first appeared in February 1915. In subsequent months (and years), clerical readers received a wide range of spiritual direction and practical advice. A citation from a letter about Joan of Arc encouraged priest soldiers to heroism: "The voice of your conscience, after you have examined before God where your duty lies, pushes you like Joan of Arc and says to you, *Son of God, go forth!* Because the church suspends, if not the censure, at least the effects of censure, and permits you to follow the call of the fatherland. Son of France, go! Go and show that the minister of God and of peace knows how to be a hero and martyr."[27] A young priest of Kremlin-Bicêtre, who perished leading his men in a charge, wrote in his last letter, published in *Prêtre aux Armées*, "I believe that with the help of God I will be strong enough to lead my men well, and so arrange their lives with the sovereign power as to give them, if they fall, a better life."[28] The journal's foremost concern was the spiritual life of the priest, including such paradoxical juxtapositions of values as childlikeness in the acceptance of death ("as a little child ought to accept everything smilingly from his beloved father"), and sacrifice of one's youthful body as a priestly sacrifice.[29]

Discussions of pure sacrifice and spiritual growth did not mask the huge spiritual risk inherent in the chaos of war. Priests sometimes set a bad example: "A soldier from my region remarked that several priests took care to avoid their duty and to leave it to others."[30] In the background always was the problem of shedding the blood of others. A clarification was necessary: "His Eminence Cardinal [Hector] Sevin, in the well-known consultation granted *Prêtre aux armées*, has responded that because of the seriousness of the defense situation and because of superior motives, the priest can obey... but *he cannot take the initiative in offering himself for the task of taking life.*"[31] It is one thing to be forced to tote guns, another to offer oneself to the task. Nevertheless, the priest could still be a moral watchdog. One priest corporal, decrying obscenities in soldiers' songs, had written "The Song on the Front" with a promise to provide more lyrics free of scurrility.[32] Here priest soldiers had opportunities that the chaplains did not have, because the men knew that these priests "share[d] their life."[33]

We can go beyond *La Preuve du sang* and *Le Prêtre aux armées* to see how the priests combined national sentiment and religious ideology, and how they interpreted their role in the *Union sacrée*. In their letters French priests tried to make sense of the war. They said the war could be a punishment for sin, motivation to return to God, and a source of salvation for France. No set of letters shows the whole range of concerns better than those written by the priests of one diocese in central France, presented and published only a few years ago by Father Daniel Moulinet, archivist of the diocese. To sustain their own spiritual lives the priests worked to arrange places and meetings where they could support one another; they relied on the Eucharistic liturgy, celebration of the feasts of the church year, the breviary (book of hours), the rosary, pilgrimages, retreats, relics, and medals.

Some devotional practices were "portable" and others were a logistical challenge, such as a leave for a pilgrimage or retreat, or celebrating Eucharist at the front (or in the trenches). They tried to meditate the obstacles to the spiritual life, ways of drawing near to God, the will of God, the presence of God, suffering with Christ, reparation for sin, sacrifice, preparation for death, and spiritual discouragement. Traditional Catholic prayers to the Sacred Heart of Jesus, the Virgin Mary, the angels, and the saints could also strengthen and console.[34]

During and after the war, biographies of priests proliferated, sometimes written as hagiographies, sometimes with substantial quotes from war letters, originally collected to support the religious nationalism of the *Union sacrée*, but later integrated into the Bibliothèque de Documentation Internationale et Contemporaine in Paris.[35] Peering through the occasional cloud of the hagiographer's incense, readers can still see the honest self-expression of the soldier priests. A middle-aged Franciscan, Father Edouard de Massat, expressed simple patriotism and belief in the saving power of the priesthood. De Massat had been in Canada for ten years following his expulsion from France. He was a perfect example of the religious order priests, who were finally appreciated by the old anti-clerical Georges Clemenceau (they returned "after we chased them away"). Explaining his motivation to his sister, de Massat wrote, "I have made the sacrifice of my life to God for my dear and beloved country." Fifty-four years old when he came back to serve in the army, de Massat went racing into battle beside the soldiers, carrying the sacred host and wearing his habit. There is a photo—which actually seems to be posed—in the de Massat biography with a quote from one of his letters: "Cross in hand, I made the attack with my Zouaves." He was there to use his sacramental powers to bring God to his fellows, and it was clear that he did it for the sake of France: "During this time, I was just about everywhere to give absolution and care to those who were falling around me. My habit, my haversack, everything up to my crucifix, were red with blood. . . . During the attack, I carried the sacred host with me, and it is to the presence of God that I attribute our success, which cost us relatively few losses." When receiving the Croix de Guerre, he concluded his remarks with "and long live France the immortal." He was even able to make his own the language of violence: describing a church service, de Massat added in, "Our last words and our farewell were, 'We will have our revenge.'"[36]

Seminarians without sacramental powers seemed more anxious about their vocation and less secure about what they could offer the fatherland. Jean

Audouin, a major seminarian and combatant, saw his sacrifice as a Mass. Writing to his family, he begged them to "pray for our poor France. She is not lost, but will make up for her sins by much bloodshed.... I will have fulfilled my role as victim and priest; I will have followed my mentor. Let us abandon ourselves to the will of God."[37] The nineteen-year-old seminarian Manuel Baillet of the Cordeliers (Franciscans) seemed a figure of goodness, simple piety, and sensitivity. He thought about family and friends while in the field, but his possibilities for future priesthood were his main preoccupation: "The first shells that reach me could also end my vocation by a canonical irregularity, or even by death." Expressions of anxiety, rather than of heroism, follow: "I suffer because my vocation is in danger and because I am alone here!"[38]

Some priests could integrate their apostolate with actual combat. Writing fifty years later, Father Maurice Grivelet remembered that he took his fighting techniques seriously: "I draw my saber remembering my fencing lessons, and pull out my revolver. Suddenly, a few hundred meters from us, we see a sortie of I do not know how many enemy soldiers in columns of four, coming toward us." Wounded in the arms and legs by bullets and shrapnel, he was resting when he heard someone call out for a priest, and he struggled to give the man absolution with his good arm. Naturally, he attributed his narrow escape from the destruction of his medical station to divine providence.[39]

Father Joseph Arlet also went about his soldiering earnestly. His bishop describes approvingly how Arlet died, still firing his revolver: "Suddenly, there he was, face to face with the enemy. Directed to surrender, he responded by pistol shots. Then grenades and other explosives were thrown at his feet. From this whirlwind of destruction he was carried off to eternity." Arlet, feeling no hesitation in associating *le bon Dieu* with bloodshed, had already said that "our good God wants us to win out over these unjust aggressors, and to inflict on them the most bloody defeats." He wanted to be "useful to France and the church"; for him, "the priest soldier has a wonderful part to play. How much consolation and help has been set aside by God in order for us, as mediators, to bring [it] to the soldiers!"[40]

One killed people, of course, in defending France. Marie-Bernard Lavergue, well into his major seminary years, was proud to be a soldier. To his mother he wrote, "I assure you that, far from being afraid, far from being intimidated by the arms that have been placed in my hands, I am happy to bear them, and I know how to use them. You should know that I 'brought down' three Prussians. That will be three who will not fire on us again." But

Lavergue envisioned his own sacrificial death more than the death of others: "To die for the fatherland . . . is an enviable fate for those who dream of the priesthood, because in the sacrifice of one's life, offered in youth for a good cause, there are many elements of priestly immolation." He understood that redemption could occur in the midst of the fighting. "A brutish life, then? No. A tough life, if you will, in its context; a beautiful life, in sum, because it is a life of total abandonment, of perfect submission to the will of God, sole master of tomorrow." He believed that in the midst of chaos a mysterious personal transformation was taking place: "If this [work] is accomplished, what else matters?"[41]

Examples of priestly spirituality abounded. For Father Pierre Babouard, the death of soldiers for France was an introduction to the mystery of Christ's death for the world: "That was a frightful death: the skull shattered, the bones crushed; machine-gun bullets ploughing into the chest, exposing the intestines, carving up the limbs with horrible wounds. But was the death of Christ more gentle? His head also was torn, his limbs pierced; his poor lacerated body appeared to onlookers and executioners as one great wound."[42]

The Jesuit priest Pierre Durouchoux was a genuine soldier who suffered from being such. A veteran and officer, he was likely to be in the thick of the fighting, which was deeply disturbing to him: "Physical suffering is nothing; the moral suffering of the priest who is forced to fight and to strike his neighbor, even though the enemy of his country, is frightful. The victory is costly. But let us pray that the Virgin of the Rosary will at length grant it to us." His mission, as he described it to his mother, was religious and national: "The war has brought God out of the churches to receive public and national worship! Dear *Maman*, I am happy and proud to be associated with this religious renewal of our French men, and, in my own small way, to be an agent of it."[43]

The Jesuit seminarian René de la Perraudière, though fascinated by military progress, was not at home, therefore effective, with the ordinary soldiers: And he was not sure whether this sentiment came from social pride or the reasonable certainty that he would simply have more influence on the officers, men of his own social level. He was less guarded in his expression of French patriotism and his specifically French spiritual ministry: "I will help to save the world and France by working actively, in taking to heart more my obligations as a sergeant. My efforts are not empty because of their outcome; on the contrary." Speaking of dark moments, he was still able to say that he was delighted to defend the fatherland, and he seemed positively excited about an important military advance: "How I would love to be with the French who enter Metz, and this is something I can perhaps hope for now." A slight wound evokes the most patriotic sentiments: "Yesterday a shell falling nearby caused some drops of my blood to be shed for France by scraping my cheek with stone fragments."[44]

A happy balance of fighting and ministry was the will of God, wrote Father Georges Sevin to his mother. "Our daily tasks ... cannot keep our thoughts from turning constantly toward France, our own people and loved ones.... Each one of us has a place marked out by Providence to contribute to *the salvation of France* during this horrible war." He considered the military camps at Salonika to be devastating for the moral well-being of numerous priests, blaming the ambivalence of the Greek government, and its lack of whole-hearted support of France and the allies: "It seems to me and everyone else that we have let ourselves be *betrayed by Greece* too long." The prime minister supported the allies, but the king wanted neutrality; for Sevin, the officials resisting the allies should be overthrown.[45]

Of all the personalities examined, however, the Jesuit novice Lucien Chabord, by his apostolic concern and his fighting spirit, seemed to embody to the fullest extent both minister of religion and soldier. Chabord combined the intense devotion of the seminarian and novice with the responsibility and patriotism of an officer: "Our riflemen were happy with the results ... with regrets, however, that they were not able to redden their bayonets! You may find this to be an awful detail, but war, as a German ambassador has been saying these days, 'is not five-o'clock tea.'" Even then, he was a devotional warrior: "We were attacking at noon, and before that there was intense artillery and infantry fire.... I was reading *The Imitation of Christ* with a priest sergeant major when I heard myself called. 'Chabord!' 'Yes, Captain.' 'Advance with your section.'"[46] For him, the French and their enemies shared a common spiritual dilemma. "That we have come so to deal with one another, O God, have pity on us! O Jesus, God of peace, you who have shed your blood for all men, grant, I beseech you, that people may offer a kiss of peace to one another and that you might be glorified by all the earth."[47]

Like many of his clerical colleagues, the foundation of his patriotism was the home territory—in his case, the Savoy. "Here I am," he wrote while on leave to his confreres in the novitiate, "in my dear Savoy, with my parents whom I so often thought I would never see again, at the base of mountains that I am now trying to hold within myself, so that I can carry their image with me more surely onto tomorrow's battlefields."[48] Chabord distinguished between dying for France and dying to attain heaven: "And the riflemen have

FIG. 14 Memento card for the Jesuit novice, Lucien Chabord, with a photo and data on his military honors. Éditions La Fontaine de Siloé.

Souvenez-vous dans vos prières
de
LUCIEN PIERRE MARIE CHABORD
Novice de la compagnie de Jésus
Lieutenant au 54ᵐᵉ bataillon de Chasseurs
Chevalier de la Légion d'honneur
Cité trois fois à l'Ordre de l'Armée
Tombé glorieusement à CLERY (Somme)
le 25 Septembre 1916 à l'âge de 26 ans

« Il regardait toujours en face l'avenir éternel... Ce que Dieu lui laissait de répit, il le dépensait à propager le règne de son amour. Il avait réussi, et il est tombé tenant haut le fanion du Sacré Cœur. »
Mgr. Castellan, archevêque de Chambéry.

responded to this call [to surrender] with their last rounds of fire. They died, hit standing up, crying, 'vive la France!' Is that not beautiful? And yet, *illi ut corruptibilem coronam accipiant, nos autem*."[49]

For Chabord and his contemporaries, a rapprochement between secularized society and the Catholic church in France was just beginning, and he accordingly displayed a combination of understanding and criticism. For him, a freethinker of his acquaintance was not aware of reality: "If he rejects every solution [to life's problems], it is because of the illusion of artificial happiness and the giddiness of the world. But there is also at certain moments of lucidity the profound melancholy of a soul that ignores what it is." On the other hand, the man appeared to have been searching: "If he hesitates to solve [life's problems], it is because of that unrest known by [John Henry] Newman while he was searching for ten years, in prayer, study, and tears, the way of life."[50]

Problems of ministry and secular ideology also preoccupied the Jesuit seminarian Jean Nourisson. Nourisson pointed to the lack of spiritual transformation of the men, observing that they were brave at the front, but nothing special when they came back—swearing and threatening one another. "Will this be the renewal of France by the young? It could be something great, but in any case, we have much work to do if we want this harvest to ripen." And his love of the fatherland was also a theologically conscious act, in the good company of Thomas Aquinas: "Is it in no way permitted to cast a look at the great sorrow of the land of France? It appears that Saint Thomas exalts the love of the fatherland." Religious ideals were in complete contrast to secular ideals: "The church is very much hierarchized, but its doctrine is complete humility, whereas the foundation of the egalitarian spirit is pride." The situation was doubly objectionable because the secular government attributed to itself messianic accomplishments. People were told that "humanity made progress and civilization finally came into the world, thanks to the Revolution and the Third Republic; and they believed it." The secularists found nothing of value in the old Catholic tradition: "'Before.' That was the old regime, Catholicism, all the retrograde institutions. One should not 'return to the past,' to the time when there was no happiness for the worker, when Jules Ferry had not invented the public school, when one burned alive the founders of unions and those who did not bow before processions."[51] Nourisson criticized also the socialist priests. Prayer, mortification, gospel living were all more important than social action of the clergy: "Do you not think that there has been a debasing of priestly consciousness among the 'socialist' clergy?"[52]

French Catholic sisters were not on the front lines, but from time to time they were not far behind. In the hospital of Senlis, in German hands, an officer came upon wounded French soldiers and took out his revolver. The mother superior ran after him and grabbed his arm: "You do not have the right to touch our soldiers, they are wounded. I forbid you to do anything to them."[53] At Clermont-en-Argonne, the Daughter of Charity Gabrielle Rosnet described the evacuation of the French and the arrival of the Germans. "The second blow [of a rifle butt] smashed the door to smithereens, which opened the way to three officers, two of them holding revolvers.... I said, 'Our wounded soldiers left yesterday. Give us yours and we will take care of them. But in return care for ours who are on your side.'" She commended herself and her aged hospital charges to the kindness and generosity of the commanding officer, and he responded, "My good woman, we will respect your house."[54]

FIG. 15 Sister Gabrielle, who, along with other nursing sisters behind several fronts, cared for and even protected French soldiers. Éditions DRAC.

Another Sister of Charity, Sister Rebondins, near Dunkirk, described the shelling and hospital conditions to her superior general. "The condition in which our poor wounded arrive is horrible! Alas! Many die. For several days now, many arrive, and each day, twelve to fifteen of them pass on to eternity." Her hospital also had to be disinfected for typhoid fever.[55]

Sister Saint-Péreuse described the destruction of Reims from a field hospital on location. "The martyrdom of Reims began again after a moment of calm." Following a French air attack on their trenches, the Germans bombarded the city. "Yesterday, at eight o'clock, there was a dreadful cannonade over Reims and violent German attacks at several points. Our artillery responded." The French soldier battalions, deploying between attacks, excited her appreciation. "An order is given, a single word from the officer, and all the men stand, make a half turn, and march away. . . . How we admired this military obedience. . . . How beautiful it is!"[56] But another sort of pride, totally different, a greater pride combined with profound religious faith, suffused her description of the tragic fate of the "*gueules cassées*" [facially disfigured] and the other dying lads. "A young amputee, dead from gas gangrene, had said simply, 'Ah, it's sad to die at 25 years . . . after having been married two months . . . it's very sad.' That was his sole complaint. A small soldier arrived one evening. He had expired en route. Removing his uniform we found in a tiny pocket next to his heart, his first communion rosary, it was stained by his blood.... The little blond seemed to smile: he must have seen the Blessed Virgin."[57] Then Sister Saint-Péreuse, with a reporter's instincts and great sympathy at the same time, listed the wounds she had seen: an eye destroyed by a flying piece of a skull, teeth buried in tongues or cheeks, wallets, even pages of correspondence, pushed into stomachs, bodies loaded with pieces of bone or clothing.[58] For all of these sisters, their combat was fighting to save lives and their religion was the alleviation of suffering.

ENGLISH CHAPLAINS: OVERCOMING THE CHURCHES' INFIRMITIES AND VALORIZING SIMPLE FAITH

When the British Expeditionary Force of one hundred thousand men arrived on the front in August, only sixty-five chaplains went with them, but a month later, there were nine hundred more chaplain volunteers than could be processed. It was a chaotic situation, not helped by the conservative and narrowly evangelical attitude of Bishop John Taylor Smith, the first chaplain general, because many Anglican chaplains wanted to reach the soldiers with communion services and church devotions, and well as with biblical preaching. It took the appointment of Bishop Llewellyn Gwynne to arrange a more developed prayer and sacramental ministry, as well as the improvement of recruiting and organization, impressing the devout General Herbert Plumer, who later went so far as to say that Gwynne did more to win the war than anyone. The Anglican priest Frank R. Barry wrote, "Many of us, I think, would have gone under or have suffered shipwreck of their faith had it not been for the pastoral care and guidance of the great and saintly Bishop Gwynne, Father in God to a whole generation of our men."[59]

The churches' deficiencies before the war were magnified all the more. Indifference to the national church made the ministry more difficult to begin with, and with the addition of the disruption and chaos of war, the result was little short of total frustration. In the words of Frank Barry, "I myself had only just been ordained priest, hopelessly ignorant and inexperienced.... But all of us, apart from a few regulars, came from academic or churchy circles.... Now we found ourselves called to serve a mass of men under intense moral and physical strain, to whom most of what we have been taught to preach seemed to be almost totally irrelevant." For a long time, the only distinctly spiritual ministry expected was the burial prayers, although some priests were called to do body identification. Edward Campbell in particular steadfastly identified over six hundred bodies of the five to six thousand, in various stages of decomposition, which had to be buried over the course of fifteen weeks. Writing letters to next of kin was the associated task, and beyond this there were sports events and entertainment to be arranged. But encountering and making sense of frontline hell had the potential to destroy even the chaplains' faith. Neville Talbot wrote:

> At the front, where all is stripped and laid bare, modern warfare is at times a furnace of horror. Its smoke darkens the heavens, thickening the "clouds and darkness" round about God, and deepening His silence. Its white head scorches out human confidence in Him. He does not seem to count. There are stars in the darkness of war—stars which are the achievements of man's indomitable spirit. But God-ward there seems sometimes to be great darkness.... Further, war, despite all the easy things said in its praise is a great iniquity. It is, as others have said, hell. As an environment to the soul it is, for all the countervailing heroisms of men, a world of evil let loose.[60]

Struggling to meet the challenge, Neville Talbot and Philip Clayton, his fellow Anglican priest, rented a house behind the Flanders front at Poperinghe as a club for the men. They installed a chapel in the loft, using a carpenter's bench as the altar and deliberately omitting the communion rail.[61]

Talbot composed a combination memoir and informal theological essay based on his experience there and elsewhere on the front, which he entitled *Thoughts on Religion at the Front*. The questions he tried to answer were "How is the Christian religion at the front? How is it with the men? Where are they religiously?" He saw beneath the rough and "inarticulate" outside were depths of goodness and self-sacrifice. Talbot vigorously rejects any demeaning descriptions of his men. "As I have hovered in seeming priestly impotence over miracles of cheerful patience lying on stretchers in dressing-stations, I have said—I have vowed to myself—'Here are men worth doing anything for.'" But he found little to commend in salvation-seeking religion, understandable as part of human nature but nothing more. There is plenty of goodness in Anglicanism, but "religion seems not to afford the slightest relief," because "religion as taught by the Church of England, has a feeble grasp on the masses." Here, biblical literalism has been a "dead weight," only made worse by "the cataclysm of war." No wonder then that it has seemed natural to the soldiers to be less religious and more sportingly self-sufficient: "the best men, richly gifted with manly excellences, tend to leave [religion] to one side."[62]

Talbot creates a theological profile of the ideal Christian soldier, who finds life by losing it. This is neither a matter of nature nor of church. This is the religion of Jesus, rooted in the Father's will. "For him the one sufficient thing was that the Father knew all things—the times and the seasons, the cup to be drunk, the will to be done and the final outcome," and "Jesus ... is the full and crowning expression of that which is hardly articulate in others." He doubles back to his natural, manly soldier and the service mission of the church. The soldiers who do not pray, the soldiers who pray out of their deep need to escape the suffering of the war, and the soldiers who detest their own fear and failures: these all deserve pastors and a church that ministers to them in the present war and effects reforms that will better serve them in peacetime. The church owes it to them, because "only second to the wonder of the Gospel of the Cross are the achievements of the souls of very ordinary men under unparalleled afflictions."[63]

P. B. Clayton featured Talbot House stories in his *Plain Tales from Flanders*. Charming they could be, but one was particularly dark in its opening theme, poison gas: a story of the "instructed and intelligent Christian," George Dewdney and the guileless, salt-of-the-earth soldier, Archie Forrest, who was introduced—to his great joy—into the Christianity positively presented by Talbot, Clayton, and Dewdney himself. Archie, on an emotional high after his baptism, and without any inclination to convert-style proselytizing, radiated a happiness that caught on with the soldiers and officers. Six weeks later he was killed, on his way back from the front line. Dewdney, his friend and mentor, survived but died shortly after the war from the effects of poison gas. For Clayton, Archie's death brought to Talbot House "a power of union which life in the world lacks ... and he grows not old; for time, which halts with none of us here, is powerless to change him, and no lines of disappointment and disillusionment are on his face, or is his hair tinged with grey." Clayton's own dedication was well known. He brought the Eucharist into the trenches and was known to scramble over to men who were on guard, so as to give them communion: "all knelt, taking off their helmets to receive Communion."[64]

The essence of these ministries was face-to-face encounter. John Groser also lived with his men in the trenches and was even agreed to lead them on one occasion when all officers had been killed—provided he himself did not have to kill or even carry a weapon. John Michael Stanhope Walker, who joined the war in 1915 and in three months buried nine hundred soldiers, struggled through the chaos of the first day of the Somme. "We have 1,500 in

FIG. 16 The upstairs chapel at Talbot House, now preserved as a museum. Photo: Maurice Savage / Alamy Stock Photo.

and still they come, 300–400 officers, it is a sight—chaps with fearful wounds lying in agony, many so patient, some make a noise, one goes to a stretcher, lays one's hand on the forehead, it is cold, strike a match, he is dead—here a Communion, there an absolution, there a drink, there a madman," the latter kicking and swearing and spitting water in his face. He combined a ministry to the disfigured with attempts to structure a Eucharist and even cared for flowers and fruits when in a hospital behind the front. Although the men were grateful for his care, they did not return to regular church attendance: "They would come as a favour to me if I pressed them, at least some would, but what is the use?" Soldiers could be profoundly grateful. As one of them was being pulled from a trench, wounded, he said, "Are you our clergy?" and then put his arms around the priest, clinging to him, "feeling [the priest thought] he was not alone in a friendless world." But they also had considerable questions. In his autobiography Frank Barry wrote about the challenge presented by the good and heroic *ir*religious soldiers. "In so evil a situation, of which the devil seemed to be in control, how could we go on believing in God at all, as the Father of our Lord Jesus Christ?" There was real perplexity in the words of the soldier who could not reconcile Christian teaching with battle: "Well, Padre, you think it all right sticking Germans. You love'em and stick'em?"⁶⁵

Oswin Creighton passed through the full range of padre experiences and is perhaps the best example of service to the last as total discouragement darkened his last years at the front. He embraced all the elements of the Church of England sacramental, evangelical, and social, out of which the clergy often selected only one or the other. But Creighton suffered because of the church's failure in each of these areas. It pained him that the men who liked him would avoid the communion liturgy, that men who loved to argue would avoid religious issues, and that men who wanted a reformed society ignored the potential of the church to help with all this. First sent to the Gallipoli front in Turkey and then to the western front along the Somme, he little by little lost all ministerial energy, finally believing that the men who fought fatalistically and without reflection had gotten it right. In Gallipoli he could still write, "Men are turning in absolutely simple faith and confidence to God, and the sense of His Presence has been wonderfully close all the time. I do think we are a Christian army; that is the great comfort." Transferred to the western front, he briefly spent some preparation time in Romsey, England, where he was invigorated by a discussion of the role of the lay people in the church but said that men who go about their work with complete dedication without any help from or regard for religion are a challenge to his own ways: "Have I learnt wrong, or is the way I have learnt it one and theirs another?" These two ways he contrasts as a "within" and a "without." "The pious, narrow, self-satisfied, exclusive, moral world within—the weak, kindly, happy, loose-moralled, generous, spontaneous, tolerant without." There are strengths and weaknesses on both sides, and he would like to bring the two together.⁶⁶

Creighton's first experience of religious worship in France was rewarding. He praised the "little services" where men were "crammed" together and "sang heartily." He could hold them in tents, in battery gun-pits, and in barns. It is no surprise that after his experiences in the first part of his chaplaincy, communion services and discussions were the primary values, and that only after he gained some experience did he appreciate the importance of preaching. He wrote, "It was wonderful how they listened. How terribly important preaching is, even though one feels that worship is the only thing worthwhile." He worked hard to convince the men that worthiness and propriety were false sentiments. "They think me rather profane when I suggest that only people who feel they are bad should go [to communion].... After all, Christ was not formal, and why should we hold formal services?" Creighton

FIG. 17 The Anglican priest Oswin Creighton, one of a number of chaplains who ministered to the English soldiers and shared their pains and religious doubts. From Oswin Creighton, *Letters of Oswin Creighton, C.F. 1883–1918* (London: Longmans, Green, 1920).

alternated between pleasure and discouragement depending upon the attendance and engagement of the men. The common feature across all religious encounters was "how few men know anything of, or take any interest in, the Church of England," and he had no solution to that either: "What religion—apart from ordinary life—is, and how to set about it, are questions I am unable to answer, and the difficulty or getting at any conclusion is so great that I often feel utterly bewildered and at sea."[67]

Arriving at the front, in Arras, Creighton found that he and his fellow chaplains believed they were all deteriorating religiously. Their prayer together was rewarding, but they were incapable of defining religion for the soldiers and unsatisfied with past definitions of it. Creighton himself was perplexed by the almost universal "agnosticism" of the generous and unselfish officers, and he evoked how an officer's "actions so often belie his words. He is a generous unselfish fellow . . . so bored with preaching and speechifying that he constantly, as it were, caricatures it in his own conversation." Creighton above all rejects the important of converting such a fellow to faith. "Christ did not demand of any one that they should believe in Him as God. He left it to them to find out if they could. Yet He said, 'Follow Me,' not as God but as Man—Son of Man." For Creighton, the war presented no religious possibilities or options. Apart from bringing men of the same side together in friendship and social exchange, the effect of war on religion was totally negative. If people pray, it is mechanical. Specifically religious thinking is unintelligent. Creighton took on the attitude of Thomas (the apostle doubting the resurrection), "who could not cut himself off from the rest with whom he had identified himself, but could see nothing plainly and had no programme." The once rewarding experience of lively discussions no longer resonates for Creighton. He writes, "Life is too unnatural and false to have any ideas of any value." Even the death of a much-admired fellow chaplain left him indifferent.[68]

Oswin Creighton never lost faith in Christianity, in the sense that he never lost faith in Christ. In August of his last year in the war (he was killed on 9 April 1918), he wrote, "I get quite alarmed at the extent of my own disillusionment. I don't quite know where I find things that stand the test. . . . I see singularly little efficacy in any of the religion I have tried to practice as performance." He believed in the bravery of the men and the goodness in individual lives and did not believe that "God can be interested in the war or in the nations taking part in it, or in the righteous causes involved, but solely in each of the individuals engaged. He looks at it all from their point of view. How are they going to take it? What will they make of it?" And here, the church is in the way, so if people don't want the clergy system it should be dropped. For Creighton, religion is, finally, an agnostic faith in an "Almighty Being," and a personal faith in "Christ *only*. . . . At Easter-time I always feel the personal note of Christianity. 'This day shalt *thou* be with Me,' 'Mary,' 'Follow thou Me.' . . . 'Ye shall be My witnesses.' 'even so send I you.'" These were the last words Father Creighton wrote before heading out to a battery position during an attack. He was killed instantly with several other men by an exploding shell.[69]

Creighton's explanation of why God permits war, and World War I in particular, was grounded in the Parable of the Prodigal Son.

> I asked [the men] to think of the father's relation to the son. Why did he not stop him leaving home? Simply because he was his father and not his boss. He wanted him, but he could not stop him and remain his father. No father can thwart his son and retain his love. The son going down the road confidently, excitedly to see the world and join the crowd, is the symbol of nearly all mankind. The trouble with the world is its thoughtlessness and heedlessness. The prodigal son wasted his substance as the world has wasted its civilization. Did his father

forget him because he had gone? He never ceased watching till he should see him coming back. So God waits for man's return from a life, not so much of evil, but of purposelessness, emptiness, riotous living without anything lasting to show, to his true home of beauty, truth, justice, honour and love—and above all of merry-making. The world is in want and pain, but as it returns in penitence, only beauty, the robe, and real merry-making await it. So though God cannot stop the war because He is our Father, He waits and longs for our return from a life without Him, which makes war possible, to a life with Him, when war will be impossible.[70]

Other chaplains offered reflections that were, in effect, variations of Oswin Creighton's search for the goodness in the men and the obligation of the church to cultivate this goodness on the soldiers' own terms. Charles Doudney, killed early on in the war, described his first experience of the wounded men, "They're so quiet. Surely down at the bottom of it all, under the rough surface and the ignorance, there must be the sense of that same sacrifice that in some manner was borne on the cross." After he had arrived at the front himself, he wrote, "One who has not been through it could never hope to understand what this war is. It is simply hell on earth but a hell through which moves a race of heroes, whose bravery and self-sacrifice make one ashamed." James Hannay wrote, "I resent the talk about the failure of Christianity and the assertion, far too often made, that our soldiers are essentially irreligious.... If indeed it is true that these men are irreligious, then religion is something other than what Christ taught." And Arthur Gray was similar to Creighton but with some subtle differences: "[The soldiers] don't believe in Church, or parsons, or pious pretensions. . . . They do believe whole-heartedly in good-fellowship, in being jolly to everybody, in unselfishness, in good spirits, and in charitable judgment. Call these things by their New Testament names—call them brotherhood, loving the brethren, losing your life, bearing others' burdens, rejoicing evermore, charity—and Tommy is 'put off.' But the things themselves he believes in with his whole heart. Believing in them constitutes the religion which he already has." Even so, Gray, a Presbyterian minister, held out for a church that makes demands on its members. For him, the God revealed by Christ "is the father in the parable of the Prodigal Son, and also the austere leader [Christ himself] who cries 'If any man will come after me, let him deny himself and take up his cross'—that God loathes sin and yet is able to love sinners—that he wants now to welcome sinners and lead them through a life of brave, happy, and exhausting service—that surely is the good news."[71]

German chaplains looked to extoll the virtues of the soldiers, while trying to minister to their weaknesses. Although seldom directly engaged in the attacks, they saw firsthand the suffering and death all around them and shared the sorrows engendered by separation from homeland and family. They brought to their men the pastoral concerns of the home churches for faith and sexual morality. Those that wrote extensive diaries could report more. Pastor Eggebrecht, although totally committed to the German cause, saw militarism as a hindrance, and the tendency to create a German God lamentable. Realistically, he knew that some men needed to hate the enemy in order to fight, but he firmly believed that Christ died for both sides. His war-chaplain ministry did not distract him from thoughts of his wife at home or from keeping watch at the bedside of his dying soldier brother. Pastor Stählin walked the high road of respect for cultural beauty and an ecumenical commitment to negotiate and enhance the liturgical worship at the front. Yet he gave himself fully to comforting and counseling the often-anguished men in the field hospitals, and he had an unusual sympathy for the folk in the occupied territories. It all became too much at one point, and he temporarily broke down. Other pastors in their writing highlighted the vital ministry of the field hospitals, the unique quality of German goodness, and the spiritual beauty of the evangelical church. The priests Berg and Kreutz exercised ministries similar to the Protestant pastors, but with minute record keeping of official religious services and pointed efforts to bolster the soldiers' morale. For these two men, connections with government and church authorities were central to their identity as chaplains. And it would appear that lecturing on Catholic history was almost as important as any liturgy or soldier consoling and counseling.

The testimonies by and about the French priests were a mixture of national sentiment and religious ideology: fighting for France could be done within the context of a priestly vocation. Saintly figures (such as Joan of Arc) and childlike virtue were the types to imitate. The priest could not choose to take life but could be forced to do so by war; even so, he must ever remain the moral guide. From God came life, and one should be willing to surrender it. It would be perfectly appropriate to do so for the sake of France—to safeguard the integrity of French soil and to share in the blood sacrifice of fellow French men and women. The importance of their sacramental powers (celebrating Mass and hearing confessions) preoccupied some of the priests and seminarians, whereas the ability to be genuine soldiers and genuine priests at the same time preoccupied others such as Grivelet, Arlet, and Lavergue. Jesuit priests and seminarians—Durouchoux, de la Perraudière, Chabord, and Nourisson—highly educated, produced more systematic moral reflections on the killing of enemies and submitting to mortal danger. They resolved the moral contradictions of killing for the sake of a greater good: enemies are enemies, but one must love them. They understood suffering and death to be for the sake of a future, better world. They believed that the coming of the Kingdom of God depended upon the realization of the mystery of the cross of Christ, a mystery that soldiers share in when the war ravages their bodies also. French nuns wrote little that has been preserved in original form, but Sisters Gabrielle, Rebondin, and Saint-Péreuse described in detail their encounters with enemy soldiers and gave graphic accounts of the suffering of the severely wounded. At the service of France, they negotiated with German officers. At the service of the church, they consoled and carefully nursed the soldiers in their care.

The key examples here of the English chaplain experience were the Anglican priests Neville Talbot, Philip Clayton, Frank Barry, and Oswin Creighton. Talbot and Clayton were able to set up a way station where a semblance of home life and pastimes could be combined with services, preaching, and serious chat sessions. But the dangers, sorrow, and dramas reported by Frank Barry and Edward Campbell show the challenge to Talbot-house solutions and underscore the uniqueness of the Talbot-house ministry. Chaplains Groser and Walker were especially aware of the need to be in the trenches with the men but doubted that even trench solidarity would lead to more soldier engagement with the churches. All of which places the personality of the Anglican priest Oswin Creighton in high relief as the key witness to the full set of chaplains' experiences. He concluded that the soldiers themselves— for all their failings—would produce the *substance* of Christianity, and that this was more important than the churches or even the war itself. Chaplains Doudney, Hannay, and Gray, a Presbyterian, echoed Creighton's beliefs, although neither they nor the other chaplains reached for the key parable of Christ on the departure, wandering, and return of the Prodigal Son, to explain the *whole* of the human struggle across the endless years.

CHAPTER 5

Jewish Chaplains and Their Soldiers
Ministry and Preaching

In Germany, France, and England, Jewish citizens were a small influential minority, men and women who were facing the challenge of preserving an identity, partly religious and partly ethnic, as they worked toward first-class citizenship in each of these nations. They had centuries of oppression and rejection behind them, making acceptance by Christian majorities everywhere a major task. In the armies, the heritage of anti-Semitism was still active. Prussia had no Jewish commissioned officers after 1885, despite legal and political maneuvers to change the situation, mainly because anti-Semites were deceptive and educated Jews were blindsided by official army assurances that there was no real problem. Only Bavaria had some token Jewish officers.[1] French Jews after the Dreyfus affair ended either remained in shock or trusted the liberal government to countermand the conservative army command. They could be encouraged, as the war went on, by the change of heart of the well-known novelist Maurice Barrès, politically a conservative and religiously an anti-Semite. In his *Diverses familles spirituelles de la France* (The Diverse Spiritual Families of France), he argued that Christians and Jews, socialists and traditionalists had come together in "a profound unanimity" at the outbreak of the war.[2] In England, the Jewish officers were few and belonged to the Anglo-Jewish elite. Jewish expressions of faith and identity paralleled those of the Christian majorities in Germany, France and England; here, though, to home-nation loyalty were added expressions of international Jewish solidarity. Even the demeaning "Jewish census" ordered by the German war ministry in 1916, which angered rabbis and activists at home, was barely noticed or went unmentioned by chaplains and soldiers. Derek Penzlar in his *Jews and the Military* explains that "the census gained significance [only] retroactively, after the Nazi accession to power in 1933, as shown in memoirs written at and after that time."[3]

German Jewish chaplains have left the largest collection of writings, engaging with and responding to the war. With only six rabbis at the beginning of the war, the number grew to thirty by the end, but they had roughly ninety-six thousand Jewish soldiers to minister to. A remarkable collection of these writings has been published in translation with commentary by Peter C. Appelbaum in *Loyalty Betrayed: Jewish Chaplains in the German Army During the First World War*, and this is the source of the testimonies here. French chaplains, studied in the broader setting of the French Jewish experience of the war by Philippe Landau in *Les Juifs de France et la Grande Guerre: Un patriotisme républicain* (The Jews of France and the Great War: Republican Patriotism), come into full focus in the stories of two leading rabbis: Abraham Bloch, chief rabbi of Lyon, who achieved iconic status for care of Christian as well as Jewish soldiers, and Jacob Kaplan, later the chief rabbi of France but during the war a rabbinical student and only informally a chaplain, who fought as an ordinary foot soldier. There were no English rabbis in the British Expeditionary Force, or even provision for them, until Michael Adler forced the issue. Rabbi Adler wrote up his experiences subsequently for publication in the *Jewish Guardian*. There are few collections of soldier testimonies because so much was lost during the Holocaust, although the few available ones can be very revealing and are presented here.[4]

GERMAN RABBIS: JEWISH CULTURE IS GERMAN CULTURE

Bruno Italiener, before leaving for the western front, preached the patriotic sermon, "We Must Win," to his home congregation in Darmstadt. Reading the verse "See I lay before you a blessing and the curse," he said that blessing and curse were never more clearly posted than in the war Germany was undertaking. The fate of the fatherland will be both; the fate of individuals will be both. Though not yet off to war, Italiener still dared to say to his congregation, "Would we wish to have missed these [recent] days of enthusiasm, when a wave of one great will took hold of our entire German *Volk*"? He evokes the wonderful German spirit that inspired people to put down scythe and pen to take up the sword. This patriotic commitment could only have come from faith: "Yes, we pray again." Not that prayers will guarantee victory or safety,

FIG. 18 Jewish chaplains who served on the western front. Standing (from left to right): Rabbis Baerwald, Italiener, Cohn, Lewin, Salzberger. Sitting (from left to right): Rabbis Wilde, Baeck, and Levy. Jewish Museum, Frankfurt.

but they will guarantee justice and truth. Italiener (from Darmstadt) was in contact with and was able to join in conferences with the principal field rabbis: Georg Salzberger (Frankfurt), Leo Baeck (Berlin), Emil Levy (Berlin, Charlottenburg), Reinhold Lewin (Leipzig), and Leo Baerwald (Munich). "Baeck was the chairman and Italiener kept the minutes."[5]

Rabbi Georg Salzberger began service as a chaplain one month after the declaration of hostilities, publishing his war diaries—redone as a memoir—in 1916, right after the battle of Verdun. He reported his service to the dying, burials, and the religious festivals celebrated at the front—a chaplain who was clearly ministering to his men. In fact, the memoir begins at Verdun, with the battle in the background and a blood-red sun sinking in the west. As the Jewish New Year began, he prayed "Our Father Our King, frustrate the design of our enemies," and "Our Father Our King, cause salvation speedily to spring forth for us." He also reported how struck he was by the words "Man is like a flower that fades and a shadow that passes, like a fleeting dream." As the days went on, the number of congregants increased, but they were still only a fraction of the Jewish soldiers in the field. The vast majority would have no services, and no rabbi to minister to them. Yom Kippur itself, the Day of Atonement and the day when, as Salzberger wrote, "Our religion proclaims a kingdom of eternal peace through this day of peace with God," had arrived. Rabbi Salzberger could only hope for the unity of nations who pray to the same Father, looking forward to "the Great Day of Atonement for all Mankind." In the army, the Jewish soldiers were, in spite of old family prejudices, treated as equals and, for some achievements, respected. This situation stands in contrast with what Salzberger understands to be English and French culture; "Whatever one can say about French spiritual flexibility and English business sense, the decisive factor is that the Jewish heart corresponds with German nature," which means that anti-Jewish stereotypes are actually anti-German stereotypes. Away from the battlefields Salzberger served, he contrived to gather several dozen soldiers for his Sabbath services. All ranks of soldier, and the full spectrum of Jewish viewpoints—orthodox, liberal, freethinkers, Zionists, assimilationists—were represented.[6]

Moving from field hospitals to the front, Salzberger wrote passionately of the horrors experienced by his soldiers. He was never part of the attacks, but he ministered to the men when they were brought back wounded and dying. The men cry out to him as he moves in their midst. He tries to write postcards home for them: "Please don't make it sound too bad, Rabbi." For him the material and spiritual ministries are inextricably mixed together, sometimes in a structured field hospital, but often in any shelter where the wounded could be gathered. "Words alone are of no assistance. The poor souls crave a refreshing drink." He worries about handing out cigarettes in straw-littered barns or churches but cannot refuse. Sacrifice is for the fatherland and Salzberger notes no bitterness but says "the spiritual treatment of an educated man more difficult," brooding about how he could help a crippled physician or a paralyzed teacher who will have no professional future. Salzberger reviews the types of wounds, from easily removed shrapnel to dumdum bullets and splinter sprays. He found that some of the most seriously wounded possessed an optimism that he encouraged, even as he prepared to write the inevitable death notice to the family. Traveling in German-occupied eastern France, he stopped at every field hospital to minister to the Jewish soldiers, moving so fast that he could not make satisfactory bed-to-bed visits. His main purpose on these journeys was to conduct services, arranging place and time by telephone or visits to commanding officers.

He conducted services everywhere, but not in the trenches because his soldiers were too widely dispersed and so had to be brought together in a hall, schoolhouse, or Christian church. He found only three Jewish synagogues; although he was not able to use them for services, he was moved to find the enshrined Torah scrolls. Staying with a French Jewish family, he participated in, led prayers, in the evening meals: "Domestic tranquility is not broken by the fact that our hosts cling to their own French Fatherland with the same fervent love as do we Germans ours."[7]

And so there were the Chanukahs, the Passovers, and back again to the New Years and Yom Kippurs. Some men did not seem to have serious religious interests or concerns but prayed to express solidarity with their fellow Jews. Salzberger describes others on the front, however, "who daily and hourly look death in the face, experience a religious rebirth. It appears simply as a belief in one living God, but their faith is deeper and more profound exactly because it is experienced." Thus, Jewish memories and customs serve as the channels for a profound experience of God. Meeting with Jewish chaplains later at Lille, he was taken aback by the destruction of the beautiful train station and business quarter, and the strict—justifiable, he thought—German control of the city, but was pleased by the preservation of the public buildings, the art museum, and the theater. He writes of Verdun with such perception that his interpretations seem to come after a long period of reflection, belying the fact that he published them in 1916. Something about the near instant accumulation of all the horrors of war made Salzberger, like so many others, feel exhilaration in the presence of the "wall of humanity" and the "incredible frenzy": "man against man, for every forest, every town, every valley and every hill." But this sentiment is paired with "Friend and foe agree: Verdun is hell, a hissing, howling, bursting, crashing, flaming hell, a suffocating, crunching, devouring hell," making endurance a "triumph of the human spirit." At the end, though, both the nonwounded and wounded could no longer muster enthusiasm of any kind, and spiritual care became more difficult. The rabbi could only work on continually writing the letters and cards for the wounded, and sending families news of the dead. The common burials were naturally presided over by Christian chaplains—with the help, when necessary—of the rabbis, which leads him to praise the "unity of faith in the face of death, which is the same for Jew and Christian." He goes back over the Verdun Passover celebration with the Seder ceremony, evoking Jewish striving, suffering, and sacrifices to get to Egypt, and sets it within the modern experience of saving the German fatherland. Later, as he preached, he realized that the men before him had just come from the trenches, mortal danger, and the shelling to silence, light, and "an atmosphere of human kindness and Godly peace." These men then returned to the battle, many to their deaths.[8]

What, then, could be learned from the war, from the experience of time and space on the battlefield? There were no masks, no defenses against reality; the men came to know themselves and their fellows. As the men gathered for prayers in what Rabbi Salzberger called his "forest synagogue," his experiences came together for him. "The deep silence of an autumn day reigned in the forest around us.... Cannons thundered on the other side of the valley. Bloody battle in the midst of the holy peace of nature. In seemingly eternally peaceful nature, powerful forces battle for victory everywhere, and everlasting Godly laws are revealed in the thundering struggle of nations. And we humans, who are placed equally into nature and in history, what else could be our ethical duty other than to overcome this conflict in our own breasts with the iron law of duty?" For Salzberger the war was a spiritual setback for all. The initial rekindling of faith died down into fatalism. For the small numbers who "found God once and for all in the silence of many a long night," there was the majority who were "gradually . . . overcome by fatalistic belief." Faith was not completely extinguished, but such resignation "has little in common with the humble confidence of the faithful one who . . . bears his fate with patience." Salzberger had here one central consolation: "Our Jewish soldiers have become more Jewish. This is a sign that outside, or rather beneath, our faith there is something that binds us together: the past, present and future, in brief our common history."[9]

Rabbi Martin Salomonski was a German patriot, who remembered a good, if sometimes unhappy, relationship between Germany and France. On his way to Saint-Quentin in northern France, he passed the towns of Maubeuge and Le Cateau that had figured so prominently in the first months of the war, finally arriving before the "glorious" cathedral of Saint-Quentin. From there he made his way toward an advance field hospital at the front. Burials were an occasion to lament the deaths, of course, but also to praise the solidarity of the men. "Clearly no extensive praise would bring the dead back; the biblical words: 'weep not for the dead, weep rather for those who remain behind' assume increased relevance. The compassion shown by our comrades in arms is a great deal more honest than that seen at home from acquaintances and so-called friends." But when a French airplane shot German observation balloons out of the sky (over French territory), he thought everyone, even the French villagers, was disgusted. "We saw a tiny column of smoke and soon the entire proud giant shell became a sea of fire. The observer [in the balloon] plunged from the basket head over heels into the depths. . . . I can still hear the crowd's cry of pain at the horrible sight of this act of destruction." Then Rabbi Salomonski launched into a long diatribe condemning the French and completely exonerating the Germans. "[German soldiers] are happy to sacrifice their lives to protect the Fatherland, and would rather die than wish to fade away in an infirm body or an enslaved Homeland. . . . Our air forces have gone to war against the armed enemy following only justifiable dictates of necessity and resistance, and they treat the enemy with conciliatory chivalry. . . . By contrast, the abuses and attacks upon our prisoners of war, especially in France, by officers, physicians, nurses and the inflamed masses, often at express command of their superiors, are well known." Such chauvinism also found its way into the liturgy: "A prayer for each comrade who had fallen or been badly wounded during the course of the week and the extended prayer for Kaiser, Princes of State and *Reich*, in which God's blessing is beseeched: 'For our army that is used to winning in battle, and is not fighting the harsh battle that has been imposed upon it by others.'" In fact, though, Rabbi Salomonski brought this same loyal dedication to his work as rabbi and counselor. "How often have I sat at the bed of a suffering man, spoken to him about an approaching good future and speedy return home, knowing that in a day, maybe in an hour, he will have crossed over into the unknown. . . . Each bed holds a new task for the chaplain. . . . One must always proceed in such a way as to gain [the soldier's] trust and lighten his spirit." Those soldiers who survived wrote back later to express their appreciation.[10]

The liberal rabbi Leo Baeck became the most renowned of the chaplains. His reports in the *Gemeindeblatt der jüdischen Gemeinde zu Berlin* (Newsletter of the Berlin Jewish Community) took readers to the front and the field hospitals. He was there for the first Yom Kippur of the war, and then, in October, he held services in Noyon for the soldiers who could get away from the front. Praising his soldiers for their sensitivity to the local population, he had a special appreciation of the "warmth," "light," and "joy" found in his small gatherings of men. He was pastorally responsible for over seventy field hospitals, some of which were converted churches. He appreciated the churches, and he also appreciated the captured French Jewish soldiers. He tried to appeal to the hearts and minds of all of them.[11]

Preaching for the Jewish New Year, Baeck told his soldiers:

> It is the deepest demand of our religion that we do not pass by any question that touches our lives. Its introductory work is therefore, always and again: "Hear!" "God speaks to you!" For our faith it is a godless quality when the ear is closed: he who has turned away stands before it as a sinner. It has given its many commandments, but they are all, to begin with, a simple word; they become reality only when these words have called to men from life quietly or loudly, and they have heard. The world around us speaks, admonishes and asks, and only insofar as there are people who hear will truthfulness and loyalty, righteousness and love descend to earth.

This sermon seems more like a meditation on a "new piety" whose bearers simply appreciate life in the face of war. "What has for so long dominated life's view has collapsed . . . belief that everything has already been achieved, that there is so much civilized behavior, education, religion in the world." Now the soldiers could see "how little faith really exists on earth despite all reigning, beckoning religions." Baeck believes that Jews in particular would not be disillusioned here: "We have known this feeling from the days of our forefathers: of standing alone in the family of nations, not understood or respected. . . . So our religion signifies hope." The settings and the services make Judaism real for his men, in all of their personal and regional variety. In August of 1915, Baeck wrote, "The former inn room in which we gather transforms itself into a *shul*, into the synagogue of a small town with its atmosphere and warmth. One of the older men knows how to lead the service, in the ancient melody of Sabbath afternoon, with ascending and descending cadences containing so much that is calm and contented. All the rest join in responsive sentences of the prayers and on their faces is reflected something of this experience." It was clear to Rabbi Baeck that the soldiers are engaged: "One of them knows how to quote a Bible text in line with the sermon as proof of his opinion and hope; another mentions a sentence from our sages, which he has heard from his grandfather. Conversation and contradiction, question and answer go back and forth, sometimes serious sometimes cheerful." This gathering had more the qualities of a service in a small German town; another had the qualities of a larger synagogue in north Germany.[12]

Rabbi Emil Levy pondered the meaning of faith in his contribution to a collection of *Sabbathgedanken* (Sabbath Meditations) collected and published later. "Without faith there is no future for the German nation; without faith there is no progress for Israel, without faith there is no happiness or individual peace." The cultural mission of the German and Jewish people means the destruction of a materialistic worldview, as in the prophet Zechariah, "Not by might nor by power, but by My spirit, says the Lord of Hosts." Levy evokes the song of victory after the crossing of the Red Sea, the joy on entering the promised land, in the confidence that they are an eternal people. "We are not soulless dust particles and machine parts without a will of their own; in each human being slumbers a spark of God, which can by a feeling of faith be ignited to become God's flame."[13]

In the same collection of *Sabbathgedanken*, Rabbi Reinhold Lewin grappled with the meaning of the existence of God and Rabbi Leo Baerwald grappled with the meaning of prayer. Lewin believes that few would doubt the existence of God if the war had been short with a German victory. He reminds listeners that the outbreak of war was met with some relief, enthusiasm, and engagement. Humans in their free will entered into war. What should they have expected of God then or now? "What does the claim mean that God, if He exists, should have stamped out the conflagration at its inception? Does it mean anything else but that God should, three years ago, have broken and violated the free will in men's hearts?" So, the person who makes God responsible for unleashing war actually ascribes to him a "theft of the crown which belongs on our heads." It would have taken a miracle, a suspension of nature's laws to prevent war at the beginning, and it would take a similar miracle to end it three years later. It is not for God to come down to "recast" human reality, but for humans to strive toward faith. Rabbi Baerwald began his contribution by quoting the Talmudic prayer, "The needs of men are many, but their understanding is short. May it be Your will, O Lord our God, to give each man what he needs for his sustenance and preservation. But, may Your will be done." Prayer is not *wishing*, then, prayer is *introspection*. One should pray for wisdom, which includes all others; one prays for shelter, food, and loved ones. It is not wrong to declare life's cares before God, but all the demands of the book of Psalms are in the context of praise. Union with God and submission to his will are the final goal: "This means, do not worry whether your prayer is heard, let that be God's concern because He knows better whether you will benefit by His answering it. Be happy that you have poured out your heart and have been able to liberate yourself from the pressure of your cares."[14]

FRENCH RABBIS: FRENCH LIBERTY GUARANTEES JEWISH LIBERTY

Toward the end of the war, there were thirty-eight French rabbis in the military chaplaincy compared to five hundred priests (not counting the large number of priest combatants), and sixty-eight Protestant ministers. Their average age was forty-one years old. The central consistory broke off relations with Jewish authorities in Germany, and the local consistories urged Jewish youths to fulfill their military obligations. The use of Yiddish was discouraged because of its resemblance to German and an obstacle to assimilation. Preaching could be pro-French for basic theological reasons. Samuel Korb of Nancy who lost three sons on the front, said simply, "God will not permit the triumph of violence over law." Use of arms is legitimate "for a just cause, for liberty, and for progress." He did not consider the armed response to "atrocities," "fires," and "devastation" an act of vengeance, but an act of justice. And preaching could be ferociously anti-German. Rabbi Maurice Liber, director of the *Revue des Études juives*, wrote, "The God of the French has nothing in common with the God of the *Boches*." The Germans represented the eternal enemy of Judaism (Amalec). Honel Meiss specifically invoked the law of the talion, "an eye for an eye, a tooth for a tooth, tears for tears, devastation for devastation."[15] Overall, Jewish authorities supported French

FIG. 19 The painting by Lucien Lévy-Dhurmer of Rabbi Abraham Bloch offering a crucifix to a dying Catholic soldier. Bibliothèque de Documentation Internationale Contemporaine (La Contemporaine).

republicanism in the context of the *Union sacrée*. As Philippe Landau notes, "The struggle was transformed into a holy war, which did not exclude a messianic hope, but was always in correlation with the republican ideal. Far from settling accounts with the political regime, the rabbis' sermons emphasized the objectives of the Jewish faith. In the war for law and justice, it mattered to define the role of Judaism in this time of trial as an heir of the Revolution of 1789 and a protector of the republic."[16]

The rabbi best remembered in postwar France was Abraham Bloch, who was killed on the front early in the war. A Jesuit reported at the time that Bloch died as he held up a crucifix before a dying Catholic soldier who had taken him for a priest, a story that gained wide currency and softened some of the anti-Semitism on the home front. Born in Paris, Bloch served in Remiremont in the *département* of the Vosges after being ordained a rabbi. He later applied for the post of chief rabbi in Algeria, meeting some opposition and antagonism, but none greater than that of a synagogue member who felt wronged when he did not receive sufficient money in charity from his rabbi. The man stabbed Rabbi Bloch, who forgave him and prevented his incarceration. The two of them were ultimately reconciled and Rabbi Bloch circumcised one of the man's children. After returning to France, Bloch became the chief rabbi at Lyon in 1908. Officially an army chaplain in 1913, he headed off to the front when war was declared. In his letters home to his wife, children, and sister, and in his diary, he spoke often about his good relationships with fellow chaplains, Catholic and Protestant. In his carnet entry for 8 August 1914, he wrote that he had traveled with a priest and a minister, with whom he got along quite well, and that even his beard did not identify him, because one of the Jesuit chaplains also had a beard. By 15 August, he was doing voluntary kitchen duty with curés and doctors but then headed off in terrible weather to help with the wounded. "I have seen the sad results of the fight, the fires, the dead, and the wounded," he wrote. Just over two weeks later he was dead. Then, on 24 September, the Jesuit Father Chauvin, sent Rabbi Bloch's wife the description of the final moments as reported by his fellow Jesuit, Father Jamin. "Before leaving the hamlet, a wounded man, taking him for a Catholic priest, asked to be able to kiss a crucifix. M. Bloch found the crucifix the soldier had asked for and helped him to kiss it. It was after having accomplished this act of charity that he left the hamlet, accompanying another wounded man as far as the closest car. The shell reached him a few meters in front of the car the wounded man had just gotten into." Abraham Bloch's widow sent this letter to the chief rabbi of France, who then forwarded it to several reviews. When the story appeared in the *Écho de Paris* of 7 November 1914, it contained added details about Bloch's efforts to secure the crucifix from a priest, coming back to the wounded man, and then offering the crucifix to another soldier, before Bloch himself died from a bullet wound to the head. Jamin's letter and the brief article in the *Écho de Paris* together were the sources of this most famous of French rabbi stories of the World War, and it inspired one of the most famous religious images of the war, *Le grand rabbin aumônier Abraham Bloch*, by Lucien Lévy-Dhurmer. In fact, details of the story remain controversial because of the incomplete and contradictory testimonies of the "witnesses."[17]

Jacob Kaplan, who later became a chief rabbi of France, was a rabbinical student in 1913 when he began the war as a simple soldier. Even when Chief Rabbi Alfred Lévy asked him to serve as military chaplain on a hospital ship, he demurred, so important to him was his membership in the "fraternity of the trenches" as a witness to his faith: "I felt that because I was a Jew I had to remain with my comrades." He led his parents to believe that he was better off with his regiment than on the hospital ship, and he firmed up his relationship with the men, who only learned decades after the war that he had passed up the chance for a much safer and somewhat comfortable assignment. Heading to Verdun after a leg wound suffered during the 1916 battles along the Champagne front, he served as a liaison between the front lines and strategists behind the lines, but he was regularly in the trenches at their most dangerous. There, even so, he managed to avoid shooting and killing. "Running the same risks as my comrades, I didn't have to shoot and kill. I couldn't stand the idea that I, a future rabbi, would be responsible for the death of a man, even if he was my enemy." He tells stories of his escapes from almost certain death, telling himself at one point after being hurled to the ground by an exploding shell, "I am dead," because, unable to move, there seemed to be no communication between his mind and his body. Always it was a question of whether to run or to hide from incoming artillery shells. After the war, when he was formally ordained, Kaplan ensured that his relationship with fellow soldiers issued in mutual respect at home. When the commemoration of the battle for Alsace at Vieil-Armand involved the official approval of a monument in the form of a cross, he gave a brief speech before a great gathering of civil and military officials, to the chagrin of the then chief rabbi. He said that as a veteran he was happy to celebrate "at the foot of the flagpole bearing the French flag," although he would not have been able to celebrate before an exclusively Christian symbol—and he was applauded by all. He also rejoiced to recall the fraternity of Rabbi Abraham Bloch and Bloch's fellow Catholic chaplain, and he rejoiced to recall the wartime chaplains' fraternity in general. "I am persuaded that the wonderful improvement of interconfessional relations that continues in its wake, is a result of the common life of Catholic, Protestant, and Jewish chaplains during the First World War."[18]

ENGLISH RABBIS: WAR, A TRIAL FOR FAITH AND MORALITY

As war was declared, rabbis in London immediately attempted to interpret its meaning for the English Jewish communities, urging English Jews to support England in spite of the moral "ambiguity" of waging war. The Orthodox rabbi Morris Joseph preached from the pulpit of the Berkeley Street Synagogue: "The lust to destroy and slay has taken possession of minds hitherto chiefly concerned to heal the hurt of the world, and to set the feet of mankind more firmly on the high-way of progress. It is a terrifying paradox, a cruel blow to our optimism and our most cherished ideals. It makes us doubt the value, the reality of our civilization, the stability of righteousness, the fixity of purpose of God himself." A year later he took all belligerents to task for disregarding their own cherished beliefs: "What faithlessness to the 'Prince of Peace' can be more flagrant than that which has plunged twentieth-century Christendom into the worst horrors of war."[19] He allowed, however, that the belligerent nations were at least officially ashamed and apologetic. "Even our chief enemy in this present conflict, while extolling war as the maker and preserver of a people's vigor, inconsistently excuses this particular war as one of self-defense. And we, his antagonists, though believing and declaring that our cause is just, confess in our inmost hearts that the means we have chosen to vindicate it are at best a necessary evil, a huge blot on our civilization."[20]

The first and most influential English Jewish chaplain, Michael Adler, was forced to cover a huge area but was instrumental in establishing the Jewish chaplaincy and reached a large number of Jewish soldiers even so. He explained in his journal that when he asked the War Office if he could minister to Jewish soldiers in France the authorities hesitated, because there was no precedent for a Jewish chaplain in the field, and Jewish soldiers were spread out over the entire front. They advised him to visit the British Expeditionary Force (BEF) to see if his services could be effective. YMCA authorities and some of the Christian chaplains, including a curé who lent Adler a car, helped him to get established. He held his first service at the Harfleur Reinforcement Camp on 29 January 1915; notices had been posted or published, and he was

FIG. 20 The English rabbi Michael Adler, second from left in bottom row, who was responsible for structuring and organizing the Jewish chaplaincy and ministering to soldiers in the field, shown here with members of the 17th London Regiment. From *British Jewry Book of Honour* (London: Caxton, 1922).

pleased with the results. Next was a synagogue in Le Havre, members of which were moved by this first gathering of Jewish soldiers to continue Adler's outreach. He subsequently activated synagogues in Rouen, Paris, Versailles, and Boulogne. In Paris, he made contact with the French chief rabbi, Alfred Lévy, in an effort to ensure Passover matzoth for the English troops; having them made was no problem, but there was a breakdown in the distribution system. By this time, he was assured by English authorities that he could operate in France as much as, and as long as, he saw fit, and another car was placed at his disposal upon his return to the front. Adler then worked out of the Mont-des-Cats monastery in Belgium, gave sermons, led services, and provided an occasional historical lecture. Headquarters provided him with provisional lists of Jewish soldiers, presumably a unique kindness, because no other denominational lists were made up. Exact location of the troops was not revealed until he was ready to make his way to them for a service. "Notices of the services were placarded in YMCA huts, and thus attracted the attention of stray soldiers. Their devotion to Judaism was exemplified by the eagerness of the men to attend these services under the most difficult conditions and frequently after long journeys." Adler said that he compiled a prayer book, with a printing of one hundred thousand copies, which served as a model for a similar prayer book in the American army. He urged soldiers who had no knowledge of Hebrew to come anyway, and he was happy to see that all those who came the first time presented themselves the second time around.[21]

Across the months of the Somme campaign, he came under enemy shelling several times, seeking shelter when needed. "Many a time, I would visit a group of men, however small, in some out-of-the-way place, much to their gratification, and a friendly chat and smoke always concluded with a brief religious service in which the men earnestly joined." Christian chaplains would request that he arrange services for the Jewish soldiers in their units. Military authorities also cooperated, suggesting that Jewish soldiers who were eligible for leave within the High Holiday period be permitted to do so. In 1915, for those still on the front, he made a broad tour to lead the services. "My first service on Yom Kippur in the Mairie of Noeux-les-Mines was most inspiring. Men marched in full-equipped straight from the lines, special orders having been issued to set them free, and we numbered about 200 congregants." On the following Saturday these same men went over the top, many to their deaths, in the Battle of Loos. When Rabbi Adler followed as far as the field hospitals and dressing stations, he "saw for the first time the dreadful sight of thousands of wounded and dying men being brought in." He also met Field Marshal John French and served as interpreter for the captured, wounded Germans, some of whom were Jewish. Rabbi Adler was called upon to conduct burial services with increasing frequency and subsequently tried to arrange for Jewish burial sections in the military cemeteries. Signs of anti-Semitism were "so small as to be entirely negligible," he said. "I received frequent letters from Christian soldiers telling me about their Jewish friends in most affectionate terms. . . . I can bring the same testimony with regard to the relations for the Jewish Chaplains to their colleagues of all other faiths. Two years in a row, Adler held services in theaters, Chanukah services in Lillers in 1915 and then New Year services in Acq, the Arras sector, in 1916, leading some soldiers to label the setting "Cinema-gogues." On those New Year days, he raced along conducting a service in Senlis, and then arranging to return to Acq and Albert for Yom Kippur. This was a style of conducting multiple services in sometimes widely separated settings that earlier earned him, to his amusement, the title of the "Wandering Jew"! Before 1916 was out there were Jewish chaplains in each of the five army areas and at three bases, a situation, in fact, that was woefully inadequate.[22]

In the spring of 1917, Adler had to perform numerous burials after Vimy Ridge and the battles around Arras: "The Jewish casualties in this offensive were very severe." He describes the scrambling across a fifty-mile area of the front, concentrating on those units that contained larger numbers of his men, such as the Royal Fusiliers, Middlesex, Manchesters, Rifle Brigade, and King's Royal Rifles. Then he settled into an "Armstrong hut"—canvas and wood— where he remained throughout the winter, until the retreat of March 1918. Proximity to medical units was excellent for his ministry and rewarding because of the interest in Judaism that he found among the medical services: doctors, nurses, and officers. For the New Year and Yom Kippur, he celebrated the services in a theater close by the ruined Bapaume basilica, before large congregations that "included, both on New Year and Atonement Day, a number of American Engineers who had recently been attached to the British Army, a party of Egyptian Jews with a Labour Company, and men from all parts of the Empire. The Shofar was blown by a soldier of the 4th London Regiment, who had been a bugler in the Jewish Lads' Brigade." Throughout this time, he conducted occasional services, even as shelling continued on the front line about 1,500 yards away. As the English were retreating from his area, he saw the cars of Marshal Foch, Douglas Haig, Lloyd George, and Georges Clemenceau outside the Doullens town hall in the Somme, the site where "the famous decision was reached to appoint Marshal Foch as Generalissimo of the Allies." Both the retreat and the arrival of American troops provided the dramatic experiences of a celebration of Passover that terminated in the bombing of a large camp of German wounded soldiers before his eyes ("near where my car was standing"), and a joyful union of English and American Jewish soldiers—Australians also—who were happy to discover one another. He wrote letters to parents in America, who were very grateful for the contact. When he returned to England in July 1918, after his health gave way, his two great satisfactions, were "that [he] found ample opportunities to perform useful work, and... that the reputation of the Jewish soldier on the western front stood very high and reflected the fullest credit upon the good name of Anglo-Jewry."[23]

SOLDIERS OF THE THREE NATIONALITIES

The soldiers whose diaries and memories we have found seemed to appreciate Jewish tradition, value the moral high road, or appreciate human love as the greatest good.

Soldiers who spent their early years in a Jewish children's home and orphanage in Berlin wrote faithfully to the head educator and administrator, Sigmund Feist. These letters provide an insight into the strength these soldiers drew from a living tradition. With so many Jewish records destroyed during the Nazi period, this collection is now of singular importance. Former boarders recalled the discipline of the place with no resentment, but rather with gratitude for its formative value. One of the soldiers, Herbert Cyapski, even assumed that Feist would appreciate some propaganda features of the war: "Included here, a flyer thrown out over our placements by the French, which ought to interest you." He and other boarders said that they were well prepared for military drill and discipline, because their training was in order and discipline. Julius Marcus was especially clear about this. "The formation in the orphanage ensured that my life as a soldier did not seem difficult. In the morning we were awakened at 4:00 and were made to put bed in order, as we learned in the orphanage." Siegbert Jungmann closed his letter in the patriotic spirit that had been inculcated there. "With German-loyal greetings." But patriotism diminished as the war went on, and within the year Jungmann was writing, "May Almighty God grant us all good things, above all that this terrible killing come to an end." And Benno Jastrow on two occasions confessed, first, "Personally I feel perfectly fine. However, I'd much rather be working at my business than stay longer in this terrible war," and second, "Hopefully this fraud comes soon to an end." No mention was made of the Jewish census in any of these letters.[24]

Clearly the orphanage years left some of the men with trust in kindness and understanding, as well as confidence in their own Jewishness. Josef Cohn counted on Sigmund Feist to facilitate official registration of a complicated situation whereby he wanted to change his family name from Cohn to Kon for the sake of his Christian wife. And Feist had signed off on it. "With your valuable signature in hand, I would like to briefly and honestly respond to your questions. I have a Christian wife, but my family and myself are as Jewish as we were at the time of my stay in the orphanage. I married my wife out of love, and our marriage contract, which had been previously recorded in the registry office, has finally resulted in the authentic processing of my papers." Letters frequently cite feast day celebrations. For example, Benno Jastrow wrote, "This is my second Yom Kippur in the trenches, and now one prays, something that for me in civil life was seldom the case." So also, Karl Levit: "There are fifteen Jews in our company. So we marched to a gathering place, where Jewish soldiers from a variety of units were gathered. A Jewish military doctor, a Lieutenant took part in the service." Adolph Wisocki was pleased to write back about his work, beyond religious services, with the rabbi, Leo Baeck: "Rabbi Baeck boarded our hospital train, which is open to chaplains on the front. I introduced myself to him and was very happy that I could be helpful to him in a number of things." Paul Wohlgemuth sent to Feist a considered interpretation, virtually a brief discourse, on the war, morality, and society. "They always say that humanity stands on a higher level of culture. Yes, the culture level is so high that all that human hands have created on the entire front, from Flanders to Alsace, has been leveled to the ground. Men who thought they had no enmity between them must now take one another's lives. The greater the horror around us, and the longer the slaughter lasts, the more do the rich capitalists and winning battle units rejoice. We win and win, and so win ourselves to death."[25]

Jewish religious values grounded the war reflections in the diary of the German officer, Bernard Bing. From Verdun in 1916 Bing commented in his diary on the overall progress of the war on both fronts. He was clearheaded about command mistakes, and he saw the war itself as an overall mistake. After the loss of Fort Vaux, he wrote on 11 March, "We have again lost Fort Vaux; so swings the battle back and forth and costs victim after victim; the insanity of mankind, an era gone mad." A month later he observed that pessimists were easier to find than optimists, complaining that while the authorities in the Reichstag argue about peace, the "little people" suffer food rationing. He was only halfway through this international war when he began to call it a sickness. "More than ever I am thinking, a war of movement never more! Grave after grave! War unto the destruction at home and on the battlefield in one of the warring countries. Sad, unbelievable time, missing out on the good will of thousands, a sickness among peoples worse than the plague." Bing's diary entries in the months that follow include his thoughts on the Paul Hindenburg–Erich Ludendorff control of the army, the horror of the Somme, the progress of the war on other fronts, and the challenges of dealing with England and the still-neutral United States.[26]

Human love as the heritage of Judaism preoccupied the French secularized Jew André Kahn, whose diary of the war was edited and published years later by his nephew. He "lived and observed the war from every angle," wrote the nephew. So then, crawling under machine gun and artillery fire, lying flat in the trenches, and sorting out the dead at the Marne, the Chemin des Dames, and Verdun, he was still able to think clearly—and subtly—about the news of military and diplomatic actions. He wrote passages on morality and on the existence of God, in ways that could be interpreted as almost anti-Semitic. Antagonistic to the French army and government, at times to the point of disgust, he regained his loyalty with the thought that at least they were fighting Prussian militarism. He spent a brief time in a prison camp and later served on a tribunal to judge deserters from his own army. A right-wing bourgeois when he expressed himself about parliamentary administrations, workers' movements, and colonial troupes, he nevertheless damned the love of money as the source of the war and the motivation to end it.[27]

The God that Kahn believed in was not a personality but was love itself, in fact, the love between his wife, whose own beliefs he respected, and himself. He wrote to her at the beginning of the war, "I laugh not at your confidence in God nor at the pleasure you find in the fragrant calm of a church. This pleasure I experience myself without letting religious faith blind my soul. Regarding confidence in God, I can admit that, far from mocking it, I envy it. I understand it in others, but pass it up myself, because I have my own God, as I told you. It is our love." He combined a respect for people who were believers with a denial of formal religious faith. He quickly reprimanded a soldier who used a nail in the foot of Christ on the wall crucifix as a hook to hang a soiled shirt. "I made him hurry up and take it down.... Why? I have no belief in the power of Christ. I willingly pass up his protection, but I thought that such a gesture profaned something—not the person of God whom I do not believe in, but something else, subtle and immaterial: the beautiful religious soul of the believer." And then he returned to the theme of the shared love between himself and his wife. "I cannot put up with the defiling of the mystical love of so many human beings, the same as I would not allow for defiling of my own love." Nevertheless, he was angered by the conversion to Catholicism of a young, highly secularized Jewish member of his family. Religion could be beautiful, provided it did not represent a defection from secularism. "The conversion of Marcelle remains a mystery... she was resistant to the Jewish religion and did not hide it and gloried in being an atheist. Was she hiding her thoughts all along? Did an unexpected event throw her into the arms of Christ? Which one? Disgust with the family is not enough to motivate such behavior. Was it the result of a failed love affair? A crisis of hysterical mysticism?"[28]

French and Belgian Catholicism was always the religion reference. At Christmas, he recalled the beauty of the carols at home ("I felt great pleasure in singing, along with the others, the wonderful 'O Holy Night'") and he was bemused to hear of the tipsy soldiers at Midnight Mass near the front. Some army chaplains disgusted him—one of them asking a dying soldier to repent of bad language—and others deeply impressed him, totally dedicated as they were to calming and consoling their wounded soldiers. "They understand their role and are the only dispensers of the divine." He had to add that many nonreligious functionaries also filled a consoling function. He admitted partial appreciation for a particularly intelligent and politically conservative (a virtue for Kahn) chaplain, and partial disdain for him when he minimized a young woman's pain as she viewed the body of her dead soldier husband. Although he opposed the conversion of a solid atheist to religion, Kahn appreciated a conversion from belief to atheism. He recounted the complete rejection of God by an elderly woman who had lost her son in the war and whose husband had been murdered by colonial French soldiers, impressed by how adamant she was in her disbelief. She had to pass in front of the parish church to get to the cemetery but would not dream of going in. This event reminded him of the basic problem of a God-image and God-talk. "The gospel says that God made man in his own image. So my old woman was wrong to reproach him for his crimes, because if man is naturally evil, then God is also." Kahn can only conclude enigmatically in the midst of war that "man and God are made to get along well together, for which reason doubtlessly one can see a renewal of religion."[29]

The German, French, and English rabbis reiterated the traditional beliefs in the unity of all nations under a common father, but they praised the special genius and cultures of their own European nations, explaining how the Jewish spirit could resonate with each. German Jews believed that German culture was the natural setting for Jewish genius. French Jews believed that France was the only land of freedom and equality where Jews could be first-class citizens. And English Jews believed that England and English-speaking countries were a home for the Jewish diaspora. Such expressions were basic but less frequent than the attempts to see past the seemingly endless conflict to a renewed world; the celebration of the festivals and the Sabbath served to protect these goals throughout history. This would continue, according to the chaplains, during the war that was upon them. Here and now, as in the biblical books, God was speaking directly to them. For Salzberger, the men could maneuver between the opposites of God's goodness and war's wretchedness by Jewish communal prayer and by individual contemplation. For Salomonski, recognition of the one-time cultural accomplishments of the French should be subsumed into appreciation of the good and dedicated German army. But for Baeck, the goodness could only come from above. Likewise for Levy and Lewin: the remedy for materialism should be worship of God. For Korb, Liber, and Meiss, God would guarantee the gains by the army. French rabbis vociferously opposed German religion, whether Christian or Jewish. In the spirit of the *Union sacrée*, they worked with Christian chaplains to offer the consolation of faith and hope. One of them, Abraham Bloch, presumably killed while presenting a crucifix to a dying soldier who mistook him for a Catholic chaplain, became an icon of Jewish fidelity to the French nation. And for the seminarian Jacob Kaplan, further Jewish enjoyment of France required postwar Jewish dedication to a full community of both Christians and Jews. Jewish chaplains in the English army were led and organized by the enterprising and influential rabbi Michael Adler, who almost single-handedly assured a genuine system of soldier care across the vast front. He compiled a prayer book, tirelessly led services, and was often close enough to the front to comfort and to bury. He was at Vimy Ridge, celebrated New Year's and Yom Kippur near Bapaume, and then celebrated a Passover that tragically ended with the bombing of a camp of wounded soldiers. His was a down-to-earth ministry formed out of personal fidelity to his formal rabbinical calling and his desire to assure the good name of Anglo-Jewry.

Jewish soldiers—the few whose testimonies survived—wrote simpler versions of their rabbis' theological formulations. Their identity as Jews was often religious, as in the cases of the alumni of that Berlin orphanage school or the German officer Bernard Bing. Even when the Jewish identity was purely secular, as in the case of the French businessman in arms André Kahn, there was respect for the love and goodness of believers, both Jewish and Christian. Love of wives and family, and solidarity with fellow soldiers personally sustained many of the men. National experience had differing effects. One man could be profoundly patriotic; another, disgusted by the war; another, concerned by an overly high-profile Jewish appearance in Christian Europe. Condemnations of governments that continued the war and of high-minded European cultures that provided no defense against war-mongering, reached high intensity in Bing's label of the war as "a sickness among peoples worse than the plague."

CHAPTER 6

Day-to-Day War Experience
The Diaries

In a sense, all diary writing that reveals human thoughts and feelings has a depth that can be interpreted as "religious."[1] Little of the writing is formally religious: a devout thought here, a prayer there; a wish, a brief report on services or a home-front festival memory. The thoughts and feelings that come to frequent expression are about life and death, suffering, the home country and its people, family; plain thoughts about faith and morality; and images of the enemy as human, inhuman, or subhuman. Authors take us across the years and the individual battles, on occasion pairing a thought with a battle. Their sensorium is grounded in mud and drowning; shell holes and exploded bodies; trenches and rotting corpses; sounds of weaponry; and the cries, the whispers, and the screams—always the screams. Day-to-day entries are shaped by the types of battles, the length of time the soldier or individual nurse has been in the war, where he or she was placed along the front, and reactions to the enemy soldiers—alternately seen as treacherous and as victims themselves.

There are three classic collections of diaries—German, French, and English—set up to report the experiences of the war, although not structured in the same way. Edited by Lisbeth Exner and Herbert Kapfer from the Deutsche Tagebuch Archiv and published in 2014 and 2017, the *Verborgene Chronik* (*Hidden Chronicle*) offers a fascinating roster of soldiers and nurses, with their writings selected for every day of the conflict.[2] A well-worked-out time table of major events and battles is partially coordinated with the diary reports contained in the main body of the text, along with the operative dates and precise location of those reports. Such a central archive containing diaries that could be systematically presented in the same way does not exist in France or England, but fortunately there are resources that can be used to similar effect. A key to French diaries (though not everyone would agree) is the remarkable catalog and study of war writings by Jean Norton Cru, born and educated in France and a professor at Williams College in the US for most of his career. The book is *Témoins: Essai d'analyse et de critique des souvenirs de combattants édités en français de 1915 à 1928* (Witnesses: An Analytical and Critical Essay of the Memories of Combatants, Published in French from 1915 to 1928). Appearing first in 1929, the book has been reissued several times. Norton Cru presented and evaluated more than three hundred publications under these headings: "*journaux* [diaries], *souvenirs* [a catch-all category for recollections of all kinds], *réflections* [meditations, thoughts, philosophy], *lettres*, *romans* [novels]," and here we follow his lead across the diaries he studied for their moral and cultural intensity. Norton Cru also presented tables at the end of the whole text, including a classification of his authors by the time periods they were writing about. For the English diaries—even though the letter-diary distinction is not always clear—our best source is the volumes of Lyn Macdonald covering the entire spectrum of soldier experience. All these collections have significant limitations recognized by the editors. Exner and Kapfer remind readers at the start that "a *Chronik* using other records would have another story-line," but the records used do make available "a many-voiced historical narrative." And we could say this about the other two collections, recognizing that Norton Cru gave preference to the vivid prose of socially and educationally elite soldiers who best portrayed suffering and fear; also recognizing that Macdonald and her research team highlighted the testimonies from all ranks that coordinated best with the chronological phases of the war.[3]

Dramatic and original insights found in high-profile diaries published before or since these basic collections bring the diary themes into clear focus. Stephan Westmann's journal surpasses the German diaries for its coverage of the role of the churches in the author's war experience. It appeared only in an English translation in 2014. Ferdinand Belmont, not only a patriotic French humanist and doctor, but also a Christian mystic, surpasses the other French diaries in religious expression. His writings, never translated, are available in a recent reprint. Arthur Graeme West's *Diary of a Dead Officer*, published in 1917 but appearing in more recent editions (1991, 2007), reveals his questioning of religion, nationalism, and the war itself, all of it with more concrete religious focus than the English diaries quoted.

DEUTSCHE TAGEBUCHARCHIV

The authors usually report their experiences stoically, sometimes sorrowfully, chronicling troop movement, wounds, death, and personal thoughts, looking across to the trenches opposite, and interacting with people in the villages and fields behind the lines. They cover the invasion of Belgium, the frustrations of the first years, and experiences of the enemy at Verdun, the Somme, and during the final advance and retreat—this last, far less stoically.

As the German armies made their way through Belgium and pushed into France on a broad front, soldiers, and nurses, chronicled their progress. They spoke not of atrocities, but of tragedies, Belgian betrayals, and German bravery: the other side of the story most recently presented in John Horne and Alan Kramer's *German Atrocities: 1914: A History of Denial*.[4] The observations come from the doctor Georg Becker, the nurse Gertrud Blanckenhorn, Corporal Karl Groppe, the field communications officer Otto Gehrke, military vehicle driver Willy Straub, the base camp record keeper Richard Walzer, a senior lieutenant with an engineer's training Richard Pilz; the field secretary Max Schmidt, the feed master Jakob Krebs, and another nurse Marie Kettler. We follow these personalities as they advanced across the Belgium into northern France, through to the end-of-the-year additions of the journal entries of Siegfried Eggebrecht, the evangelical chaplain, and the farmer Peter Weber—both of them with a special sensitivity to the physical and moral realities of war. Save for a dramatic closing witness at the end of the war, the story of Eggebrecht is found in the chapter on churchmen in the trenches.

Georg Becker had reported in early on 5 August for assignment to his proper field hospital, and Gertrud Blanckenhorn, waiting for the first news of the inevitable injuries on the front wrote, "Time to return to religion, then, in this time of uncertainty. This is the beginning and the inevitable casualties still have not arrived." At least the situation would be better if the battle were joined. "The uncertainty is enough to kill us." Karl Groppe, already passing by a Belgian monastery by 6 August, lunched there, and then with some pleasure chatted with the locals. "The people were shy at first, but little by little they came out of the houses. We stayed with the people, it went so well. Some of us know French, and so all shyness vanished." No doubt but that it was

FIG. 21 German soldiers during the taking of Liège, a major moment in the campaign across Belgium and northern France, the morality of which was defended in soldier diaries. Photo: INTERFOTO / Alamy Stock Photo.

war, however: such was the confusion that some observers thought that more Germans were shot by Germans than by Belgians. There were already a number of dead and wounded, six officers and around fifty of the men. After his encounter with some good Belgians, he turned to damning the other Belgians for their falsity: "The white flag was raised, a sign they wanted to surrender. When we stood up in order to accept it, they began again to shoot. The German response was to shoot them all, no mercy considered, whether they put down their weapons or not. Blanckenhorn continued to monitor reports of German troops, who by 7 August were already engaged in the siege of Liège. She is still wondering who is dead and who is wounded; so, again, the uncertainty.[5]

Groppe was deciding, 7–8 August, that good Belgians were only bad Belgians in disguise. In Louveigné, shots came from behind bushes and out of houses, which, then, were immediately torched. He did not minimize the damage, "From a distance we saw that Louveigné was burning. But when we got there a more horrible sight greeted us. The houses were shot up and burned out; those still standing were looted and corpses lay everywhere." For Groppe, Belgian treachery knew no bounds. His list of the Belgians' atrocities includes cutting the soldiers' throats after plying them with food and drink, nailing one soldier's hands and feet to the floor, covering another with tar and burning him alive. And the women join in, throwing hand grenades from the houses, offering a soldier a glass of water with one hand and shooting him with the other. It would appear that the local pastor and a local land aristocrat were not only in cahoots on this action but were putting the simple people up to it. Soldiers set their houses on fire, then shot those fleeing, and then killed those already taken prisoner. "Mostly because of these horrors, our troops, the Cavalry in particular exacted a frightful penalty." On 10 August, still in Louveigné, Groppe found further evidence of the wickedness of the Belgian clergy, two of whom were retained by his men. "In the parish houses we found a bloody bed, and a German military boot." Nothing to do, then, but to burn it all down. "The house was quickly set on fire, as were those who were barricaded inside." As the women stood by in horror, Groppe was softened by the sight—and moved to prayerful gratitude—of an old, eighty-year-old woman seated on a log and eating a bread crust. "Many quietly thanked God that the war was not in our homeland." Though God was thanked, the work had to be completed, the soldiers blowing up everything within reach. Finally, the local chateau had to be dealt with: the Count had gotten away, but the troops took along with them his horses and part of his livestock. On 14 August in the next town, Hermalle-sous-Huy, Groppe got immediate hold of the priest and the mayor. As the ultimate hostages, they had to help find food supplies and "at the same time let the people know that in the case of an attack on us or with the firing of only one shot even, the pastor or the mayor would be immediately shot, and the whole place burned down."[6]

A note on enemy piety was made by Georg Becker on 16 August when he saw that wounded soldiers wore both identification and a religious medal. "A small metal religious image." But the communications officer Otto Gehrke found such a high percentage of treacherous Belgians that brutal reprisals were perfectly in order on 21 August. Approaching Héron, they reached Andenne, where the troops who had been attacked along the way set themselves to destroy and plunder, and then shot 130 men and women. He evoked the mass destruction: "Everywhere we encountered smoking ruins and corpses. The inhabitants had fled." "Not a pretty sight," he wrote. Some of the diarists had passed through Belgium to France, and some had simply crossed the border from Alsace into France. Approaching Tellancourt in France, on the march toward Saint-Pancré, the driver Willy Straub justified the soldiers' severity because they were fired upon. Destruction and despair, everything afire. Here the Germans were encountering genuine evil, he thought, pairing the notions of Satan and sniper. Stark images of individual Belgians and their original perversities imprint all the details on Straub's imagination. The enemy: "Hidden behind a hedge, I saw him, a guy somewhere in his twenties, peeking out from behind the door of a house, who then leveled his rifle and took a shot." Straub fires back, hitting the Belgian in the left hand. Inasmuch as he cannot see Straub, he takes aim with his rifle again, but Straub fires first and kills him. Then, of course, the entire village was set aflame. For Richard Pilz in Alsace a week later, both village destruction and church worship seemed to be works of justice. "On account of the shots fired by civilians on our troops, the following places are slated for destruction: Nomeny, Port-sur-Seille." These decisions did not seem to cast a shadow on the religious service held at 10:30 by the chaplain for the first and second reserve militia in the chateau courtyard of Chérisy on the first free day in a week and a half. Gehrke, near and in Namur, was finding that along with all those bad Belgians there were some good ones. In the suburb, houses that shots came from were plundered and blown up, the women and children begging the soldiers not to hurt them. But in Namur itself, "We greeted them as good friends. They were pleased and gave us tobacco, cigarettes, and chocolate. All with strong characters, Walloons. With some you can get along. They were unwillingly pulled into war."[7]

Straub, in Longuyon, came upon a French priest as treacherous as Karl Groppe's Belgian clergy. By 24 August, a whole town, it would appear, was put on defensive footing by a priest. At a signal, shots came from every direction. "The pastor during the night had gotten ammunition distributed to the people in church. He also betrayed our positions and shelter to the French." Even the French artillery had been given exact position information, so by the end of the episode, both the Germans and the French were bombarded by French artillery, killing soldiers and setting the town ablaze. Arriving in Bévillers, France, from Tournai on 25 August, Karl Groppe was amused to find that some took him and his companions (they were wearing Gibralter bands!!) to be English at first; then German troops in their easily recognizable uniforms arrived. The villagers, having offered food and wine, quickly disappeared. The next day, he was in a long skirmish in Beauvois-en-Cambrésis, which left him with dramatic memories of bodily destruction. Otto Gehrke, still in Belgium, talked to Belgians who complained that the French had stolen from them, so the Germans tried to recruit them. Reaching France, he bemoaned the life of the soldier: fighting spirit was gone, as they were treated like school kids, rather than family men. But Becker, the doctor, was sorting out French and German destructiveness. With the French, garbage everywhere; the Germans (especially the Bavarians), though not as bad, wasted and destroyed their supplies.[8]

As the Battle of the Marne began, Willie Straub was pleased to see on 7 September several German breakthroughs along the French line, a brave stand against the French in spite of their many losses. "The French had broken through somewhat. We came to Èvres, which was completely burned down. Two kilometers from the village we stopped again... various villages around there were burning." Otto Gehrke wrote up the destruction and carnage he had seen near Châlons, where fierce fighting had occurred the previous day. "Germans and French were mixed up with one another: a dead Saxon with a bullet in the head; Frenchmen sitting where they had been killed, one with the top of the skull torn off." However, Max Schmidt had come upon a priest who seemed generous, yea even trustworthy. This was 10 September, when the battlefront was beginning to look quite good for the French; they heard rumors everywhere as they marched back through Tours-sur-Marne. The priest there was a Luxemburger who spoke good German. He and his sister served the soldiers fries and beer. Said Schmidt, "All this is very kind, but caution is necessary!" Even as French leaders and soldiers were beginning to see or suspect their victory (grounds for Catholic celebration), Jacob Krebs recorded a German Protestant service near Baccarat. "After twelve, the infantry choir begin to lead us in song, first with 'A Mighty Fortress is our God,' truly uplifting." Fighting was merciless all about, however, and Willy Straub was horrified to see huge piles of dead French and Germans. No quarter could be given to the enemy soldiers, even when the "red pants" wanted to surrender. The Germans shot down anyone they could get to, as they remembered that wounded German soldiers brought to a local church had not been spared by the French. "The worst thing we saw in the bullet-riddled church itself. A field hospital had been set up in the church: a lieutenant and nine men from the 69th field artillery regiment lay wounded inside. A grenade was thrown in and the poor fellows must have been burned alive." By 14 September, Willy Straub heard fighting only in the distance. It was raining when they moved on, "God be thanked," and they came upon a "beautiful valley" with its untouched surroundings. Villages were still intact; inhabitants still there. Otto Gehrke's situation was the opposite on 18 September: daily losses in the "bedlam"; nerves on edge with the sound of explosions, feet freezing in the shelters, no food or drink. "Each man was nervous because of the continuing noise. Across the day we sit in our shelter with feet freezing. We still have nothing to eat and drink." As his armies were pushing back (19 September), Max Schmidt found the French villagers timid and untrustworthy at the same time. He and the other soldiers had to closely watch them, an impossible task at night especially, so they gathered them all into the church, elderly and kids included. "War is a hard job," said Schmidt. Meanwhile, Marie Kettler was rejoicing in the comforts of a French house, writing on 20 September that all the necessities, good wine, and best of all, the realization that they were in France and that the situation was not reversed! "But how thankful we must be that the war does not playout in the slightest way on German soil."[9]

After the Battle of the Marne, the German troops retreated to positions along the Aisne River, soon to compete with French units in a race to preempt mastery along the river and beyond the river to the sea. As the armies reached the Aisne, Georg Becker continued to record thoughts on churches and medical field stations. Sometimes the two came together, as in the report on a medical station in a church; sometimes not, as in his praise for the cathedral of Saint-Quentin. On 18 October, he was able to witness to the alternation of Catholic and Protestant services in the same church. As the fighting concentrated in Flanders, Marie Kettler, though attentive to French Catholicism, reporting on a curé and a service in Latin, highlighted the day of repentance and prayer in Germany. At about this same time, we have first reports from the diaries of Peter Weber and Siegfried Eggebrecht. Weber meditated solemnly on graves and the fallen and then, looking about him at Longwy, was reminded of the destruction of Jerusalem when he saw the church with only its pulpit intact. Krebs was troubled by the report received in Lens that Louvain was in flames. Pilz stood before fifty graves with "pious" crosses raised on them. But Becker was present in a French home for the celebration of Saint Martin's Day with the pastor present. By the middle of November, both sides dug in for a war that was ever in place on a virtually unchanging front. The theme that dominated all others was, of course, the weather, not only in Flanders but all along the Aisne. Groppe also noted the national day of repentance and prayer. And Krebs found himself celebrating the first Sunday of Advent in the village (Lens) church. The Artois offensive, north of Soissons began in the middle of December. In the days before Christmas, the writers continued to expand their battle and deployment reports with Christmas and weather notes. Then came the feast itself, with its brief and uneven cease-fire actions and fraternizing that became the great religious story to close 1914.[10]

The second volume of selections made by Exner and Kapfer from the Tagebücher Archiv covers everything after 1914, with some of the same diaries as volume 1 and with many new ones. The salient pages of eight writers in particular provide moral reflection or specific church experience. About Josef Kollmannsberger we know little, other than that he fought in France from August 1914 until his death near Verdun in 1916. Bernard Bing, the Jewish officer (whom I give separate coverage in chapter 5) and member of the Landwehr, was stationed near Lille and then saw action on the Somme and in the 1917 battles around Arras and Douai. He experienced the prejudice that prevented his promotion and the humiliation of the Jewish census. Martin Werner was a construction supervisor and fought in the Argonne after helping to set up a field hospital. He was at Verdun for the first and last months of the battle. August Gieselmann spent time on both the western and eastern fronts, in Belgium, then on the Somme, and also in the environs of Reims and Verdun. Josef Bindrum also fought near Laon and later Verdun. Gottlieb Frank was a lawyer who had responsibilities as a surveillance officer, then at Verdun, and during the 1918 final offensive. Herman Kell was a career officer and engineer whose competence was at play in a wide variety of services across the war; he wrote his diary as a set of communications to his family. Reinhard Lewald fought both at Verdun and on the Somme; he was wounded in the last months of the war. In the first part of 1915, Josef Kollmannsberger, clearly an engaged Catholic, wrote up the circumstantial details of sacrament of penance near the front: instruction in a small barracks room, followed by individual confessions, all of which went quickly, although some of the men let it be known that it had been years since their last confession. Afterward, all the men returned to the room for prayer and, finally, Holy Communion. In May, he reported that he succeeded in getting to Mass, something he had been unable to do for months.[11]

Some of the salient religious observations of 1917 include Josef Bindrum's May meditation on the unreason of natural beauty and the so-called reason of human beings. With military music and hymns sounding, Bindrum writes up his sentiments on 27 May for the Feast of Pentecost. "All kinds of feelings pass through my mind. I think of the past year and the New Year, and I am in a melancholy mood. 'We Enter in Prayer before the God of the Just,' goes the hymn, and the artillery growls and thunders, and the earth shakes with the shots fired. This is my Pentecost, Pentecost in the field." Bindrum reports on services near the village church later in the year. The story was that the church had been burned and so religious services had to be in a school hall. A Catholic service with Latin hymns that afforded Bindrum the minor amusement of the French way of pronouncing the vowel "u"—just like the German "ü." The worshipers seemed not to make the sign of the cross or strike their breasts at any point. In 1918, Herman Kell celebrated Easter away from the front, on leave with his family. He was happy to begin the Easter season that way but made it clear that he was supposed to use the leave to study poison gas techniques: with the family in Leipzig, in Berlin for the gas seminar and two trips to the theater, and finally back to the family in Berlin. Gottlieb Frank was clearly out of emotional resources. "I am no longer a human being." Each grenade explosion increased the sense of helplessness, and the need for calm, for the good, the pure, the beautiful, and the peaceful. In June, Reinhard Lewald lamented the deaths of two brothers and swears that his family could do no more. "How hard it hit our father: after all the misfortune in his life, now this! There is nothing more we can do as we submit ourselves in silence to God and further fulfill our duty to our fatherland." The last word, the most agonized admission of defeat, belongs to Siegfried Eggebrecht, who had returned to Dresden from the eastern front: "The war is lost! Farewell: German greatness, German hopes, German victory! Germany becomes the servant of England. Why the more than two million dead? It is once again too much for me. I sink into mourning. . . . I must forget everything so as not to despair. My soul seems frozen in ice. I strive no more. How paltry are we humans! A life is built up by work. Now on the heights. Suddenly it is all gone—ruins."[12]

Stephan Westmann reported for service in the German army months before the war as a medical student, but he officially became an MD in the course of the war. We do not have his original diary entries, because he wrote up a memoir-like version some years later (after he had emigrated to England) and had it translated into English. Some of his reflections on human nature and the role of the churches in the war were obviously added years after the war, but we can follow reasonably well his battlefield experiences as a doctor and his discussions with officers, clergy, and the men in the trenches. He and his battalion attacked on 23 August near Lunéville. "The padre gave all us soldiers absolution in front of a makeshift altar in a field near a village." Then, as the battle began his commander was killed and a young officer came over bleeding profusely from severe wounds to head and knee. At daybreak he found him dead, "holding a small gold crucifix in his hands." In spite of the army's reputation for atrocities, which developed quickly, Westmann found that the troops he fought with treated civilians very humanely. "When we entered one small town the mayor met us with his red, white and blue sash around his middle. With tears in his eyes he begged our company commander to order us not to cut off the hands of the children." But, writes Westmann, "Nobody ever saw a single child whose hands had been cut off." In fact, he helped the villagers when he could. Once near Loos, before the famous battle, he was billeted with an old couple, who gave him their son's bed. "I helped them draw water from the pump, carried coal for them and swept the yard." The woman "often said, 'Oh, Monsieur, the war is a great misfortune for you, for us, for everyone.'" After the battle of Loos began, this house and all the others around it were blown away.[13]

Westmann made what he could of the merciless killing in war, asking himself "how civilized and educated men could hurl themselves at each other like mad dogs, savagely thrusting bayonets into the chests and stomachs of their opponents." He recorded one scene where he bayoneted an enemy soldier to death and vomited afterward. After the same battle, his companions—a teacher, a farmer, a student, and a chimney sweep—reported their achievements: "One had killed a Frenchman with a pickaxe, another had strangled an officer and a third had crushed the skull of a *poilu* with his rifle butt.... So

FIG. 22 Stephan Westmann, third from left, who became an army surgeon in the course of his service, shown by a hospital train with army officers. From Stephan Kurt Westmann, *Surgeon with the Kaiser's Army*, ed. Michael Westman (South Yorkshire: Pen and Sword Books, 2014).

now we were all murderers. However, it seemed to me that while we were all now standing on the brink of insanity, . . . without people such as us wars could not be waged." And for months afterward, he had nightmares of the dead soldier staring at him with glassy eyes.[14]

Wounded, though not gravely, Westmann was sent to a hospital set up in the Palais de Justice at Saint Quentin. There he and the others were especially happy to be washed and dressed by young women until they found out, to their chagrin, that the young women were nuns. There also, he also met a group of Franciscan brothers and priests, whose medical and religious help he highly appreciated. A hospital orderly, Brother Ludovicus helped him with a man whose amputation needed draining, with another who was choking from a throat wound, and with yet another who needed a catheter. Westmann appreciated in particular the father superior, often called in to administer the last rites, who had doctorates in theology, philosophy, law, and medicine.

> He was a man full of worldly knowledge, in no way confined to the narrow life of a monastery. We would often end our duties back in the officers' room, at which point he would invariably produce a bottle of wine from under his flowing brown robes. We talked over the day's or rather the night's, events, and the discussion would turn to the utter futility of war. He was a pacifist at heart and we both condemned the useless slaughter of men in the prime of life. He reminded me that wars had been fought since time immemorial and that the Holy Book was full of stories of bloody fighting between various peoples and tribes. . . . I remarked that war was the antithesis of love and that the arrival of Christ's brotherly love should have prevailed. Instead, look what happened. One war after another was launched in the name of God . . . but which one, God, Allah or Jehovah? Weren't the crusaders sent out by the Pope, i.e. Christ's representative, to recapture the Holy Land from the infidel? Yet who were the infidels and who the believers? What about the Thirty Years War in the seventeenth century which reduced the German population from sixteen to four million and all this for religious conviction? Perhaps there were other more sinister motives behind all this. Now there were priests of all denomination in the armies who implored the Almighty to help their own side, and the Almighty was at a loss whom to favour. All we had to do was to walk through the wards and to see the mess we were in! Every German soldier had the inscription "*Gott mit uns*" on the buckle

of the belt holding his ammunition pouches, hand-grenades and bayonet.... We sat and discussed the abyss into which mankind had fallen. Sheer blasphemy was being preached from the pulpits by men dedicated to the fostering of Christ's gospel of brotherly love."[15]

In 1916, Westmann spent time on both of the great western battle fronts, Verdun and the Somme, lamenting the complications of gas masks, flame throwers, the arbitrariness of stretcher-bearer choices, the sufferings and destruction of horses, and the burning villages: "an awe-inspiring and infernal vision, in which men had to fight and die." He could not avoid irony when reporting a civilized gathering of men at a way station after the Somme battle, a group including industrialists, a major publisher, and university graduates in archaeology, economics, and literature, the latter writing poems on the blessings of peace: "We would gather in our mess, sing and drink together and one could hardly wish to meet a happier group of young people, whose job it was now to devise the most ingenious ways to kill other men."[16]

In several of his assignments, a principal duty was the regulation of prostitution and the care and protection of soldiers with venereal disease. Seeing the worst health results at close range, he was not attracted to sexual satisfaction in this context. So, when billeted to a luxurious house in Lille, where he was set upon by the middle-aged wife (her husband was away), he compared himself to the biblical Joseph in Egypt, accosted as he was by Potiphar's wife, the whole scene doubly surprising because "the house gave out an aura of chastity and respectability and seemed almost like a nunnery." He was proud that he resisted but was then crestfallen to find out that the lady was well known for nymphomaniac behavior and so was not especially attracted to him. No stern moralizer, he could see the expediency of sexual images for some of the men. "I do not like pornographic books and magazines. However, I honestly believe that they are a necessary evil for large sections of society of all ranks. They seem to fill a gap in the mental structure of our society and to condemn them out of hand is nonsense."[17]

One of his last postings was to the Richthofen Squadron of the air force, where he quickly adjusted to the almost old-fashioned codes of honor and chivalry still possible in those days of aerial dog fighting. Given the virtual certainty of death, the men tended to be terrified before taking off and very cool once in the air and in combat. Westmann did insist on grounding some from time to time because of obvious nervous strain. There he engaged in intense religious arguments with the base chaplain, who did not see the war in the same light as his good friend, the Franciscan superior. This man "would insist on blessing the fighter aircraft, bristling with machine guns, before they went up for the kill.... surely this is not in keeping with the Sixth Commandment, 'Thou shalt not kill.' The Chaplain answered that the German airmen were fighting for their Fatherland, for freedom and for a better world." Westmann would have none of it. For him, soldiers who had high ideals were perverted by politicians and war propaganda. After demobilization with its complexities, he finally made it back to Berlin, and he concluded with a damning observation that he may have written down then but maybe added in the expanded English memoir-style version. "Almost five years had vanished since I had put on the Kaiser's uniform in Freiburg. Nearly all my pals lay buried in foreign soil, together with nine million soldiers who had lost their lives in the Great War—and for what?"[18]

THE *TÉMOINS* OF JEAN NORTON CRU

Doctors, university professors, lawyers, leaders in industry and commerce—all educated and successful members of society: Norton Cru promotes what for him are the clearest and most honest diaries. Here follow a few of them: Maurice Genevoix on the bloody horrors of the first years, Paul Cazin on the Meuse battles of 1915, Maurice Deauville on the Flanders battles of 1915, Charles Delvert on the war detritus of 1915–1916, Louis Mairet on the Somme, Henry Morel-Journel on Verdun, and Gaston Top on the later battles in the Champagne region.

Maurice Genevoix, scholar and author, published several volumes based on notebooks covering his war experiences from 25 August 1914 to 25 April 1915. "The genius of Genevoix is unique in our history," writes Norton Cru, choosing long quotes such as this: "The wounded drag on, without equipment, shirts open, in rags, hair soaked in sweat, gaunt and bloody. They have improvised their slings with checkered handkerchiefs, towels, sleeves from shirts; they walk bent over, mournful, pulled to one side by an arm which hangs loose, by a broken shoulder; they stagger, they hop, they waver between two staffs, dragging behind them a lifeless foot wrapped in bandages." Then Genevoix describes their waxen faces, twisted in fear, blood dripping from stretchers, saying that for the soldiers waiting to attack next, fear bordering on despair was their fate. The sad returnees were at least able to get back, but there were countless wounded and dead still out there. The next wave of soldiers knew what was awaiting them. Some officers were willing to drive the men at first but then held back, only to finally press the troops foolishly on. Total panic resulted when there was no rhyme or reason to the fight: no goals to be seen, no defenses to be had, with men piling in on one another. If it was not possible to form ranks and fire, the firing could itself be meaningless, bullets into the void. Later, soldiers would mumble their total despair, "not possible, not possible," scarcely believing, then, what they had experienced and witnessed. "I prefer not to live than to see again a single night like this last." And Genevoix had his own special thoughts for Christmas. "Have mercy on our dead soldiers! Have mercy on us, the living who were among them, on us who will fight tomorrow, who will die and who will suffer as our flesh is mutilated. Have mercy on us, the galley slaves of war, who have not wanted it, on us who were men and despair of ever becoming men again!"[19]

Paul Cazin was an intellectual who began his odyssey as a Franciscan seminarian, continued as a student of ancient and modern languages, received his license at the Sorbonne, and finally set himself after marriage to a life in letters—with language instruction on the side. His *L'humaniste à la guerre* (A Humanist in the War) was subtitled *Hauts de Meuse, 1915* (Heights of the Meuse, 1915) and covered a period from 9 March to 20 July 1915. Reflections on Christian festivals, Homer, and the despicable essence of war were essential to the narration. He pairs the idea of ringing of bells on the feast of the Ascension with the psalm verse, "I am a worm and no man," attributing the notion of dying happily for the fatherland to Homer (a precise and famous quote comes, rather, from Horace, whom he cites further on in the book), and countering it with the opposite notion that living a long and happy life is better. His condemnation of war was savage and unconditional: "Whoever does not curse the war be cursed. Amen. By blood and by scars, by screams of fright and agony, from which the darkness still trembles; by the icy wind and the shell that makes the hairs stand on end, and the horrible flame which reddens them, by the tears which dry on the faces of the dead, may he [who does not condemn war] be cursed!" Cazin began his *L'humaniste à la guerre* with epigraphs from the *Odyssey* and the book of Psalms, finding consolation in both: "Masters of the sacred and profane lyre, I brought you along in my knapsack between my handkerchiefs and biscuits, or kept you in a corner of my cartridge pouch. You have helped me out of a real fix, enabling me to suffer this trial with dignity." He thanked, praised, and loved the texts—but nonetheless labeled them "grandiose fictions." Yet, Norton Cru says of Cazin that this is not literature to be read for entertainment, because "this is the cry of anguish and horror of a soldier coming out of the unforgiveable attacks of spring 1915 that he describes for us in living prose."[20]

Maurice Deauville, the nom de plume of the medical doctor Maurice Duwez, wrote two books on the war that could be considered diaries, *Jusqu'à l'Yser* (To the Yser) for the period from 16 August 1914 to November 1915, and *La boue des Flandres* (The Mud of Flanders) for the period from October 1915 to February 1919. Working behind hedges, in hovels, behind piles of debris, and in a "precarious" shelter for medical service, Dr. Duwez describes the gamut of wounds he worked on, from virtually destroyed bodies through light wounds, and the psychological states of the soldiers suffering these wounds. Norton Cru believes the book to be "the most blood-filled narration in all the war literature." The endless variety of country scenes, along with the beauty and charm of home interiors, are presented alternately with the horrors of war. In those earliest days, the news of the Belgian invasions, the destruction and the cruelty, quickly sank in, as the wounded came back with legs destroyed, chests torn open, fingers shot off, gangrene setting in for some. Then for all of them, the shelling continued to grind down such psychological strength as they possessed. The doctors put some back on their feet and sent them out of the shelter, others could only be left on the ground, often despairing, "To have suffered for so long, and to finish by dying even so." The second book, *La boue des Flandres*, is the fulfillment of the war pessimism of the first. "We are artisans of the lie.... What we fix in our memories is deformed immediately by a rigid cast of words. But if we remain silent, others will come and denature the facts much more than we have.... they will paint the war in glowing colors." Duwez fears that too many will enhance their relative lack of true horror experiences with tales of bravery and heroism, creating a lie for future generations.[21]

Charles-L. Delvert was a lycée professor who wrote five books on the war, three of them more diary-like in style than the others. Norton Cru highlights the narration from 11 November 1915 to 26 June 1916, written in notebooks that Norton Cru considers more honest than the books later published, one description in particular. Stiff and decomposing bodies, blood sprayed or pooled, the flies, the smell, the trash piles of food jars, torn packs, punctured helmets, and broken rifles lay all about, as Delvert and his companions thirst and cower under a shower of bursting shells that cover them with dirt.[22]

Henry Morel-Journel started his adult career with a licentiate in letters but quickly moved to business and banking; he was well traveled and fluent in several languages. He was at Verdun, although he spent the greater part of the war as soldier and interpreter on the Italian front. His diary, *Journal d'un officier de la 74e division d'infanterie* (Diary of an Officer of the 74th Division of the Infantry), covering more than fifty-one months of the war is the longest of the texts presented by Norton Cru. If he admitted to emotions, reaching pleasure sometimes in his experience of the war, he was unremitting in his condemnation of the suffering inflicted on the men by foolish generals, none more wasteful than Charles Mangin at Verdun. "The Generals should know that one does not play with the blood of France," he wrote, quoting a friend of his who said of one general in particular, "They should put him in charge of an army of Orangutans." He scoffed at the bayonet stories that were then current in a long diatribe on the uselessness of every weapon except the rifle. How could the regular guys, all wrapped up in their coats and equipment, have the slightest idea of how to make use of the bayonet or fight effectively hand-to-hand? And of course Robert Nivelle, Mangin, and the rest of them were the ones really responsible for the rebellions of 1917. His last hundred pages contain the reflections on the damage done to the young by the heroic stories of the great French victories of history, and, although basically a traditional Catholic, he rejected the use of the Sacred Heart image on French battle flags.[23]

Louis Jean-Émile Mairet had just been admitted to the École normale in 1914, when he was called up. He was killed in 1917 and his *Carnet d'un combattant* (Notebook of a Combatant) appeared right after the end of the war. Norton Cru notes the contrast between the pessimism of his notebooks and the optimism of his letters home, across his soldier years, 9 February 1915 to 15 April 1917. Mairet writes, "Let us die here! Nothing more interests me, neither the sun nor letters nor eating. I still have a certain attachment to life, so however we die, let us die quickly—with last thoughts of light, the green countryside, and dear friends. If the gentlemen at headquarters were to take account of the ground situation, they would be struck dumb at the sight of us."[24]

Gaston Top had a minor seminary background but finally chose medicine as a career. He was horrified to hear violent phrase insertions in several pious hymns. During winter battles in the Champagne region, he wrote, "One cannot think without trembling that in the time it would take to put a dog outside, these poor brothers in Christ are going about tearing one another apart with bayonets." As a doctor powerless to prevent the decomposition of the living bodies rotting away with gas-produced gangrene, he remarked to an officer, "Man is a sorry animal" and was absolutely depressed by the reply, "He is lower than an animal. You have never seen, Top, a regiment of pigs battle another regiment of pigs." Doctor Top's pity for the soldiers extended to Germans—almost equally. He reflects on a German soldier who had been mortally wounded in the battle: "Can you imagine the last ten days of this man, alone in the midst of corpses, without eating or drinking or shelter? Can one create a word stronger than 'horrible' to qualify such wretchedness. You, poor man, go, you merit respect and sympathy. You have done your duty! Poor Boche!"[25]

The letters, diary-like in regularity, of the young French doctor, Ferdinand Belmont display a depth of religious reflection rarely found in the Norton Cru ensemble of diaries. To begin with, Belmont engaged himself as a fighting officer rather than as a member of the medical corps. Few war writings express religious engagement more than his letters to family and friends, published right after his death in 1916. It was clear that his piety and resignation came out of religious meditation. All Saints' Day—1 November—was the occasion for thoughts on faith, prayer, duty and God, "It is one of the feasts I prefer, because it is among those that best recall to us all the force, all the profound peace that one can find in the faith." One needs "to seek out the courage, the resignation, and the hope that are necessary for all of us to go all the way, without weakening in the trial that God requires of us." God challenges; this is a trial, an occasion to "unite us more closely in prayer, which admits of no separateness." Spirituality belongs in the trenches as much as anywhere else. "I will pass my Feast of All Saints in my trench; our good God hears our prayers, whatever the place from which they are addressed." War does not have to shake one's trust in God. "We need only avoid anxiety, and submit ourselves to Him who loves us and takes care of us at every second." Life can bring us nothing "more consoling and more sure than this blind submission to the will of God." The evil that we see is not the real evil, because God has to demand this suffering for his greater purposes: "The sorrow that it pleases him to demand from us is a mysterious ransom from more authentic misfortune that our veiled eyes cannot see." God can be compared to a sculptor, with war as one of his tools for sculpting. "Each cut of the chisel little by little makes us less grand, purifies us, separates us from our original encasement and leads us toward perfection. Ah! If we only knew how to let ourselves be carved by the cool of the heights, and to make more abundant the first flows of Spring." Full happiness comes only through total and perfect submission: "We must desire neither life nor death, since we know neither what awaits us in this world nor what is reserved for us in the next."[26]

FIG. 23 Ferdinand Belmont, a medical doctor and a religious mystic, who served as an officer in the regular army. From Ferdinand Belmont, *Lettres d'un officier des Chasseurs alpins (2 août 1914–28 décembre 1915)* (Paris: Plon, 1916).

Belmont fights no theological battles in defense of his beloved Catholic liturgy. True, he was writing to his own family, but it would have been natural to defend official Catholicism, inasmuch as French Catholics were just coming out of a period of great national controversy over religion. On family and religious identity, there is this reflection: "It does us good across the inevitable monotony of our earthly existence, to find again in such a peculiar setting, the old practices of that religion that as little children, we learned to love—before penetrating the meaning of it and feeling the benefits of it." Expressions of national identity are virtually never explicit and are always subordinated to nostalgia for family and home ground. For his fellow officers, national identity is local identity. "The words, 'Fatherland,' 'ideal,' and even 'duty' themselves designate only abstractions. It is good to concretize them by colors and forms; one should speak to them of their church tower or their own roofs when dealing with the fatherland, speak of the flag when symbolizing honor and military duty." Still and all, he showed great respect for his comrades. He was touched by the reverence for bodies of slain comrades, often nothing more than "a mass of decay." Burial of these dead was more than a health measure: "There is a simple, profound faith that comes out of an ancestral soul. There is an evangelical tenderness of mortal man for his own kind; there is also perhaps a vague awareness of the silent mediating role that is established between the men and the families of their comrades.

This was a bond sealed by the immediacy of shared existence. It is not inaccurate to say that this reunion of men, grouped in front of the enemy and danger, forms an authentic family and binds everyone together by the same duties as brothers; they are brothers in arms." For him, France was not so much a matter of greatness or immortality, but simplicity and perseverance. "France is an eternal child; one can neither wish for nor hope that the lesson of the events she traverses transform her in her tastes or her affinities; it is sufficient that she orient and discipline them."[27]

THE "VOICES" OF LYN MACDONALD

In Lyn Macdonald's collections of soldier response to time and place, themes emerge across the days, months, and years of the war, with the name, rank, and military units of the numerous men listed.[28]

We can follow the soldiers' observations beginning at Mons, through the post-Marne German retreat to the Aisne, with subsequent fighting in Flanders that quickly centered on Ypres. New arrivals in 1915 were labeled "happy warriors," though the reality, even for the most naïve, became tragically clear on the killing ground of Loos and during the months-long battle of the Somme. Arras, Messines, and Passchendaele were their own kind of hell. And the last year of the war brought the widespread German breakthrough that was finally arrested, with the war only ending when the English regained the ground lost.

What It Means to Wage War

At *Mons*, Lieutenant K. F. B. Tower saw his first German soldier shot and the surrender of a self-proclaiming aristocrat but seemed oddly mesmerized by the beauty of the morning, the ringing of church bells, and the Belgian country folk heading for church. He lost all will to fight during the retreat from Mons back to the border. "And so the great retreat continued, all through the next two days and nights. No rest, no food and no excitement. We walked as if in a dream." Lieut. E. H. T. Broadwood, under German shellfire for three hours, could barely think: "I kept wondering what it was going to feel like to be dead, and all sorts of little things that I had done, and places I had been to years ago and had quite forgotten, kept passing through my mind. I have often heard of this happening to a drowning man but have never experienced it before and don't want to again."[29]

Encountering the Enemy

Pushing the German forces back from the Marne to the Aisne, Corporal T. North was already using the expression, "slaves of the war machine" to describe himself and his men. Captured, he saw that the Germans could be considerate to prisoners, and so when the tables were turned—quite soon in fact—he tried to oblige in the same way. He saw French and German doctors working together to care for the wounded. Lieut L. A. Strange even went so far as to save two German airmen, whose plane had crashed, from a French farmer who was fixing to shoot them, handing them over subsequently to an English patrol. In contrast, Lieut. H. S. S. Henderson, captured by the Germans, saw only hate on their faces. In this setting, English soldiers saw only aggressive hostility, and cruelty. Henderson could not help but notice that these Germans treated the French prisoners much better.[30]

Death and Normal Life

In rural Flanders, Captain Maurice Mascall remarked on the churches and the farms and found it amusing that he, an English soldier, was giving fun lessons in French to the Flemish-speaking Belgians. Four days later, he was in the midst of artillery fire and trench warfare, noting the deaths around him, bullets through head and chest, and the steady stream of miserable wounded men coming back in the darkness, some of them hit by their own artillery. At Christmas, Gunner Herbert Smith was intrigued, in fact puzzled, by the truce. He had a conversation with a German who had been a waiter in London and said that he did not want to fight. Surely, Smith thought, the Germans will get more than they bargained for. And Captain Bryden McKinnel was able to celebrate in relative comfort with good food and the small gift packages sent by the king. He wrote, "'Peace on earth and goodwill among men.' How incongruous it all seems."[31]

Horrors

Near Ypres itself, Trooper Sydney Chaplin was disconsolate to lose a horse who had raced across the battle area, saving Chaplin's life and dying from his own wounds: "I shall never forget him." For Sergeant Britten, the horror symbols were the decaying bodies and roofless houses, and across several encounters, the dead and dying all around, and a near escape from poison gas. Sergeant Bill Hay was not so lucky with the gas: "The gasping, the gasping! And it caused a lot of mucus, phlegm. . . . You couldn't stop to help anybody." Even with this, Hay felt that his own tragedy was interior.

> I'll tell you this much, I might not have been wounded in body but I was wounded in my mind. I don't know if you can imagine it but obviously when there's shell fire, you get down to get cover, only an idiot wouldn't get down, so you get down and you can't get your nails into the ground and your head under the ground, you can't get down because you can't go any further. You're on the ground and your nails are dug into the ground and there you are and the shells are bursting round and there's screaming bits of shells and they're not just bits of metal, they're hot metal flying all over the place and there are machine guns going and pandemonium all round.[32]

(Un)happy Warriors

Lyn Macdonald collected a few testimonies of new arrivals in 1915 that she curiously entitled "The Happy Warriors." 2nd Lieutenant Ewart Richardson personified what he called "the Line," finding it "ugly and lovely by turns." Sinister during the day, at night "it changes to a thing of delicate beauty. Flares, glowing and white, rise and fall continuously. . . . A stranger might well believe he had come to some fete save that, for accompaniment, [there] is a steady rattle of rifle fire, and now and then the rat-tat-tat of a machine-gun. . . . These are quiet times. But sometimes the line wakes to fury. . . . The Line alone, a moody giant, stretches his sinister length unmoved across the country." Sergeant W. F. Low, seemingly little bothered by the marching and the weather, was horrified by the destruction of Ypres. "I believe that I am a kindly-natured man, yet that sight made me madder than anything I have seen or suffered in my life and gave me a real feeling of bloodthirstiness. . . . It makes me impatient of anything but real work against the Huns who have desecrated Ypres. Churchyards, altars, monuments, all that has been revered for countless ages even among savages, still receive their senseless spite and I think nothing of the man who after passing through Ypres could lay down his rifle before avenging it."[33]

Of course, there could be no happy warriors after the English soldiers experienced the killing fields of Loos and the Somme. At Loos, endless screams during the battle and endless empty ranks after. Private Harry

Fellowes saw the advance where "men began to stumble and fall, machine-guns were firing from the front of us and enfilading from the left-hand side from some Germans. . . . I'll remember the sight until my dying day, the whole slope was full of prone figures." He repeats the report he heard soon after that German machine gunners refused to fire after all those corpses littered the field, and Fellowes believes it. Private Carson Stewart recalled that during the rollcall after the battle, the number of deaths sunk in; when new recruits arrived not long after, there were a great number of parcels sent to the pre-Loos regiments that were distributed to the new men.[34]

The Somme and After

The Battle of the Somme was the central story of the English experience of the war, even more than the dramas of the retreat from Belgium to the Marne at the beginning of the war and the full-spread push back of the final German advance in 1918. Major H. F. Bidder recorded the initial optimism: "There was a wonderful air of cheery expectancy over the troops. They were in the highest spirits, and full of confidence." As the charge came, he saw them "all walking over the top, as steadily as on parade." Corporal W. H. Shaw reported what happened next. "We never got anywhere near the Germans. . . . Our lads was mown down. They were just simply slaughtered. The machine guns were levelled and they were mowing the top of the trenches. You daren't put your finger up. The men were just falling back in the trenches." Sergeant J. E. Yates detailed one typical scene, where men tried to save badly mutilated companions. "His left hand wandered over his chest to the pulp where his right shoulder had been. 'My God,' he said [to Yates], I've lost my arm.' The hand crept down to the stump of the right thigh. 'Is that off too?' I nodded." They ended up putting him on a ground sheet and dragging him to the medical station, after which Yates simply fell exhausted into a bed of ferns and flowers, wondering how there could still be flowers in the world as he passed out. Corporal H. Diffey was one of the soldiers who marveled at the early reports of the battle in the home newspapers, when there were so many wounded that the stretcher-bearers could in no way keep up, when the only scenes were of total devastation, when men were ordered to forge on without stopping to help the wounded, "and newspapers in the UK wrote of tremendous victories and killing Germans as sport similar to ratting. We could laugh aloud at their reports, plagued by lice and living amongst the debris of war and the legends that sustained our armchair patriots at home." Private W. Hay wrote that the men knew that advance into the area of High Wood meant certain death. "It was hell, it was impossible, utterly impossible," and he added the general sentiment that the higher ups were to blame: "The higher the rank, the fewer the brains." Moments of respite alternated with dark moments, literally. Gunner Frank Spencer found bodies, English and German, in the darkness: guns and dead gunners covered with ammunition and debris, shell holes and random corpses. As the shells arched over them, they leapt into nearby dugouts. Spencer wrote, "Oh, the ghastly sight that met me. (I often see it in the dark now) for just inside the entrance, which, in the dark, was only a black hole, was a corpse—that ghastly face and glassy eyes against the inky blackness of the interior was sufficient. It was as if death himself and I had met." Going across the gas-polluted valley, he evoked the scriptural "valley of death." 2nd Lieut. Ewart Richardson saw the flowering of chamomile and poppies, immediately thinking of the red blood–stained white bandages, but this helped him not at all. "Every attempt to move forward meant certain death and useless sacrifice, while No Man's Land and our trenches behind us were plastered by the enemy's artillery. . . . If someone was wounded he was better off dead since no help was possible during the day. And who would find him at night?" Private Charles Cole remembered the title of the book *God in the Trenches* when trying to explain how his colonel standing at the top of the trench, thereby consolidating the men, got through it alive.[35]

At the Somme, then, virtually all was death. CSM W. J. Coggins wrote, "The Somme was the worst. That's all I dream about, mostly, now. I never saw so many dead." Shocked by the triage the doctors were forced to make, he helped by placing red tags on the men who had no real chance of survival and taking them to a tent to moan and cry for water until they died. When winter arrived just before the end of the Somme campaign, Corporal H. Holbrook was disgusted by a sign in the warm hut of a general: "Oh Death where is thy sting? Oh grave, where is thy victory?"—made especially troubling because it was wet, muddy, and freezing outside. Private J. Bowles reacted to a chaplain's sermon to the effect that mortal danger made men think about religion as the only source of comfort. On the contrary, wrote Bowles, "Men go to their deaths with curses on their lips and religion is never mentioned or thought of. . . . being killed is spoken of as being 'jerked to Jesus.'" Conclusion: "In war there is no place for a God of Love, no time for the softer emotions, and no inclination to worry about a future when the present is a hell that the devil himself would be proud to reign over." As Private Lawrence moved away from the center of action, he noticed a burial ground had placed a sign in German, "Here rest in God 17 British warriors," and then mournfully described the war debris of weapons, coats, helmets, rifles, and the sickening smell of decay.³⁶

Arras was the setting for the English part of the Nivelle offensive, and in the middle of that was Easter. Rifleman Ralph Langley then wrote, "Being as how we were in the Church Lads Brigade we were supposed to be very religious," describing two souvenirs, a German belt with "*Gott Mit Uns*" ("God is with us") etched on it and another badge sort of thing imprinted with "*Dieu et mon droit*" ("God [is] on my side"). "It made you think," he wrote. Private Reg Lawrence wrote a longer commentary on the Easter sermon. "Today the Padre preached on the text *Love your enemies, do well to them that do spitefully used you*. Afterwards the Colonel gave us a little heart-to-heart talk on the desirability of remembering that we had bayonets on our rifles and using them accordingly. No encouragement to take prisoners unless they can be of value for information. Dead men tell no tales and eat no rations, etc. ad nauseam." There is no doubt as to which of the two talks he agreed with: "The Church cannot be allowed too much rope lest we lose the war!" Ralph Langley did not solve his dilemma as easily. "I don't know what the Generals wanted to do that attack for, because it was murder.... They had a job to do, of course, but there were too many lives lost."³⁷

Passchendaele and the 1918 Denouement

In the latter part of the war, no battle was more absurd and tortuous than Passchendaele—Third Ypres—with its back-and-forth across the sea of mud created by the rains and the destroyed drainage system. No other option but to leave men behind, wrote Lieut. H. L. Birks: "We had to leave the chap with his leg off to the stretcher-bearers." This was the result of a subsequently described direct hit—by either German or English artillery—of a tank, rendered useless anyway by the mud. Passchendaele being an outlying district of Ypres, Private Reg Lawrence saw the city, "majestic, though in ruins, and silent but for the echoes of marching feet on the stones." Then in the battle itself, "I felt myself drifting away into a great quiet, almost as if I was in church. I kept thinking of the words of the litany—*Good Lord, deliver us. From lightning and tempest, from plague, pestilence and famine, from battle and murder and from sudden death.*" Some days later he summed up: "Of our Company only thirty-two men answered roll call. Puckrin has shell shock. Engels leg is broken by a shell. Hands is wounded. Roscoe is dead. I am the last and I have no companions left." His condemnation of it all is unequivocal: "I see no excuse for war, unless it is in defence of home and dear ones. Otherwise it is just legalized murder conducted on a large scale.... But, of course, we are fighting for national honour. How absurd! A soldier when he bayonets a man does not nurse the nation's wrongs in his breast." For Rifleman V. Shawyer, Passchendaele was even worse than the Somme. "Sooner or later the stretcher-bearers would get to you on the Somme, but at Passchendaele the wounded didn't stand an earthly chance. At one aid post a doctor said to the stretcher-bearers, 'Only bring back men we've got a hope of curing. If you get a seriously injured man, leave him to die quietly. Too often you bring men back here and before we can help them they're gone. You're wasting your time and ours.' I thought that was a terrible thing to say. But that was Passchendaele." And for 2nd Lieut C. D. Horridge, winter fixed the land into a horror-scape. "The front line is really an elongated shell hole," where flares reveal "tree stumps and branches, bare, black, broken on what was once a road ... like bony old women's arms, stretched out to heaven in silent imprecation." The dead "hang on the barbed wire like grotesque figures carried round the streets on Guy Fawkes night." Then, "here and there the ground bulges into a head, booted feet, khaki covered arms. A dead man is lying on his back with his knees up and his arms outstretched as though lazily reclining in a field in the heat of a summer day."[38]

The great German breakthrough the last year of the war was broad and determined but bore within it the seeds of its own destruction. At first, though, wrote Sergeant E. Davidson, they "were coming down everywhere and they were so confident that they weren't taking the slightest trouble in concealing themselves." A sign of deterioration, if not self-destruction—a tipsy version of the shared humanity of the first Christmas—was an Australian regiment's discovery of a winery full of totally drunk Germans. The first group of men joined in—drunk in their turn. It took the arrival of a second regiment to drag the Germans out by the feet to a prison compound and place a guard on their own wine lovers. But Capt C. M. Slack was totally humiliated by his forced surrender to the Germans (after he buried brigade and division orders), but he saw no other option. He saw fit to note that he was able to keep a watch his girlfriend had given him because one of the German officers would not let a private remove the watch. Gunner George Worsley was angered when a French man, mistaking him and his cohort for Germans, cried in French, "We are French, not English." It was too much like "Don't blame us," thought Worsley. But another French fellow who had to be pulled away from his wife, children, and an elderly relative, all of them killed by shell fire, personified the reality of the French tragedy. From the sky, Balloon Observer Bernard Oliver saw the disastrous widespread destruction of the frontline villages: "Dranoutre village was wiped out. Locre Church, just inside our lines was burning, the village itself was slowly being wiped out by shell fire." He felt deeply about it: "It was like seeing my own home village in ruins."[39]

No soldier quoted in the Lyn Macdonald collections expressed himself more strongly than Arthur Graeme West, whose graphic questioning of religion, nationalism, and the justice of the war issued in a solution more negative than the others. The war was not only evil, but church support made it worse. Volunteering in a fit of patriotism, West quickly came to hate the training and regret the loss of the good life back in London. After he began his service in the water-soaked trenches, death became a grim prospect, quite different from his earlier benign and abstract thoughts about it. But even then it could be an escape from the loathsome trenches, salvation from an unproductive middle age, and the elimination of a fate he had earlier feared—a mediocre intellectual life. Even so, he clung to life, writing that "it was the animal that hated death and clung passionately to promise of life . . . there were instants when the pride of my flesh and the lust of my eye rose up in all their manifestations from highest to lowest, and willed majestically to life."[40]

Lenient and without hatred when it came to the enemy, as when he sighted the poor German soldier who would be happier at home "with his wife and his books," West was quite dismissive of the religion of his fellow Englishmen: "They go to church, a lot of them, on Sundays, partly, I think, because they like the service out of religious sentimentality, partly to feel themselves a part of normal civilization again, partly to get off with a choir-girl." (Clearly, he was not talking only of religion in the trenches).[41] He also dismissed his own earlier benign philosophy. "Stoicism's fundamental assumption was the positive one that only the good is good, and for that we should live; whereas I sometimes think rather that nothing is good or has any permanent value whatever." In which case, what difference does it make whether England wins or loses or how the war develops? Though he could at one time, perhaps, make a logical case for faith, he now writes, "I reject the presumption that I worship a God by Whose never-wronging hand I conceive all the present woe to have been brought upon the now-living generation of mankind. If there is a God at all responsible for governing the earth, I hate and abominate Him—I rather despise him. We only fall into the habit of calling down curses on a god whom we believe not to exist, because the constant references to his beneficence are so maddening that anger stings us to a retort that is really illogical."[42]

Thereafter, he renounced belief in "Christianity as a religion" or "Christ as an actual figure," now ashamed of himself that he had tolerated "conventional religion... all emotionalism and religious feeling."[43] He writes that after having traversed "Christianity, Theism, Paganism" to arrive at "Atheism and Pessimism," he finds that each system, even the last two, wears down. He remains open to further development, because he appreciates what older men have gone through and the wisdom they have acquired, especially those who managed "to defy the whole system, to refuse to be an instrument of it."[44] For all that, he remains an atheist, claiming that the two groups that have "really occupied their minds with religion" are mystics and atheists.[45]

In the end, for West the horrors of war are an absurd reality, not to be preempted into a religious, or any other, abstract discussion. There was only the destruction in the trenches, men dismembered, buried alive, as the others "sit like animals for market, like hens in cages."[46] He found himself agreeing with a religious believer, a "nonconformist," who returned from a military training session saying that "he had really come to the conclusion since he had been away that the war was really very silly, and we all ought to go home."[47]

The collections of diaries, individual diaries, and the strings of letters resembling diaries reveal moral judgments and sometimes casual, sometimes earnest observations of church presence. The writers, their lives passed in the mud and wretchedness of the trenches, alternated between hope and despair.

On invasion morality, the German diaries collected in the World War I diary archive in Emmendingen give us "the other side of the story." The Belgians commit the atrocities and the German soldiers are simply fighting back and punishing the evil, attributing the greatest treachery to the Belgian priests, very few of whom could be even partially trusted. Accounts of church services, Catholic and Protestant, highlight the makeshift features of church use, though there are random vignettes of violence to men and architecture. The nurses combined hope for Germany and pity for suffering inhabitants. But stoicism gave way to lament over the death and dying, especially in the final months. More pointedly, Stephan Westmann, a doctor and a humanist from a Jewish family, was a focused commentator on European Christianity. He saw the bloody destruction, partial and total, of the men and defended the humaneness of the German soldiers interacting with peaceful civilians. But he was disgusted by the delight some of the men took in mangling enemy soldiers. When he himself had to kill—apparently only one time—he was thereafter haunted by the memory of the moment. His long and learned conversations about Christianity as an ideal were filled with evocations of the history of Christian rulers and clergy who waged and blessed war. Westmann witnessed major battles in the field; chatted behind the lines with farm families, learned monks, nursing sisters; and brought humor and humanity to everyday living.

In the French diaries, collected in the decades after the war by the veteran and scholar Jean Norton Cru, well-educated and professional men meditate with sensitivity and often disgust, the blood and despair. They graphically detail the butchery of war, pairing this with scandalized condemnation of it as a breakdown of the Christian morality taught at church and at home. Loss of Christian morality at the center of total loss of humanness! They pair regular expressions of sympathy for the suffering of enemy soldiers with violent condemnation of war and its perpetrators. Consolation, if there was to be consolation, could only come from the glories of French culture, literature and art, sacred and profane. Ferdinand Belmont combined classical resignation to the will of God and striving for generosity and greatness of soul. All of this he placed at the disposition of his fellows and their families. The faith of his own family and the faith derived from the culture were essential elements of his identity, but in this war each trial was the hand of God newly fashioning his self and his existence. His writing is marked by formal meditation and a literary craftsmanship that seems natural and spontaneous, however practiced it may have been.

The great collection of English voices, masterfully coordinated by a leading English historian of the war, Lyn Macdonald, contains the widest range of soldier expression, revealing less about formal religion and more about specific agonies, hopes, and interpersonal experiences. Less given to stoicism than the German writers, less given to moral condemnation than French diary writers, the British "voices" were from all levels of society: down–to-earth commentary, with thoughts from an occasional devotion-inclined personality. They felt immediately transformed by the war's indiscriminate violence and their encounters with both fair and hateful Germans. They observed destruction of bodies with a horrified fascination seemingly unmitigated by repetition. War challenged whatever moral sensibilities they had developed and kept intact—"In war there is no place for a God of love"—despairing of life and barely clinging to faith by Passchendaele and the last major German advance. Alternately angered by and sympathetic to French civilian behavior, some of the men could openly express their natural sympathy for the German soldiers when the Germans were driven back beyond their starting point and an armistice request was their only hope. With Arthur Graeme West, fears of bland mediocrity were the prequel to his wartime conduct and thoughts. Patriotism moved him to war, and he came to see death as the grim salvation from wartime horrors. But without belief in eternal life or a God who caused the world's suffering, he clung to human life and wished the good life for his fellows and his enemies. Appreciating the efforts of philosophers and mystics across the centuries, he nevertheless chose atheism as his response to World War I.

CHAPTER 7

Behind the Lines
Religious Traditions at War

At home but in contact with the western front, German and English clergy carried on their own polemics—a war of words about a war of weapons! German and English Protestants and Anglicans decried one another's base motives and evil actions; German and French Catholic bishops and priests attacked the errors and the injustice of the other side. Yes, these were fighting words and a clear expression of religion and nationalism together: sometimes ingenious, sometimes melodramatic, and sometimes a remarkable combination of righteousness and humility. An intense, informal theology of right and might appropriate to the war was the result, echoes of the sermons and send-offs of 1914.

Two books published within a year of one another were perfect incarnations of the Catholic French and German debate behind the lines. *La guerre allemande et le catholicisme* (The German War and Catholicism), published in 1915 by the Comité catholique de Propagande française à l'étranger (Catholic Committee for the Promotion of French Interests Overseas) under the direction of Monsignor Alfred Baudrillart, rector of the Institut Catholique, was aimed directly at German Catholicism, and indirectly at Lutheranism and secular philosophy. German bishops and priests responded to the French accusations in a book edited by Father Georg Pfeilschifter: *Deutsche Kultur, Katholizismus, und Weltkrieg* (German Culture, Catholicism, and World War) in 1916.[1] Seventy-five years after the war, Arlie Hoover outlined the Protestant German-English debate, in *God, Germany, and Britain in the Great War*, which remains our best orientation to the individual books, essays, and sermons produced by German and English churchmen.[2]

GERMAN AND ENGLISH "JUST WAR" THEMES

With the traditional Christian theological justification of war fought in self-defense inferred more than referenced, German and English churchmen severely criticized the moral failings that grounded the unjust attacks of the enemy nations.

The Germans fired the first salvo in this behind-the-lines war with a formal declaration, "Address of the German Theologians to the Evangelical Christians Abroad." They said they had no choice. "We know that we are one with all the Christians among our people, that we can and must repudiate on their behalf and on behalf of their Government the responsibility for the terrible crime of this war, and all its consequences for the Kingdom of God on earth. With the deepest conviction, we must attribute it to those who have long secretly and cunningly been spinning a web of conspiracy against Germany." For them, the fratricidal war was the work of "Christian brothers" from other lands, and "Asiatic barbarians." They considered it a duty, stemming from their work across the centuries, to propagate the gospel to justify the German war action against an attack on "Teutonic Protestantism."[3]

Within a few weeks, English theologians issued a caustic response, saying that it has been necessary to wage war in the interest of the peace that has been destroyed by German expansion. German imperialism was the ground cause of this war. If it were a defensive war, the Italian allies would have been bound by treaty to join them. And to call the war an attack on German Protestantism when so many Germans are Catholic made no sense. It was true that England had called up colonials—that is, non-Christian troops—but a nation must have diplomatic relations with the colonial countries. Indeed, England has shown care and benevolence for all peoples throughout the world. German destructiveness (the library of Louvain and the cathedral of Reims) has made the English churchmen certain that "until saner elements of German public life can control the baser . . . the contest in which our country has engaged is a contest on behalf of the supremest interests of Christian civilization."[4]

SINS OF BRITAIN ACCORDING TO EVANGELICAL GERMANY

Pastor August Pott of Königsberg said, "We hate England the most because we were bound together in culture and heart and blood. A brotherly love that has been betrayed will become a burning hate." Other pastors were more moderate. Imperialism was the essence of England, according to Ferdinand J. Schmidt and Reinhold Seeberg. Schmidt invoked Luther's opposition to the absolutism of Rome as the model for Germans, and Seeberg wanted Germany to stand on its own, a new, independent, and strong nation," neither submitting to nor imitating Britain.[5] Hypocrisy characterized English war politics. England, so concerned now over little Belgium, had suppressed India, Persia, Egypt, Armenia, Tripoli, the Boers. Britain had alliances with non-Protestant countries, the most dangerous of which was Russia, not only Orthodox but not even European.

Adolph von Harnack, Germany's leading church historian, received a letter addressed to him personally from a committee of English theologians. The letter was a simple exposé similar to the general English address to German theologians as a group and was filled with compliments for Germany's contribution to the study of Christianity. But it began with an indirect quote from Harnack to the effect that the conduct of Great Britain to the present war made the country a traitor to civilization. Harnack begins his response with a rejection of the claim, saying that his original sentence was "Our culture, the great treasure of mankind, was primarily three peoples, and to them almost alone: ourselves, the Americans, and the English. Beyond that I said nothing." Then Harnack attacks instead the English defense of the Serbian and Belgian behaviors as "self-deception." Serbia's horrible assassination of the Austrian archduke was unforgivable and was of a piece with the Russian and south Slav enmity against Austria. Austria was, therefore, the bulwark against Pan-Slavism, and Serbia was simply the extension of Russian power. Harnack introduces a comparison with the England-Ireland situation and wonders what the English response would be if the Prince of Wales had been on a mission in Ireland on behalf of England and had been assassinated there. The Serbian deed was a "crime crying out to heaven."[6]

England's defense of Belgium, in Harnack's view, was even more anti-German than the defense of Serbia in the face of the Austrian invasions, simply because the political and military decisions of Germany impacted England more. Germany was threatened on two fronts, Russia on the east and France on the west, with Belgium as a satellite of France on the west. French airplanes had been permitted to fly over Belgium, and, in fact, France had turned Belgium against Germany. Harnack finds the German chancellor's response to the enraged criticism of the Belgium invasion incorrect. Chancellor Theobald von Bethmann Hollweg, in evoking the dangers of the two fronts, had appealed to expediency: Germany had to do it but would make up for it later. But for Harnack, Germany was right to invade, and he wonders what England would have done if France had invaded Belgium. So, he proposes a scriptural citation in place of the expediency argument. It involves the story of King David allowing his soldiers to eat of the showbreads that were the prerogative of the temple priests, a legalism that could be bypassed for the sake of important goals (1 Samuel 21:6). For Harnack, the English government was clinging to the legalism of an old treaty with Belgium, so what could the government's motivation have been if not to "annihilate Germany"?[7]

Lamenting what Germany and England and America could have accomplished together, Harnack wonders unrealistically—it was 10 September 1914—if England could reverse course. At least the English churchmen could take up the defense of Germany against the lies repeated in the international press about Germany's guilt in pursuing the war.[8]

Other German clergy expanded Harnack's polemic. Serbia was the killer of monarchs (reference to a particularly gruesome assassination of the royal family at the beginning of the century), evils that seemed to be no problem for hypocritical England. Egoism dominated the English mind and idea of freedom, inasmuch as England wanted a fragmented political universe so as to dominate the individual countries. According to Ernst Troeltsch, the leading German theologian, national consciousness was a collection of separate egos and not a unified experience of the *Volk*. Several clergymen believed that the betrayal of Anglo-Saxon Germany was made worse by the English alliances with Africans, as well as the Slavs. All the old stereotypes were rehearsed: the English were simply envious of the broad success of their German kin, they had the penny-pinching mentality of the shopkeeper, and they thought only of utility instead of duty.[9]

Justification of the Belgium invasion dominated the early clergy responses, echoing Harnack. It was militarily justified, England would have done it, and Chancellor Bethmann-Hollweg should not have apologized for it, as he did in the 4 August meeting of the Reichstag. Given that the war was a fight for survival, the German cannot "concern himself overmuch as to whether one or two flowers are trodden down in his neighbor's garden," wrote one preacher. Necessity knows no law. English support of France was particularly disingenuous (because the French would have invaded through Belgium if it had been necessary). Certainly, the English saw the need for militarism when they were threatened by the campaigns and goals of Napoleon. Back then, militarism was a necessity that the English appreciated. War had a moral value, best

FIG. 24 Adolph von Harnack, preeminent German church historian, who argued the justice of the German invasion of Belgium. Photo: mccool / Alamy Stock Photo.

articulated during the Franco-Prussian war by Pastor Karl Köhler: "While war was declared on us from the outside, God bestowed peace on us from the inside." Monarchism as embodied by the Hohenzollerns and the peaceful Kaiser would be the strong defense against decadent republicanism. German culture, then, has a superior destiny and is coming into its own in the new century. A few preachers even promoted a world mission; "space" [*Raum*] was needed, more than "fame" [*Ruhm*].[10]

The theologian Reinhold Seeberg also bemoaned England's betrayal of Germany while arguing the righteousness of the German cause. In his *Geschichte, Krieg, und Seele* (History, War, and Soul), he relies on the biblical resume of world history found in the book of Daniel, chapter 2, with its vision of the empires, the last being the eternal kingdom embodied in Christianity. Seeberg reviews the changes that occurred across the early centuries of Christian history, the church-dominated Middle Ages, and the early modern histories of France, England, and Spain. The Reformation was the saving grace; modern nationalisms and industrialization are the basic challenge. With the developed nationalisms of the other nations, "a sphere of hate and mistrust of German was produced, which like a poisonous breath corrupted international relationships." English imperialism had the most deleterious results: "Everyone knows how impressive the unique mixture of external religion, exclusive morality, violent national arrogance, of organizational timing and commercial self-confidence have operated so often on the people of the continent." England had set itself to world dominance politically and economically, saying that it had a right to this power, working all this out with its old rivals, France, Russia, and Japan, and the result was the present war. In this light, the German alliance with Turkey has taken on a new importance, both for the war and for the development of culture and religion together. "But now a power arises, which in every direction and outlook is the born opponent of England and Russia: Turkey, and behind it the world of Islam. Turkey has placed itself on the side of Germany, thereby becoming a political channel that lies open to Germany, marked by new guides and better focus at the same time." In this war, Germany's awareness of its mission and destiny "is the hope and proud consciousness of our national character, and it is the heartfelt and rightful recognition of our state. A people and a state, how often they seem to be treated as enemies of one another. Freedom and authority, government and popular representation are opposites that from time immemorial had been dragged into political strife."[11] For Seeberg, Germany is the model of a people incarnated in the government.

German nationalism was a source of religious pride for other preachers who used the example of Jesus's patriotic words about Israel and the priority of the Jews: his words to the Samaritan woman (salvation was of the Jews), to the Phoenician women (on throwing the children's bread to the dogs), and his words of mourning for the capital city, Jerusalem.[12] In fact, by World War I German writers had produced a full theology of nationalism. For Pastor Walter Lehmann, the will or life instinct of the Nation, implanted by God, was the basis of truth, which could not be obtained by the abstract use of reason or logic. The ultimate injunction would be, "Do whatever serves the realization of the life-will of your *Volk*." According to Lehmann, even the four gospels were written ethnically, an indication that each nation should have its own special perspective on the message of Christ. Historian of theology Hans von Schubert believed that German Christianity could take its place alongside Greek or Roman Christianity as a datum of history. Others made Luther and the German reformation the key to the new era: that Germany is the conscience of the world is clear, because God raised up such great moral and religious thinkers in Germany. Biblical ideas applicable to Israel or the early church could appropriately be applied to Germany, the heart of which,

Chaplain D. G. Goens noted, was the evangelical church. Otto Dibelius, member of the Evangelical Supreme Church Council, wrote that "everything truly holy and noble is native, growing up from the ground of solid nationality."[13]

SINS OF GERMANY ACCORDING TO ANGLICAN AND PROTESTANT ENGLAND

Church of England bishops and priests soon began to list and classify the sins of Germany, joined by clergy of other denominations and engaged members of the laity. The bishop of London said that Britain was engaged in a "Holy War" against them, and William Sanday, the king's chaplain, pointed to the exaggerated ambition of an otherwise admirable people. Sanday's lengthy and considered *Meaning of the War for Germany and Great Britain* was more restrained than most of his colleagues' writings, but he held government leaders and nationalistic ideologues responsible for the war. He wanted to write the book so "that a German reader, if it should ever have one, should not feel injured and insulted at every turn." He reviews the nineteenth-century events that were crucial in the formation of a united Germany in 1871, which was accomplished by the wars of 1864, 1866, and 1871, under the guiding hand of the Prussian prime minister, Otto von Bismarck. Sanday accepts the *raison d'état* of all these wars, reserving his strong criticism for Harnack and Seeberg, the psychologist Wilhelm Wundt, the classicist Ulrich von Wilamowitz-Moellendorff, and the others who justified the present war. Nor does he accept the superficial German criticism of English national character: given to jealousy, frivolous, hypocritical, and obsessed with empire building. He says that the English foreign minister, Edward Grey, now excoriated by Germany for evasiveness and dishonesty, actually negotiated tirelessly to avoid the war. Sanday does not believe that the German people in general felt great kinship with the English, and the English "had reason to think that Germany was the most restless, the most ambitious and the most dangerous power in Europe." Given the English-German state relationship, there was no reason for a quarrel, so the political breakdown was the result of hasty and ill-considered German political and military decisions. "[Britain] formed a friendship with France, and when it became clear that German policy involved the crushing of France, she was not going to stand by and see it done. Along with France was the small neutral state Belgium and we were among the guarantors of Belgian neutrality." In the end, Sanday reaches a religious—a

FIG. 25 William Sanday, Anglican priest-theologian and royal chaplain, who argued that Germany was responsible for the war without indicting the average German citizen. Image from *The Lamp* 29 (1904–5): 328. Photo: Hathi Trust.

moral—judgment: "The tragedy remains. And, at the bottom of this tragedy is really the desertion of Christian standards and the acceptance for the time of standards that are fundamentally not Christian."[14]

Other preachers, less philosophical than Sanday, were repulsed by the Prussian military temperament, the most dramatic expression of which, just before the war years, was Friedrich von Bernhardi's *Germany and the Next War*. Bernhardi proclaimed that Germany had for too long lived a culturally generous and politically virtuous life and should begin the struggle to secure Germany's power and borders. Given Anglicanism's Reformation connection with Lutheranism, the arrogance and other defects in German Protestant Christianity had to be handled carefully, so English clerics distinguished the younger Luther, still with a Catholic orientation similar to Anglicanism, from the older Luther with his reliance on the power of the state. German philosophers and theologians, they said, were guilty of a reprehensible *Realpolitik*, a combination of the war mongering of Bernhardi, the nationalistic philosophy of Heinrich von Treitschke, and the atheism of Friedrich Nietzsche. The nineteenth-century historian Treitschke, was a collector, if not a creator, of evidence to show that Germany was the superior nation and Britain was the enemy. Lawrence P. Jacks, the philosopher and Unitarian minister, wrote that "it is but a short step from the 'morality of Nietzsche' to the massacre of Louvain."[15]

The powerful words of Heinrich Heine on the return of pagan gods formed the irresistible and favorite quote of English preachers: "And when once that restraining talisman, the cross, is broken, then the old combatants will rage with the fury celebrated by the Norse poets.... Then the old stone gods will rise from unremembered ruins and rub the dust of a thousand years from their eyes, and Thor will leap to life at last and bring down his gigantic hammer on the Gothic cathedrals." Heine's vision, anyone then or now would have to admit, was eerie in light of the German cannonading of Reims Cathedral. German militarism was the besetting sin, so obvious after Louvain and Reims. John Oman, a Scottish Presbyterian theologian, said that this went beyond a military preparedness common to all nations, to rejection of peace as an acceptable state of affairs. The Kaiser himself was an easy target. Joseph Dawson, a vicar in West Yorkshire and author of *Christ and the Sword*, decried the combination of militarism and Bible-demeaning theology: "As a scholar you may cut the Bible into shreds, but as a citizen you must not snip a button from the Kaiser's uniform." Theodore A. Cook wrote in *Kaiser, Krupp, and Culture*, "We have to destroy the Kaiser, his dynasty, and his kingdom as if he were a mad dog." Austin Harrison proclaimed it all to be "political elephantiasis" in *The Kaiser's War*.[16]

The Kaiser's War was one of the shrillest English attacks on the German ecclesiastical establishment. Harrison, an Anglican journalist, blames Harnack for being the ecclesiastical champion of the Kaiser and criticizes the English fascination with German culture and commerce because it overlooked the all-embracing militarism. Harrison pointedly attacks German Protestantism with its hymns, mysticism of nation and state, and with its combined memories of Lutheran and Catholic complicity in the Thirty Years' war. He rehearses all the mistakes of the Kaiser in planning for war, his approval of the destruction of Louvain and Reims, and the murderous march through Belgium. This was all the heritage of earlier political confusion. The fall of Antwerp forced the English government to fully reckon with its neglect of the German war mechanism and forced Harrison himself to reckon with the immorality of the German war. It is an evil that must be crushed totally. Harrison emphasizes the "immorality" of Germany as over against English military-political "carelessness." He imagines a German professor gasping "Immoral! How so?" and then further arguing that "for years ... Germany has proclaimed the intention of war. 'If a man has the chance, is he not to take it?' Even Charlemagne said that. There can be no immorality about a policy explained in every German newspaper for the last fifteen years, in every professorial chair, in every responsible utterance." What is immoral, Austin ironically observes, is "for a nation, like the English, to pretend that they were the friends of a people whom they now denounce as wicked for doing the very thing they have proclaimed to the world as the national policy and religion, and so leading the German people astray." England now has no other choice in the face of the German militarism designed for the destruction of England than conscription and all-out war against Germany. Austin also counters any lingering sentiment of Anglo-Saxon solidarity by stating that Germany is "Teutonic" and not Anglo-Saxon.[17]

Other clergymen derided the German elevation of national *Kultur* in light of the atrocities that began with the invasion of Belgium, wanting to explain why even the superior traits of the German people had their dark side. Some found answers in the German need for system and philosophical abstraction; for others it was, of course, that militarism. Whatever it was, the demon needed to be exorcised. Dawson wrote that Christ would have said of Germany, "Depart from me, I never knew you." All are guilty in the sight of the Lord, but Germany was guiltier. The only hope was that Germany's reprobate state would be temporary, like the tantrum of a child or demon-possession or madness. Frank Ballard, the Methodist theologian, concluded that one could show love for a madman only by throwing him in a padded cell.[18]

In direct responses to German attacks, the justification of the English empire was a central task: the empire was really an international government with minimal compulsion and maximum freedom. The vicar of All Saints Church in Cambridge wrote, "We believe that we are a nation wondrously favoured by God, and we like to think of ourselves as a chosen people, whose name stands in the world for righteousness and peace, for honest dealing with other nations, and respect and protection for small states and weaker peoples. There are people of all kinds under the *Pax Britannica*." With a bizarre twist of interpretation, the minister of the London City Temple showed that Britain learned tolerance from the experience of the American Revolution, caused by the excesses of the "German" king, George III! English defense of Belgium was a luminous example of Christian charity, and probably the greatest source of national and religious pride for the English clergy in the first year of the war. Several quoted the lines of the American poet, James Russell Lowell:

Once to every man and nation
Comes the moment to decide,
In the strife of truth with falsehood,
For the good or evil side ...[19]

FRENCH CLERICAL ATTACKS ON GERMAN CATHOLICISM

In *La guerre allemande et le catholicisme*, the Catholic religious expression was modified by the personal nationalism of the ten bishops and the four priests. We can trace this theology-and-nationalism relationship in the individual essays of the book and in the career and war writings of Alfred Baudrillart. In response, the German bishops and priests, under the editorship of Father Georg Pfeilschifter and supported in particular by Bishop Michael von Faulhaber, produced *Deutsche Kultur, Katholizismus, und Weltkrieg* the following year. After the war, both Baudrillart and Faulhaber were made cardinals, a development that makes it all the more appropriate to compare the political views of each man in World War I.

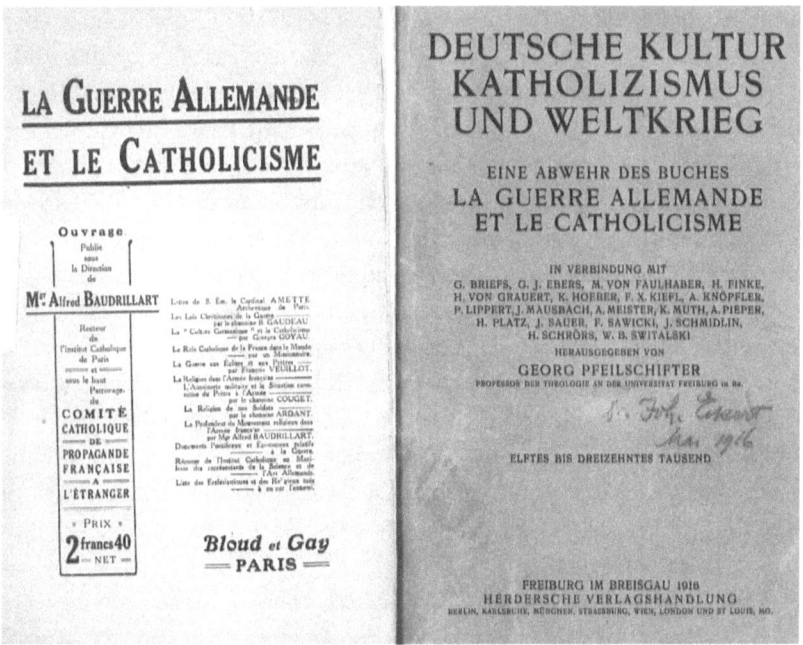

FIG. 26 Covers of *La guerre allemande*, the essay collection of French clerical attacks on German Catholicism, and *Deutsche Kultur*, the volume of German responses. Photo: author.

The French priestly and episcopal voices were stridently anti-German, mitigated very little by religious expression. On one hand, they apparently had an easy case to make: Germany had invaded France, and by the time they were writing they had the devastation of Belgium and the occupation of northern France behind them. On the other, they were attacking German Catholicism: the fellow bishops and priests, the coreligionists. There were many things wrong with the Catholic cohort in Germany, they said, best summed up under the vague heading of submission to German militarism and Protestantism. These French clerics and lay Catholic intellectuals asserted, proclaimed, or implied the right of Catholic France to judge German Catholicism. Sometimes reasons were given and sometimes not, but they were justified by the use of vague and glorious old label, "Eldest Daughter of the Church" by Léon Amette, the cardinal-archbishop of Paris. "In spite of her errors and her faults, she [France] has not ceased to be worthy of the title that Popes from Anastasius through Leo XIII, Pius X, and Benedict XV have granted and maintained: She remains the Eldest Daughter of the Church."[20]

In his introductory notice, Alfred Baudrillart tries to set the record straight for the Catholics of the neutral countries, who might be taken in by German and Austrian statements that France had ceased to be a Catholic nation. But in his presentation of the contents of the book, he is genuinely careless. He says there were two cardinals, whereas there were five. He says that with the exception of Amette, all the bishops rule dioceses that have fallen under the control of the Germans, but the four bishops of the Lyon province, plus the ordinaries of Versailles and Albi, were far from the western front. He does not mention the priests at all, of which there were four, but speaks only of the senators, deputies, and publicists who contributed to the volume. In any case, they were all lined up to answer the question: "By the teaching of its intellectuals, by its manner of pursuing the war, and by the acts of its leaders and soldiers, and in spite of the religious declarations of its sovereign, how does Germany not show itself to be the theoretical and practical adversary of Catholicism, and often of all of Christianity"? And just before he concludes, he uses the old put-down, not otherwise highlighted in the writings that follow, comparing Catholic France, to a "Germany of the Kaiser, 'the friend of Luther.'"[21]

In "Le rôle catholique de la France dans le monde" ("The Catholic Role of France in the World"), the author, identified only as "a missionary," writes, "I would like . . . to try to remind those who forget it, the Catholic role of France in the world." He then attacks the Germany of the Kulturkampf, the nineteenth-century attempt by the German chancellor Otto von Bismarck to limit Catholic influence. He derides the hypocrisy of Germans presenting themselves as virtuous in comparison to French and especially Parisian decadence. "The German Catholic press has particularly distinguished itself for a long time now, by this manner of writing history [pretending that the Kulturkampf was of no importance]. The Kulturkampf has had more success than one ordinarily thinks." Yet it is only by a certain rearranging of his own stereotypes that the French missionary author can say that an "artificial" and "decadent" France has been eclipsed by another France that is a combination of generosity, disinterest, valor, and goodness that Joan of Arc would have recognized. The tone never changes. French missionaries have gone throughout the world, and France itself has been the setting for apparitions of the Virgin Mary (La Salette, Pontmain, Lourdes), whereas Germany speaks of *Unser Gott* as if "control of the earth no longer sufficing, she aspires to [control] of heaven." The author offers a long list of French saints and foreign mission efforts, cites the church's self-sacrificing refusal to play along with the government in the 1905 separation of church and state, and several times labels the antichurch efforts of the French state a "Kulturkampf, imported from Germany." Naturally, the missionary efforts, coordinated by the Society for the Propagation of the Faith, founded at Lyon in 1822 and advanced by the Holy Childhood Society, get full consideration; worthwhile, he said, to review the enormous amount of money contributed to these groups. More important was the large number of French priests, brothers, and nuns who have gone to the missions—18,500 according to a count made in 1900, and perhaps up to twenty-five thousand according to a recent count.[22]

This same unnamed "missionary" imagines a sublime social order and religious culture should France be victorious, and the contrary, should Germany be victorious. He warns of *Macht ist recht* (Might is right) and presumes "the definitive triumph of Lutheranism and Islam" in the case of a German victory! France, however, would end more unified than ever before. Anglican England, already so important to the French and to the Catholic population of Flanders, is quickly losing the old antagonisms to Catholicism, and Orthodox Russia could eventually develop a relationship with Catholic Poland. The basic question, finally, is "will the Greco-Latin civilization, penetrated by and crowned by Christianity, continue to serve as the intellectual and moral nourishment of the world, or must we foresee its absorption by a notion of German Kultur?"[23]

Baudrillart himself explored in detail "La profondeur du mouvement religieux qui s'est manifesté dans l'armée française et comment les oeuvres catholiques de jeunesse l'ont préparé" ("The Profoundness of Religious Action Revealed in the French Army and How Youthful Experience of Catholic Action Prepared the Way"). First, he quotes the anonymous compliment of an unnamed cardinal who told him, "Your army is the most religious in Europe, and perhaps the most religious of all that we have seen in the course of history." Baudrillart admits that the statement astounded him and motivated him to offer a more refined evaluation of the army and reminds readers that not long before the war, outsiders emphasized French decadence and softness. There can be no denying the damage done by a spirit of irreligion and the *école laïque*, but now there are "unquestionable signs of rebuilding." Young people were returning to the patriotic and religious ideas of the preceding generation, "for these two things seemed bound together and they remained bound together: soldier and Christian." He tries to explain this historically by the vaguest of terms: currents, actions, reactions, and agents of renewal. Of "agents of renewal" he has an equally vague list, though he scores a direct historical hit by noting the spirit of fidelity to the pope on the part of those Catholics who, after the law of separation of church and state, refused to work with the state reorganization of the church maintenance responsibilities. He is also explicit about the schools where many of the army officers were formed in their youth, such as the Collège Stanislas and the École Sainte-Geneviève.[24]

Testimonies of officers and soldiers, whose Catholic formation inspired their ways of soldiering, constituted the greater part of Baudrillart's article: he calls them poetic, enthusiastic, and of a certain nobility. A young lawyer formed at the Institut catholique wrote, "I depart with a joy that you can surely believe in: what an honor for our generation to begin life this way. What a triumphal era for France and for Christ if we are the victors." From a Catholic student society member: "I see an officer who is really religious, *the basic good Christian*, and this is what I want to be." A former student wrote, "France must become herself again, the true elder daughter of the church that formed her." A young officer reported reconciling a catholic in the German army who had been mortally wounded in a bayonet charge that the officer himself had ordered. The dying soldier—particularly handsome according to the writer—simply uttered, "Polish Catholic" and took out his rosary with an image of the Virgin and Child. "Having returned my men to their post, I came back to him, made him understand that I was Catholic myself, and that I wanted to solace his last moments. He seemed to understand me and with one of his hands lifts up his rosary. I understood what he wanted and I recited with him a decade, to which he answered feebly in German. After that he brought the rosary to his lips." The French officer then, in his turn, kissed the rosary, which seemed to make the dying man happy.[25]

Baudrillart presents letters that describe heroic action, worship, and devotion. "The mass was said at the field hospital of the Moroccan division that was on our left.... While the men chanted with full voice the Credo and the Adoremus, they were accompanied not by a classic harmonium but by the powerful voice of the cannons and by the peculiar sound of the machine guns." This letter, written actually by a seminarian, concluded on a joyful note: "The life of a soldier is depressing, and we have great need for prayer that aids us *to immerse ourselves a little in the supernatural.*" In fact, liturgical references predominate. "Warmth and sunshine, it was a veritable Spring day, and my heart was filled with happiness; it was the most beautiful day so far. At 3 o'clock, I headed into Vespers and Benediction; a church filled with soldiers, where we all sang, 'I place my confidence, O Virgin, in your help; be my defense and watch over my days.' . . . Today, then, armed with courage, I await the future with calm and abandon myself into the hands of God."[26]

To conclude his collection of testimonies, Baudrillart addresses himself to the Germans! "Catholics, our brothers, you have heard the voice of our Christian soldiers. Do you still believe that France is an atheistic nation? . . . Do you not believe that the institutions that formed them have given the Catholic church, who is the mother of us all, children worthy of her and worthy of the best among you. I appeal to your good faith and I do not doubt your response."[27]

Members of the French hierarchy whose writings were included in the *Guerre allemande et le catholicisme*, were more belligerent than Baudrillart, because they were responding to German atrocities and German occupation. The book contains a brief address signed by all the French Cardinals, and a longer set of reflections from all the bishops of the Lyon province. The tragic and powerful figure of Cardinal Désiré Mercier, primate of Belgium, was the special object of their concerns. Mercier had remained in place when all others had fled, he had proclaimed the Christian right to war in the face of injustice, in the face of the German atrocities: "Churches burned, priests massacred, Louvain set fire, villages leveled, young woman outraged, children and old men shot."[28]

The reprinted pastoral letters from the bishops of occupied territories highlighted the sufferings endured with the coming of the Germans. Bishop Charles-François Turinaz of Nancy was overwhelmed by the size of the war and the armies that made it. He highlighted a statement made by a Bavarian colonel: "This is not an ordinary war; it is a war of extermination, so we must find out if the Latin and Slavic races are going to claim a continued existence in the face of the Germanic race, that is, in the face of a superior culture and civilization." Reviewing accusations of French atrocities, he flatly denies them: "There is not a diocese in France that has not looked out for the sick and wounded Germans." Without actually making the case, he insists that this war of extermination is ultimately geared to "the destruction of the Catholic Church, its authority and its doctrines, and the destruction of all religion." He says that regions of France and elements of French society that have attacked religion are very few, and in spite of—really because of—these trials, Catholicism in France is stronger than elsewhere. War has made heroes of the sensual and indifferent. And although "the enemies of the church do not want to abandon their projects and experiments, . . . sincere souls among them recognize that a change is necessary." Turinaz concludes with the personal observations that he is an old man, that he cannot live with the German lies propagated through the world, which are supported even by clergy and lay Catholics, and that suffering will be the ultimate salvation of France. "We place our hope in the near infinite treasures of noble actions, suffering, and sacrifices, which will obtain for us the mercy of God. . . . What an incomparable and sublime holocaust, and what a force for expiation, redemption, and salvation."[29]

Bishop Émile-Louis Lobbedey of Arras, made two principal points in his Lenten pastoral letter for 1915: (1) providential action gives war-caused sufferings the power of expiation, and (2) providential action can procure a truly glorious peace. Those sufferings begin in the trenches and in the attacks but are found everywhere the invader has a foothold, because "[the enemy] violates all laws worthy of respect, based as they are on natural law, on the most elementary principles of humanity, and on international conventions." As he looks about his diocese, with houses burned, chateaux and farms abandoned, he is reminded of the prophet Jeremiah weeping over the ruins of Jerusalem. He hopes to lift up his fallen people of Arras by relieving their suffering and promoting their repentance, as did his predecessors at the time of the Vandals, of Attila the Hun, of the Normans, and of Louis XI. Growth in virtue can bring about a glorious peace. Here Lobbedey specifically exalts fidelity to the nation, dramatizing the greatness of the sufferers: they "declare that they could never suffer too much for France," and that other countries cannot but recognize French valor. This includes the valor of those left behind, the elderly and the spouses and the children, and the valor of the mediators of "divine goodness" who care for the wounded. The priests are on the front with Mass and confession in a war "where the priest mingles his blood with the blood of the soldier."[30]

Lobbedey is sure of the revelation of the divine will, as clear now as it was in the interventions of the heavenly Michael and the earthly Joan of Arc. The divine will again reveal itself in "the irresistible" and the "unforeseen." And given the evil designs of the enemy, who could doubt that "God will judge in our favor." God cannot possibly look with favor on the other side, even though the enemy calls upon God also. Lobbedey judges them only by their actions: "Without pronouncing on their intentions, without affirming that their conscious goal is to impose on the world a materialistic civilization, a civilization of egoism and severity, it is certain that the war began with an unjust aggression of which they are the authors and we are the victims." A just war is necessary to tear the weapons from the hands of the enemy.[31]

Eudoxe-Irénée Mignot was the bishop of Albi, far from the western front. He began his 28 December (1914) pastoral letter with a historical review of war atrocities. His cast of characters included Sargon and Nabuchodonosor from the ancient world; Attila, Tamerlane, and Alaric from the period of the barbarian invasions. Mignot comments that contemporary cruelties have been of the same order as putting out eyes in the days of Sargon. He is especially troubled, however, when Germans reference the Old Testament to justify their actions. "I believe that the God invoked by our enemies is a God not free of the crude anthropomorphisms fashioned by the ancient Semites, rather than the God of the prophets and above all the God of the gospel." The Germans are guilty of erroneous interpretations of both the Old Testament and the war. "False mysticism and the lie," he says. Purporting to attack all German theologians in this regard, Mignot attacks only the Protestants: "Are they not all more Arian than Christian?" And the loyalty of all to the Kaiser gives a totally Protestant quality to the German cause; it could ensure that the old Holy Roman Empire reconstituted would become the "Holy Roman Protestant Empire." Mignot's last page or two highlight a brochure issued by women in Westphalia, *Hate or Love?*, a bizarre (and one wonders, how influential) publication with the line, "Looking fully at you, I say, my hate will not give way to your love." He responds with lines from Psalm 108 (109), wherein evil is automatically punished in the divine order of things.[32]

Charles Gibier, the bishop of Versailles, no more a direct witness to the invasion than Mignot, stays with the role of Protestantism in German history. France has always been a major force for civilization and religion. If France were to fall, "the best features of humanity would be undermined.... [and] the gospel would suffer a set-back." He, too reviews the foreign mission accomplishments of French priests and nuns, saying that France has spread the reign of God in the world better than any other country, and ending with the punch line: "In any case, if she were to lose her place of honor in the avant-garde of Catholicism, it would not be Germany who would replace her in this function." To put it simply, he blames Prussia and Protestantism for the inferior religious condition of Germany. Although France—occasionally official France—has stumbled along the path of fidelity to Catholicism, it has always righted itself. Right now, he says, nine-tenths of the soldiers pray and there are twenty-five thousand priests in the army, and in face of mortal danger, France has retrieved her essence and origins. "It seems that without Catholicism France could not continue to be herself."[33] Gibier's theological acumen was cited by Stéphen Coubé, who in the preface to the *Missel du Miracle de la Marne* credited him with the insight into absolute and relative (e.g., the Marne) miracles.

THE GERMAN CATHOLIC COUNTER-ATTACK

German clerics and laymen met the accusations, almost point by point in *Deutsche Kultur, Katholizismus, und Weltkrieg*. By way of introduction, Joseph Mausbach (like Baudrillart, a domestic prelate, or "monsignor") said that the declaration of literary warfare by French Catholic clergy and intellectuals required a response. National loyalty is understandable, he said, but why this religious antagonism against twenty-four million German Catholics? Why are the evils of war declared German? Mausbach ignores the constant theme of a France that is Catholic at heart, asking how the French war can be just when it is promoted by religion's worst enemies. He expects his French colleagues to deal with the false idea that German Catholics surrendered to the Kulturkampf, a French theme.[34]

The authors of subsequent chapters recognize the huge complexities involved in the decisions to go to war but argue that it is just and necessary. According to the Germans, French authors ignored the Russian danger to

Austria and Germany when they said that Germany planned the war, which in fact the Kaiser had always resisted. They wonder why priests of the "masonic" French republic criticize the German-Turkish alliance that brings together Christian and Muslim worshippers of the one God. And what is the point of the French intellectual attack against Kant and Nietzsche when the goodness and religiousness of the German army as a whole is the issue? Germany's treatment of Belgium was not unjust or immoral. Politically and historically, Belgium was set up in 1830 by the European powers so as to guarantee independence and neutrality, but not integrity and inviolability. Belgians had violated neutrality anyway by supporting English espionage. Atrocity reports are misleading, suggesting perversion, whereas it was a matter of blood and iron; it was war, after all. The priest Joseph Sauer responds at great length to the broader issue of art and sacred buildings in the war. Reims Cathedral and the Louvain library were not shelled wantonly or out of perversity, but because they were being used for military purposes. He reviews the other major buildings destroyed, making the case that monuments are not to be compared to human lives in measuring the war's destructiveness.[35]

The editor, theologian Father Georg Pfeilschifter, develops the preferred German theme that religious life and the care of souls by the clergy flourish in the German army. There is none of the anti-Catholic spirit assumed by the French. There are the same proportions of Protestants and Catholics in the army as in German society in general. Both Protestant and Catholic churches support the army, and a full range of prayers and devotions is assured at and behind the front. In the occupied area, the German Catholic soldiers are more church going than the French general population. Pfeilschifter takes on the five French cardinals, who believed a false report about the mistreatment of Cardinal Mercier; the five bishops of the Lyon province, who went further and evoked a Cardinal Mercier in chains; Bishop Turinaz of Nancy, who said that France has obeyed all human and divine laws with constancy; the bishop of Arras, who was sure that France never willed the war and now takes it up for moral reasons; Archbishop Mignot of Albi, who wrote untrue and injurious accusations; and the bishop of Versailles, who saw in the destruction of France the destruction of European civilization.[36]

Pfeilschifter is horrified. "Thus do the French bishops dare to talk to their people in the face of the saddening religious conditions developing before all eyes in France, in the face of the serious blows which the Church in France has received within the past decades and is still receiving up to this hour from the Masonic government." Should they not rather "tell the reader how the

Church in France is being maltreated by the government and is separated from the State, nay enslaved by it; how the people are systematically dechristianized; how the religious instruction has been banished from the school; how the placing of crucifixes is prohibited; how monasteries are suppressed, their inmates dispersed, and how the churches were secularized and profaned?" In contrast, says Pfeilschifter, the archbishops of Bamberg and Freiberg and Munich, and fourteen bishops offer a completely different teaching. Accordingly, he submits a comparison to his readers. [On the French side] "The most one-sided national chauvinism permitting itself to even attain to the vilification of the opponent; [on the other] profound religious feeling which not even to the slightest degree wounds the enemy. Every sentence, nay every word breathes forth a Christian spirit and also the commandment to *love the enemy* finds due recognition."[37]

The leading religious figure among the German writers, Michael von Faulhaber, at the beginning of the war the bishop of Speyer, responded eloquently, if not emotionally, to the French pretensions to a superior Catholicism. "Barring the fact that the mother's eldest daughter is frequently her greatest source of sorrow, it is to be borne in mind that in the testament of Jesus we find no rule of primogeniture, no exclusive individual enfeoffment of his kingdom. As the sun shines for all, so the truths of Christian faith in their fullness belong to all nations, and no nation can claim: I alone walk in the light." His themes are the general esteem for religion in German public life, and the very workable union of church and state because of a variety of Concordats with individual Catholic regions, and the perfect cooperation between church and government in the school system. He lists (1) forceful representation of religious interests and the rights of the Church in public life, (2) the union of state and church, (3) well-defined and positive confessionalism as the product of the coexistence of Protestantism and Catholicism, (4) the German understanding of, and perseverance in, the tasks of religious culture, (5) the tenor of the religious life and pastoral practice, and the (6) the school system. And he concludes: "On the mountains of religious culture at least, let us welcome the heralds of peace! There is a time for war and a time for peace. The messengers of religious truth must, above all, serve the works of peace, and pave the way to international conciliation. It does not behoove them to carry war in the name of religion to a new front, and to widen the breach which hatred has made."[38]

Faulhaber's eloquence, then, was a commendatory finale to Mausbach's rejection of French clerical belittlement of German Catholicism, Sauer's justification of German destruction, and Pfeilschifter's contrast of German and French bishops—German openness in place of narrow French chauvinism.

BAUDRILLART AND FAULHABER: A POSTSCRIPT

In his meticulously kept *Carnets*, Baudrillart cites *Deutsche Kultur, Katholizismus, und Weltkrieg* only twice, both times in reference to Eugenio Pacelli, the papal envoy to Germany and future pope. Baudrillart reported, 15 May 1917, a long, serious discussion with Pacelli about the book, identifying it simply as the Pfeilschifter text. He criticized the way "confessional parity, the tendencies of the imperial family, and the way the atrocities committed by the Bavarians are explained." Pacelli left a good impression, which means that he must have been open to Baudrillart's position.[39] In a collection of essays published in 1917, *La France, les Catholiques et la guerre* (French Catholics and the War), Baudrillart takes on some of the authors who contributed to the Pfeilschifter text, in particular one noncleric who had severely criticized the chauvinism of the French bishops published in *La guerre allemande et le catholicisme*. In his essay, "Le clergé français a-t-il péché par excès de nationalisme?" ("Did the French Clergy Sin by Excess Nationalism?"), Baudrillart insists that the French hierarchy carefully avoided speaking as a unified witness; they were simply "authorized witnesses of events and deeds in their own territories." In another essay he refers to Pfeilschifter without attacking him, because he was trying to make the case that France served Catholicism by working with Anglican England and Orthodox Russia. Pfeilschifter ("who is above suspicion [in this matter]") had vouched for the goodness of Orthodoxy, thus serving Baudrillart's own purposes.[40] Otherwise, Baudrillart was not pastorally engaged with the armies.

Bishop Michael von Faulhaber, however, was more pastor than polemicist.[41] He preached directly to the soldiers, when, as official head chaplain (*Feldpropst*) of the Bavarian army divisions, he visited the front. Instead of that pointed opposition to the French Catholic attacks on Germany, he urged his soldiers to the basic military virtues and was the most eloquent and clear-headed of the rostrum of churchmen who took part in the war of words that continued across the hot war years. He visited the front near Saint-Mihiel in Lorraine, 9–14 March 1915, and he visited the troops in Flanders, 22–29 April. His last visit to the western front was to northern France, in and around Arras, 11–26 February 1916. He received no monetary compensation from the

FIG. 27 Bishop, later Cardinal, Michael von Faulhaber visiting the trenches as part of his wartime ministry. He wrote that the German cause was just, but that hatred of enemies was not. From *Kardinal Michael von Faulhaber, 1869–1952: Eine Ausstellung des Archivs des Erzbistums München und Freising* (Munich: Archiv des Erzbistums München und Freising, 2002).

Bavarian army for his trip, traveling on his own funds as would a private citizen, but he was received with the honor accorded the highest officer level. Posters and programs were printed up, and the soldiers themselves took numerous photographs. He wanted them to realize, however, that the chaplains in the field were more important than he.[42]

Having done his military service as an infantry man in his youth, it was natural for Faulhaber to climb into the front trenches, and he insisted on doing so in order to symbolically share in the soldiers' and chaplains' experiences. During his 1915 visits to the front, his chaplains emphasized the problem of venereal disease, clearly as much a pastoral concern for them as for the Protestant pastors. One of the chaplains reported that an estimated seventeen thousand prostitutes were working the area around Lille, and the Catholic chaplains did not have enough clout to insist on greater control of the soldiers. Back at Speyer in 1915, he made an official visit to the military hospital of Saint Magdalena on 28 June, and to other military hospitals also. The Bavarian army had about 950 military hospitals and convalescence centers with more than thirty thousand beds.[43]

Faulhaber's sermons, if not fighting-words, were a clear expression of religion and nationalism: sometimes ingenious, sometimes melodramatic, and sometimes a remarkable combination of righteousness and humility. At the beginning of the church year, Advent, he naturally highlights the figure of the forerunner of Christ, John the Baptist—for soldiers. "He is the born key-saint for our engineers with their building and road work, because his voice calls out, 'Prepare the way of the Lord.'"[44] In "Die Rüstung des Glaubens" ("Armament of Faith"), he worked to put the chaplains' ministry to the soldiers in a military perspective. Spiritual ministry, he says, is its own kind of military service. This was a response to the occasional sharp criticisms that chaplains were playing no real part in bringing about victory: but without the chaplains, the advancing soldiers would lose their dedication. Faulhaber adds that the French have as many priests in arms as Germany has priests in the entire country, rejecting any comparisons there.[45] In "Soldaten tugenden und Tugenbilder" ("Soldier Virtues and Virtue Images"), he praises the men for their fidelity, which is greater than all previous wars, including the nineteenth-century wars of liberation. They are the saviors of the fatherland.[46] Then in a strong final sermon in this "Soldier Virtues" series, he displays the biblical figure of the centurion of Capharnaum, in effect, an army captain. "With this biblical story I have the feeling that the Centurion, with his hand on his helmet would have presented himself as the representative of soldiers to the savior." Christ did not then say, "Go first and take off your uniform and pound your sword into a plowshare, because I will have no saber bearers in my kingdom.... In the way that Jesus received and dismissed the Centurion, it comes out that a man can wholeheartedly be a soldier, and even so every inch a man after the heart of God.... the Centurion did not fear that he would be disowning his officers uniform when he discounted it [as an authority symbol] in his profession [of faith] in the presence of the people, his own soldiers, and even the enemies of the cross."[47]

Faulhaber was every bit the loyal subject, not only of the Bavarian king but of the Kaiser, who telegraphed after a victory in Lorraine, "God was with us. Honor to him alone." This would be a basic reason, and a theologically proper one, to honor the Kaiser, wrote Faulhaber. "Comrades! Thus does the bearer of the crown teach us to give to God what is God's, and the bearer of the cross teach us to give to the Kaiser what is the Kaiser's. A ruler who keeps the second commandment [honoring God] of the ten has by this a right that we keep holy the fourth [honoring father, mother, all authority]. True love for fatherland and the father of the land! Let us pray for our Kaiser and his royal house and his empire. A difficult burden, difficult as half the globe, lies today on his shoulders."[48]

From church leaders and writers on the home front came condemnation, alternately sober and angry, of the enemy nations, giving equal time to God-talk and nation-talk, undistracted by the chaos and wretchedness on the war front.

The German Protestant writers consolidated the preaching eloquence of the Berliner Dom clergy and the long sermons of the field preachers. Adolph von Harnack gave voice to the often-held German sentiment that England betrayed its Anglo-Saxon heritage, even bringing up troops from alien and conquered colonies, and that England's defense of Serbia and Belgium was disingenuous, given Serbia's murderous behavior and Belgium's duplicity. He called on Christian ministers in England to at least defend Germany against the false propaganda coming from other countries. Reinhold Seeberg eloquently championed German folk-nationalism, which was crucial, he thought, to maintaining the unity between culture and religion. Pastors and theologians grounded their folk nationalism in Luther and the Reformation and counted on the Kaiser to guarantee its continuation. English thinking, they said, was a cacophony of separate egos, to be countered by German reverence for the mystical essence of a people uniquely blessed, for God in modern times raised up the great moral and religious thinkers in Germany.

The gamut of English Protestant religious expression included everything from the irenic, if severe, writing of William Sanday through the diatribes of Austin Harrison, all of which hearkened back to strong and eloquent send-off sermons of London's bishop, Arthur Winnington-Ingram. Sanday reviewed German self-promotion, militarism, and unjustified aggression in the light of earlier German accomplishments and virtues to conclude, even so, that the Germans had initiated an unjust war. Harrison listed the German evils that began with Luther, his Catholic opponents, and the Thirty Years' war and came to fruition with the militarism of the Kaiser and the devastation wrought by the Kaiser's armies on the subject peoples, the library of Louvain and the cathedral of Reims. The writings of the reprobate philosophers such as Nietzsche, the mindlessness of the "mad dog" Kaiser, and the attack on biblical truth by liberal German critics rounded out the English list of German religious perversions.

Alfred Baudrillart and his fellow Catholic clergymen reprised Cardinal Amette's dicta that the French cause was just and French soldier heroism could merit heaven. They laid out what they took to be the religious heritage of Catholic France. This comprises, they said, generosity, disinterest, valor, and goodness, which are the specific Christian and military virtues developed to embody the French civilizing mission to all parts of the world and within France itself (never having submitted to a Kulturkampf). As the war progressed, the reception of the sacraments was the clearest sign and guarantee of the continuing dedication. The ecumenical dialogue with Orthodox Russia and Anglican England gave further opportunity for Christian witness. The French bishops' contribution to the discussion was an overheated presentation of France as the standard bearer of Western civilization. Turinaz and Lobbedy, near the front, wrote that the French soldiers' spirituality was embodied in love of enemies and holocaust-like sacrifice. Mignot and Gibier, in more academic messages (they were far from the front), wrote that the soldiers were living out New Testament love, as over against the denatured Old Testament mythology embodied by the Germans, so influenced by liberal Protestantism.

The German Catholic clergy responded indignantly, noting that Catholics had suffered from and resisted the Kulturkampf, and that Germany had no option other than to defend itself against the enemies surrounding the national territory. They accused the French writers, especially the bishops, of believing numerous false reports about the war and about the German soldiers, and of conveniently ignoring the de-Christianization promoted by the French government for decades. The French Catholic claim to be "the eldest daughter of the church" was disingenuous at best.

In the end, the editor of the French polemic, Alfred (later Cardinal) Baudrillart tried to claim a moral high road of simple truth, and Michael (later Cardinal) von Faulhaber, in addition tried to work out a Catholic spirituality specifically for the German soldier.

In essence, both German and English clergy were promoting the theology of a "chosen people," and did not shrink from using that exact expression to label the citizens of their own nations. They constructed a war theology from biblical passages proclaiming the justice and necessity of the sword, as did the German and French Catholic writers, bishops, and priests, who attacked the morality and motives of churchmen on the other side. To the French diatribes Germans responded in more theologically measured tones, with Bishop Michael von Faulhaber explicitly condemning the whole enterprise of religious traditions warring behind the lines instead of serving the cause of peace, because such action would only deepen the hatred. Faulhaber, more than the other churchmen, combined the mystic, the hard-headed theological rationalist, and the engaged pastor of souls.

CHAPTER 8

Theology Out of War Experience

Living through the tragedy of war and in their own ways feeling the presence of God there, the Jewish reconnaissance officer Franz Rosenzweig and the Christian chaplains, Paul Tillich, Pierre Teilhard de Chardin, and Geoffrey Studdert Kennedy refashioned religious thought for the twentieth century. Rosenzweig's all-embracing theology of creation, revelation, and redemption was written on the southern front (the Balkans) and in dialogue with another great Jewish thinker of the period, Eugen Rosenstock, a convert to Christianity, then fighting on the western front.[1] Among the many Christian chaplains who were in the trenches, sometimes in the over-the-top attacks, caring for the wounded and burying the dead, three men stand out: the German Lutheran pastor, Paul Tillich, the French Jesuit, Pierre Teilhard de Chardin, and the High-Church Anglican, Geoffrey Studdert Kennedy. Each presents a different picture: Tillich, living and creating a dogmatic theology; Teilhard, living and creating a mystical theology; Studdert Kennedy, living and creating a pastoral theology. So, we can make the case that from out of World War I emerged twentieth-century theologies for living with the death of the religious imagination (Tillich), seeing beyond the random destructiveness of evolution (Teilhard), and for engaging the meaninglessness of human suffering (Studdert Kennedy).

Other intellectuals of "the generation of 1914" had immediate influence during and after the war, but nothing compared to the enduring influence of the four men shown here.[2]

FRANZ ROSENZWEIG: THE UNIVERSAL ROLE OF JUDAISM

In September 1914, Rosenzweig began service in Belgium with the Red Cross. The next year, he entered the army and, ever the scholar, continued work during his training period on a treatise about Hegel and the state. Then, after a brief ballistics school stint in France, he joined the anti-aircraft unit that brought him to the Balkans. In May of 1916, he began the correspondence with Rosenstock, writing with equal seriousness to his parents in the meantime. In a letter to them, dated 17 August 1916, he summed up his initial philosophy of war: "War is no more immoral, i.e., irreligious, than peace. It is the *men* who are good or evil. . . . The religious doctrine of peace, insofar as it is not simply an allegory of the condition of the individual soul, is an idea of a concluding era: peace appears at the moment when world history has run its course. Consequently religion does not regard this ultimate peace as man's work but as a direct act of God to be prepared by a final and incredibly terrible series of wars." Although he could be cavalier about his duties—"My solitary tour of duty as an aircraft observer has made a romantic childhood dream come true: to be 'alone' on a high mountain with a magnificent view"—he continued to explore the theme of human responsibility and divine power. "War is a 'divine *judgment*.' . . . Within each nation a judgment falls upon internal politics, and between nations, upon the nations themselves. The touching thing about the 'just' is that they place themselves fundamentally under the same law as their opponents."[3]

Rosenzweig's correspondence with Eugen Rosenstock on Jewish identity provided the clarifying energy for *The Star of Redemption*, which he wrote out on postcards during his time at the front. Rosenzweig resists all of Rosenstock's sporadic efforts to make himself out to be truly Jewish, although a convert to Christianity, as an attack on what he considered to be true Jewishness in general and his own Jewishness in particular. "You are directly hindering me from treating my Judaism in the first person, in that you call yourself a Jew too. That is to me equally intolerable, emotionally and intellectually. For me you can be nothing else but a Christian; the emptiest of Jews, cut off root and branch and a Jew only in the legal sense, is still an object of concern to me as a Jew, but you are not." For Rosenzweig, Christianity exists to guarantee the development and spread of Judaism. "Christianity is like a power that fills the world according to the saying of one of the two scholastics, Yehuda ha-Levi [Juda Halevi]: It is the tree that grows from the seed of Judaism and casts its shadow over the earth; but its fruit must contain the

FIG. 28 Franz Rosenzweig at the front with others trained in ballistics. He wrote his magnum opus on the eternal mission of Judaism, in dialogue with his colleague Franz Rosenstock, who was serving on the western front. Photo: Image Bank / Alamy Stock Photo.

seed again, the seed that nobody who saw the tree notices. This is a Jewish dogma, just as Judaism as both the stubborn origin and last convert is a Christian dogma." He quotes a legend to make his point here. "The Messiah was born exactly at the moment when the Temple was destroyed, but when he was born, the winds blew him forth from the bosom of his mother. And now he wanders unknown among the peoples, and when he has wandered through them all, the time of our redemption will have come." In this sense, Christianity prepares the way for Judaism, an inversion of the traditional Christian view.[4]

"The election of the Jews is something unique, because it is the election of the 'one people,' and even today our peculiar pride or peculiar modesty, the world's hatred or the world's contempt, rejects an actual comparison with other peoples." In fact, Christian hopes for the transformation of a people, a nation, or an ethnic group morphed into the pseudo-messianic notions of 1789 for France and of 1914 for individual European nations, without significant results. Rosenzweig insists that "the forms of inner Jewish life are . . . quite distinct from all apparent parallels in civilizations. The art of the Synagogue does not enter into living relation with other art, nor Jewish theology with Christian theology, and so on; but Jewish art and theology, taken together, build up the Jews into a united whole and maintain them in their form of life (which isn't any living movement but just life, plain and simple), and only then do they work as a ferment on Christianity and through it on the world." Rosenzweig concludes this letter with the sentence "Before the Throne of God the Jews will only be asked one question: Hast thou hoped for the salvation?" Presumably, all further questions would be addressed to Christians, because Christianity identifies itself with the "empires" or "the world of today, and . . . Judaism is the only point of contraction and of limitation and is, thereby, the guarantee of the reality of that Christian world. Everything must vanish in order to become everything." So, Judaism, via Christianity, is the all in all.[5]

The Star of Redemption is a more expansive working out of these ideas and can be considered, with the provisos offered by the leading Rosenzweig commentator, Nahum Glatzer, a "war book." Glatzer wrote that "The *Star of Redemption*, written by *Unteroffizier* at the Macedonian front, in hospitals, and after the collapse of the front line, on the march of the retreating army, is the most curious of 'war books.'" It is clear from the first page of the book that Rosenzweig is aware of the horrors of battle. "That man may crawl like a worm, into the folds of the naked earth before the whizzing projectiles of blind, pitiless death, or that there he may feel as violently inevitable that which he never feels otherwise: his I would be only an It if it were to die; and he may cry out his I with every cry still in his throat against the Pitiless One by whom he is threatened with such an unimaginable annihilation—upon all this misery, philosophy smiles its empty smile." It is the individual crying out but "philosophy dupes him of this should when around the earthly it weaves the thick blue haze of its idea of the all." Philosophy makes the "something" of death, which all men fear, into a "nothing." For Rosenzweig, the goal is to prioritize, even absolutize, the individual human being in the face of death.[6]

The individual human being, Man, is part of the whole, Man—World—God, linked together in Creation—Revelation—Redemption.

Creation establishes the connection between God and the world, bringing God out of the unknowable beyond, "from the nothing to the 'something,'" but leaves the human being subject to death.[7]

Revelation is necessary to get beyond the finite and temporary essence of the created human being, because in Revelation God comes across as love, and the role of the human being (the beloved) is to receive it. Rosenzweig writes, "The lover who surrenders himself in love is recreated in the faithfulness of the beloved, and from then on, it is forever," so it is no surprise that the biblical book that best provides the essential teaching here is "The Song of Songs," a canticle and parable of the divine-human love relationship.[8]

Redemption comes to reality when the human being transforms love of God into love of neighbor, which "complete[s] the surrender." Rosenzweig emphasizes that this is "not a singular act, but a whole series of acts; love of the neighbor always newly arises; it is always a new beginning." It is subject to all the challenges of living with other people, who tend to turn back and be engulfed in their subject-to-death beginnings. God, at every moment, leads global redemption forward and, finally, to eternity.[9]

Rosenzweig returns in the final section of *The Star of Redemption* to the two views of the world (and so, two interpretations of Creation—Revelation—Redemption), displayed in the teachings and liturgies of Judaism and Christianity. Nathan Glatzer sums it up this way: "Both are representations of the real world (and as such equal before God) and spell the end of the heathen view of the world. Judaism, which stays with God, stands in contrast to Christianity, which is sent out to conquer the unredeemed world and is forever marching toward God."[10] And yet, ultimately, for Rosenzweig, both the Jew and the Christian are "workers on the same task. . . . We both have only a share in the whole truth. We know, however, that the essence of truth is to be shared and that a truth that is no-one's share would not be truth; even the 'whole' truth is truth only because it is God's share. So it does damage neither to the truth nor even to us that only a share falls to us. Immediate sight of the whole truth comes only to him who sees it in God. But this is a seeing beyond life." Meanwhile the vision of truth leads "INTO LIFE"—the last two words of *The Star of Redemption*, and the antithesis of the goals set for the warring soldiers on the front.[11]

PAUL TILLICH: FAITH AFTER THE DEATH OF THE RELIGIOUS IMAGINATION

Son of a Lutheran pastor, Paul Tillich was born in 1886 near Berlin. He received his secondary schooling in Königsberg, the city of Immanuel Kant, and in Berlin itself after his father received a church appointment there. He received his doctor of philosophy degree in 1911 (University of Breslau) and was ordained the following year. He married just as the war was beginning and almost immediately left for the front as a German army chaplain.

The major Tillich biographers, Wilhelm and Marion Pauck, write that the World War I years "represent *the* turning point in Paul Tillich's life—the first, last, and only one." Transformed by the war, Tillich the monarchist had become a religious socialist, the traditional Christian a cultural pessimist, and the morally strict boy a "wild man." Appointed an official chaplain, he arrived on the western front two months after the outbreak of the war, at times conducting services under fire but otherwise in a position more toward the rear, near Soissons. He was joined at the front by a Roman Catholic chaplain, with whom at least on one occasion he set up an imitation barroom for some officers and troops. When there was little action, he was bored, writing to one friend, "True experience has its roots in suffering, and happiness is a blossom which opens itself up only now and then." There was a brief time of joy at his birthday in August, celebrated by the division soldiers, and even a general. That evening he could hear cannons in the distance as he read Psalm 90, a birthday custom: "Lord thou hast been our refuge from generation to generation." Then, on October 1915, he was into the trenches, surrounded by obliterated villages, with the usual mud and rats underfoot, for all practical purposes a frontline soldier. At the end of the month, his division suffered serious losses by Tahure near the Marne, and Chaplain Tillich became gravedigger and preacher of ultimate happiness and interim sacrifice: on one hand, highlighting Second Corinthians, "Our troubles are slight and short-lived; and their outcome an eternal glory which outweighs them far," and on the other hand, "We must remain responsible to ourselves and to all others: for the sake of love for and devotion to the homeland, for the sake of pride, pride in being Germans, and for the sake of the bond of community which ties our spirit to the spirit of our nation, for the sake of the glory of the German fatherland." November brought yet more casualties, including some of the top officers, but for Christmas, the Seventh Division was in a small village in northeastern France, where Tillich managed to decorate the church for Christmas Eve and preached a sermon designed to give the men strength to live through hope for peace.[12]

After a brief interlude back in Germany, he returned to the same region, quieter this time, where he was able to help set up relatively comfortable quarters for officers and men, and, at the same time, developed a feel for the common soldier—a man subject to the aristocracy, the army, and the church—and his usual appreciation of philosophical argument. This was 1916, and in May Tillich led both Germans and the local French in a remarkable discussion. French women, more than a hundred of them, gathered at Blanchefosse, with its castle well behind the lines, working to clean the building and groom the grounds. They gathered excitedly around the few German soldiers who came to see the castle, especially the chaplains. Each side justifying its action because the other "started the war," they came to talk quietly under the guidance of the calming Tillich, who helped them understand the interpretations of the other side.[13]

Paul Tillich's sermons to soldiers during the war were admonitions and consolations in the standard, pious Lutheran God-talk of his day. These wartime sermons were oases of devotional meditations on a spiritually barren battlescape. His soldiers were fighting for God and Christian civilization. Mathew Lon Weaver reviewed Tillich's ninety-three published sermons from the war years, finding there five themes: Christian devotion; military virtue; the fatherland and sacrifice; war, peace, and reconciliation; and power and weakness.[14]

Evoking the suffering and bleeding Christ, Tillich recommends a path of Christian devotion. "He accompanies you also in the darkness of death, because no one is closer to you than He is. That is the message of Christianity, in particular the experience of the Last Supper, that God cannot be happy for all eternity without me and my soul. Human evil continues the crucifixion. Only by humility, becoming weak in order to be strong, can Germany bring God's righteous judgment into the World."[15] Love of enemies has to be a greater challenge for a soldier, to military virtue, than for anyone else. One can love enemies but hate the enemy's destructive goals. "Is not your enemy at the boundary of love?" Does not love leave off where the fight begins? No. "We do not hate the individual, we hate the popular will, which rises up against us to suppress us, we hate the power of evil and envy.... Love is not weak ... but love is the stamping out of evil."[16] Sacrifice for the fatherland is for all the brethren and for Germany as embodied in the Kaiser. "Honor the king. Love your brother. Fear God. Those are the triple roots of true fatherland enthusiasm.... King and fatherland belong together. We and the fatherland belong together. God and the fatherland belong together."[17] Tillich at times looked at the evils of war, but thought it to be God's war in that it can lead to peace and reconciliation. "We cannot live next to misery without wanting to help ... and we are not able to hate with good conscience ... when he the guiltless lifted up in his prayer for his murderers and mockers, the destroyers of his happiness, of his work, of his life, saying, forgive them, for they do not know what they are doing. No, we cannot sing along with the song of Hate with a good conscience, we who stand before the cross must say, Forgive them."[18]

And soldiers who must maintain strength in battle should pray when feeling weakest, as Christ did at Gethsemane. "He implored God that he might possibly be spared suffering and death. And God's answer was the cross. He offered himself for God's great plans and eternal goals, and so was he heard because his soul became tranquil and his will became one with God's will, his soul one with God."[19]

Tillich completely rethought this sermon Christianity of his day, even as he rethought the fundamental Lutheran Christian theme of faith alone. At Verdun in late May, he wrote to his father, "We are on the west bank of the Meuse. . . . Hell rages around us. It's unimaginable." Endless casualties, with the wounded to somehow succor and the dead to bury. He later wrote that the epic verses of Paul (Romans 8:38–39), were his support amid the sounds "of exploding shells, of weeping at open graves, of the sighs of the sick, of the moaning of the dying"— "For I am sure that neither death, nor life, nor angels, nor principalities, nor things present, nor things to come, nor powers, nor height, nor depth, nor anything else in all creation, will be able to separate us from the love of God in Christ Jesus our Lord." Having been transferred to Verdun from another area of the Champagne front, he was soon surrounded by more slaughter; racing from soldier to soldier, he helped them as best he could. Faith was no simple psychological defense for him here. He wrote, "I have constantly the most immediate and very strong feeling that I am no longer alive. Therefore I don't take life seriously. To find someone, to become joyful, to recognize God, all these things are things of life. But life itself is not dependable ground." As the Paucks put it, "More and more he grappled with the awareness that the concept of God which had crumbled on the battlefield" had to be replaced by *"faith without God,"* which he came to "by thinking through the idea of justification by faith to its logical conclusion." Here the Paucks are citing a letter to Maria Klein, but they are also making passing reference to Tillich's November letters to Emmanuel Hirsch, which contained three pointed arguments for a faith without God.[20]

First, Tillich observed that the thought of God is the setting for the opposing thought (no God), and so God cannot demand the operation of this God-thought of someone he wills to justify. This philosophical and theological argument turns on the paradox that if God implants the concept of Himself in a human being, he must also implant the antithesis of this concept. If the person is then taken over by this antithesis—atheism, in effect—it is not his or her fault. Secondly, he engaged Hirsch on the necessity of getting beyond the scientific "God concept," noting that for the nineteenth-century theologian Martin Kähler the "absolute" was an idol. One is obliged to be skeptical, then, of any proof attempt. For phenomenologists the relativity of this concept puts a limit on all results; religious certainty cannot be based on them. This mystical argument turns on the paradox that the God-concept itself is not God. The infinite can only be encountered but cannot be contained in a concept, which necessarily becomes an idol. Thirdly, he insisted that faith cannot be made dependent on a mechanism—that is, the affirmation of the God-thought or the function of the God-experience. This pastoral argument follows from the other two, that Christians cannot be required to come up with a faith profile determined by any particular thought or experience.[21]

Tillich survived it all, even the last-ditch German effort of 1918. He felt broken, incapable of going on, and in May asked to be relieved of army service. This was refused, but in the last months of the war he was assigned to Spandau prison in Berlin. Even in May, however, he wrote with hope, "Today or tomorrow our troops will reach the Marne, and we follow behind. The wounded are in good spirits; everything is different, everything entirely different, and much, much better than before. Our regiments are magnificent and I am grateful to the chief of chaplains for forcing me to experience this." After the 11 November armistice ending the war, Tillich was back in Berlin, but spirits were good no longer: the left and far left demonstrated against the hierarchical forces within Germany that, they believed, caused the war. And Tillich was with them.[22]

PIERRE TEILHARD DE CHARDIN: BEYOND THE DESTRUCTIVENESS OF EVOLUTION

Teilhard's *Écrits du temps de la guerre* (Writings in Time of War) and the letters that he wrote to his cousin Marguerite Teillard-Chambon across 1914–1918, *Génèse d'une pensée* (Genesis of His Thinking) strikingly reveal his World War I experience; his *Journal* of the period is less well known but casts light on the *Écrits* and the *Génèse*.[23] Teilhard's ability to experience, as a stretcher-bearer, frontline destruction and agony as a disintegrating and recomposing complex of atoms ("monads") which could only issue in a transfigured cosmos was the foundation of his major writings, *Le milieu divin* (The Divine Milieu) in particular. This composite of experience and religious reflection produced a "war mysticism."[24] He was born in 1881 in the old family château just outside of Clermont-Ferrand. Jesuit educated from age twelve on, he entered the order's novitiate in 1899. He continued his studies in the Jesuit house on the island of Jersey, was sent to Cairo for his teaching residency, and was brought back to England for his theological studies. After ordination in 1911, he studied and worked as a paleontologist in France, England, and Spain. During the entire war (mobilized in December), he served as a stretcher-bearer, writing the following essays along the way.

"La vie cosmique" ("The Cosmic Life")

In his letter to Marguerite of 27 March 1916, he promised to tell her more of his "*vie cosmique*" project because it related to her thoughts about music and poetry, but in the text he portrays himself scrambling across the front line, not so much in horror as in wonderment. Like the mythical phoenix that lives in fire, he saw himself in the middle of an exploding and recomposing world. "I feel it still—and this time much more clearly—a multitude of independent and spontaneous realities, atoms, molecules, cells acting together in the unity of my own body." He said that no brutality or tenderness could compare with the contact of the person with the universe, no matter how banal or ordinary that experience, because this awareness of the universe—feeling one with the cosmos—reflects the feeling of a child in the arms of its mother. Teilhard reviews a range of ancient philosophical visions of human participation in—really, oneness with—nature. The cosmos is the great whole, enticing humans into a realization of oneness with it and constant participation in its continuing existence. Human beings are, then, atoms, the monads who, each one, possesses his/her own existence within matter. "Socially speaking, the human monad, presents itself as a sort of molecule or cell, essentially destined to integrate itself in an edifice or superior organism. This combination of concrete philosophical ideas and the hints from experience lead to a vision of 'the spiritualization of the universe.'"[25]

The first fifteen pages of this essay contain no hint of the horrors of war around him, until he says that suffering, logically inexplicable and odious as it might be, has the greatest role to play in the cosmos. In the related *Journal* entry he uses the expression "LA SAINTE ÉVOLUTION" to label Christ's suffering and the cross at the center of human becoming, and to place this "progress of the whole world, the social phenomenon on the way to development" above everything else in importance—including the "Fatherland."[26]

In the essay he manages to make suffering a usable positive force, saying that it "excites," "spiritualizes," "purifies." "It is the very blood of Evolution, because by means of it the Cosmos awakens in us." Pantheistic mysticism has been superseded for the Christian believer. The reality of the universe is not Impersonal, Unknowable, and Unconscious (Teilhard uses capital letters for each word); it is rather "Being, Living and Loving." Compelled by reality, because called by grace, all human beings converge on this All. "In this relative dependance, completely similar to that which ties together material systems, lies the mystery (one could almost say the phenomenon) so astonishingly cosmic, the *Communion of saints*." Teilhard addresses himself to this totality as the body of Christ. "You are the cosmic Being which envelops us and completes us in the perfection of its Unity. Thus it is, and for that reason, I love you beyond all things!" In Christ, the heavenly Jerusalem descends to earth, but Teilhard says, the heavenly kingdom develops sometimes as part of and sometimes in opposition to human progress. It is this progress of human civilization that he works for, and for him the norm for human civilization is his own—European and French—a standard of civilization that he is risking death to maintain. "I believe in a Surhomme when I become enthusiastic for a war of cultures, and consider it a favor of God to be able to risk my existence in an abominable death to bring about the triumph of an ideal of civilization." There it is; even in Teilhard the "ideal" is represented by the nation he is fighting for, and the Church he represents. And so we come to the Cosmic Christ. "World is in ongoing creation; in it, it is Christ who is accomplished." One needs only to accept the role of working within, of making the effort, and being, Corporal Teilhard finally says it, "the soldier of the first [attack] wave." Christ is "the center of confluence and easing of all earthly suffering." And the same must be said of cosmic suffering. He concludes, "To live the cosmic life is to live with the dominating consciousness that one is an atom of the body of the mystical and cosmic Christ."[27]

"Le Christ dans la matière" ("Christ in Matter")

In his letter to Marguerite of 20 October 1916, Teilhard says that the tales of Robert Hugh Benson moved him to write in this quirky way. "You will have the good sense. . . . to see in these lines a fantasy of pure imagination—where I have put much of myself."[28] That same month, Teilhard produced "Le Christ dans la matière." It is a strange work of quasi-fiction, in that he assigns his own ideas to an anonymous writer and spells them out in three very brief tales, based on the imagery of Christ in the New Testament and in the Christian Eucharistic liturgy. Christ appears not as a limited body but as radiating the infinite, an appearance that parallels the Transfiguration. "The whole Face radiated thus, following this law. But the center of this radiation and shimmering brilliance was hidden in the eyes of the transfigured image." In a second tale, the white host in the ostensorium, the golden vessel of exposition in the liturgical churches, is transfigured into the cosmos and then contracts back into the plain white host. The third tale is an impression, rather than a vision, with the host again at the center of the tale. Holding it in his hands, he saw that it "hid itself underneath its surface, and left me to battle with the whole universe reconstituted from it [the host]." At the end, Teilhard graphically looks forward to the next step in the battle of Verdun. "We are going to be ordered to retake Douaumont,—it is grandiose and almost incredible, and by it will be manifested and symbolized a definitive advance in the world of the Liberation of souls. —I tell you. I am going to this in a religious spirit, with all my soul, borne onward by one great élan in which I am incapable of distinguishing where human passion ends and adoration begins."[29]

"Le milieu mystique" ("The Mystical Milieu")

Teilhard recognized that it would take a mystic to see Christ in the cosmos and the cosmos in Christ. In his letter to Marguerite of 19 June 1917, he wrote that Dante, who moved beyond his passion for Beatrice to his passion for reality, can help us understand how "a single object or reality can lead to the universal." So, he continues to work on his attempt to "place in relief the Realism by which the mystic lives."[30] In his *Journal* entry for 10 July, less than a month later, he sketched out, in fact at some length, his understanding of the "Mystical transformation: the gratuitous work by which God prepares the [human] faculty destined to perceive him and pursue Him at the center of Creation." Pages later he says that the passion for union with God "forces the mystic to give to things their maximum reality," still using Beatrice as his prime example of a symbol conducting a person—that is, Dante—to maximum reality.[31]

The person who is a true mystic "can see behind the music, behind the art, and behind all else that strikes the eye ... the Presence that is everywhere." He offers a label "the seer" (*le voyant*) as a clarification of, or a parallel to, "mystic." The basis for the mystical experience of the cosmos is the "inborn love of the human person, extended to the whole Universe." The mystic *sees* that the Universe is not summed up as unlimited space, because space with its multiple realities is comprised of creative actions that culminate in the pure action of the divine spirit; only the Spirit creates continually across the ages, making it possible for incomplete creative actions to progress together, beyond diminishment and death. One Reality; one Spirit. The mystic, then, is the consummate realist because he or she receives and transmits and conserves and uses the reality as it is communicated. "Here I am," proclaims the mystic in a total submission to the transforming Fire of the divine. Teilhard uses the scriptural image of the consuming fire of the holocaust as it descends on the sacrifices offered by human beings, thus accomplishing the union of God and matter. The mystic is not isolated but is united with all other elements of the universe, converging on the Center. Teilhard concludes in his own persona as the mystic who achieves contact with the Center—Christ. "When I think of You, Lord, I cannot say if I find you more in one place than in another, if you are more for me Friend, Force, or Matter.... Every affection, every desire, every possession, every light, every depth, every harmony, and every ardor is equally resplendent at the same time, in an inexpressible *Relation* that is established between myself and You."[32]

"La nostalgie du front" ("Nostalgia for the Front")

Life at the front was integral to these spiritual experiences, justifying, then, what he called his "nostalgia" for this life. Teilhard completed "La nostalgie du front" in September 1917, but he wrote to Marguerite the month before, "It seems to me that one could show that the front is not only the line of fire, the corrosive face-off [*surface de corrosion*] of peoples who attack one another, but also in a certain way the 'the wave front' that brings the human world toward its new destinies."[33] In the text, he attempts to analyze and justify a feeling that he had at the front, "of plenitude and the superhuman," and fears that he will miss this experience after the war is over! He reviews his front experiences: memories of the plains of Ypres of April 1915, as gas filled the air and the shells were destroying the poplars along the Yperlé; the slopes of the Souville in July 1916, charred by the battle. "These hours beyond the human impregnate life with the tenacious and definitive perfume of exaltation and initiation, as if one had spent them in the Absolute." And so, in his own life, "all the enchantment of the Orient, all the spiritual warmth of Paris does not equal ... the mud of Douaumont." He combined a passion to venture into the unknown, to overcome fear and suffering, and to rejoice—post-battle— in the open sky and the open fields behind the lines. It was all "the great work and sanctification of a Humanity that is born in the hours of crisis, but can

FIG. 29 Pierre Teilhard de Chardin, Jesuit and stretcher-bearer, shown here, far right, with fellow French soldiers, wrote his essential treatises on evolution and the Cosmic Christ during the war. Fondation Teilhard de Chardin.

be fulfilled only in peace."[34] In his *Journal*, he wrote that nostalgia results because the front "brings us <u>to the LIMIT of things</u> (of what is known, of what can be objectively experienced; and to the limit of war itself)."[35] He says that there is no "chivalry" in war but rather gas and metal, which seems not to animate as much as chivalry.

"La grande monade" ("The Great Monad") and Its Foundation Essays

Teilhard reviewed these mystical ideas and his war experience at the beginning of 1918, saying that this high integration of philosophy and theology was given a push by his work on those fanciful three tales in the style of Benson. He would here seriously replace "mystical pantheism with Love of the earth based on the Creator-God."[36] In his text he evokes the moon rising over the neighboring trenches, a star rich with symbolism. He saw that the war had menaced only a fallen civilization; in fact, after every war and every revolution, humankind develops positively, becomes more coherent. But the universe of thinking human beings continues to rely upon itself to self-enclose. Teilhard says, "When the thinking Earth closes in on itself, then only will we know what is a Monad." Individual men come to discover the beings outside them, but when the human community finally comes together in unity, they can feel and concretize what it is to be an ensemble. National effort will become human effort. He evokes a universe of human consciousness that permeates matter, and the unity "superior and without limit of the Universe." Of course, the Center of this universe, "the Great Monad," is God. Teilhard concludes—the war is not yet over, of course— "On this war evening, all is enveloped for me in the fullness of the Great Monad—in the brightness of the moon."[37]

"Mon univers" ("My Universe")

Teilhard at the end of the war published this text to eliminate possible misunderstandings on the part of his friends. Finished on 15 January 1918, according to his biographer Claude Cuénot, and simply referred to in his letter to Marguerite of 15 January 1919, he wrote that his appreciation of the greatness of the universe moved him to meditate further the greatness of Christ.[38]

For him there could be no limitation of Christ, or he would be smaller than total reality. Wondering how he could best express this, Teilhard writes, "Having admitted that Christ coincides with the Universe as a *universal Center* common to cosmic progress and gratuitous sanctification, it remains for us to explore if we can go further in the explanation of divine coextension with the World, that is to say get an idea of the *law of transformation* of everything *in Ipso* and *per Ipsum* [*in Him* and *through Him*]." He then tries to show that created being, from the moment of its origin out of nothingness, through the forming of rational souls, to the gathering together of the elect into the mystical Body of Christ passes through a series of progressions that will gradually eliminate "primitive plurality."[39] In effect, then, Teilhard baptized this universal tendency in order to preserve the truthful, Christian elements of it, believing that the church has provided the means necessary to accomplish this with its teachings on the universal presence of God and the reality of Christ in God.

GEOFFREY STUDDERT KENNEDY: ENGAGING WITH THE
MEANINGLESSNESS OF HUMAN SUFFERING

Studdert Kennedy was born in 1883 in England of Irish stock on his father's side; his father and grandfather were, both of them, Anglican priests. He received his university education in Ireland, obtaining a degree in classics and divinity at Trinity College, Dublin, and was ordained a deacon in 1908 and a priest in 1910. He joined the English army as a chaplain when the war began, quickly proving to be an eloquent and indefatigable soldier pastor. Known as and immortalized as "Woodbine Willie," he made his own the standard ministries in the chaplains' repertoire: leading church services, distributing New Testaments, playing the piano in the canteen, giving out cigarettes ("Woodbine" was the brand name!), and offering to write home. In a letter to the chaplain Theodore Bayley Hardy, he wrote, "Live with the men; go everywhere they go. Make up your mind you will share all their risks, and more if you can do any good. The line is the key to the whole business. Work in the very front, and they will listen to you; but if you stay behind, you're wasting your time. Men will forgive you anything but lack of courage and devotion." More often behind the lines, though living with the men there, he advanced across the fields with the men in the battle of Messines Ridge in 1917.[40]

He was both a frontline chaplain to strengthen and console the men, and a frontline theologian who explored the mystery of suffering—finding its ultimate meaning in a suffering God. Out of the orthodox Christian tradition, he created his theology of a God actually suffering in the suffering of human beings. Not a professionally trained theologian, even less a university-faculty theologian, Studdert Kennedy was, in the years after the war, respected as a great priest and spiritual writer but not avidly studied for his theology. It seemed clear that he had been trying to make sense of the war for his men, rather than enliven twentieth-century theology. *The Hardest Part* (1918) was a collection of essays that were more finished versions of sermons composed while he was on the front. In the introduction he wrote, "When a chaplain joins a battalion no one says a word to him about God, but everyone asks him, in a thousand different ways, 'What is God like?' his success or failure as a chaplain really depends upon the answer he gives by word and deed.... This is what I have tried to do in this book." For Studdert Kennedy, a God who could stop the war and does not would be a "passionless potentate," a conviction that left him, of course, with the challenge of explaining the creedal label for God as "Father Almighty." "I don't know or love the Almighty potentate—my only real God is the suffering Father revealed in the sorrow of Christ." For traditional Christian theologians and preachers, Catholic and Protestant and Orthodox, the idea of a suffering *God* as such (and not the suffering human nature of Jesus) is dangerous territory. For Studdert Kennedy, Christianity made no sense, indeed would be perverse without a suffering God, God suffering in Christ *and* in human beings.[41]

How can God be in nature, he asks when "nature's many voices seem to contradict one another. Its tenderness and cruelty, its order and its chaos, its beauty and its ugliness . . . mar the music of its message to the soul of man." He amusingly reminds his readers of the cobra and the shark and recalls how Haeckel's *Riddle of the Universe* shocked and tried him with statements like "The cruel and pitiless struggle for existence which rages through all living nature, and which must forever rage. . . . is an undeniable fact." At least materialists recognized "Nature's horror chambers" as real. Endless numbers of animal species have failed along the line, and. . . . human history is a history of ceaseless war.[42]

None of these evils was more challenging to faith than Studdert Kennedy's actual war on the western front, and his awareness that human history has been nothing but war. He introduces his "God in History" with a front-line setting—as he does for all the essays in *The Hardest Part.* "In a German concrete shelter. Time, 2:30 a.m. All night we had been making unsuccessful attempts to bring down some wounded men from the line. We could not get them through the shelling. One was blown to pieces as he lay on his stretcher." War, then, he says, is "the final limit of damnable brutality . . . the silliest, filthiest, most inhumanly fatuous thing that ever happened," but "it's the rule with man, not the exception." Though religion may have appeared to be the root cause of numerous wars, it simply was camouflage for political, social, and economic rivalries and hostilities. He admits that many theologians, following out their own lines of thinking, have been forced to state that war is the will of God. "If it is true, I go morally mad. . . . I hate war, and if God wills it I hate God." Or more explicitly, "If God does not suffer agony because of war, and if He does not will that men should live at peace, then I cannot and will not worship Him." Studdert Kennedy cannot help but attribute worship of the God of power to the Germans, from Luther to the Kaiser. The Germans are honest, at least, because where power is an absolute value, a simplistic belief in an "Almighty" God makes perfect sense. His response is deliberately outrageous: "It is the Almighty God we are fighting; He is the soul of Prussianism. I want to kill Him." "God, the Father God of Love, is everywhere in history, but nowhere is He Almighty. Ever and always we see Him suffering, striving, crucified, but conquering." But no one escapes Studdert Kennedy's discerning eye, least of all himself, because all are hypocrites; all, who can only try to be fully human, Christian, and saints. Humans are doomed to failure, because their destiny is infinitely high. He finally evokes those good-hearted everyday folk, who "long for and fight for brotherhood and peace, and therefore, consciously or unconsciously, they long for and fight for the suffering Father God of Love revealed in Jesus Christ."[43]

But then what happens when you have Bible-based proof that God will protect the just and destroy the wicked? Studdert Kennedy provides a scene for his "God in the Bible": "Sitting at the door of the regimental Aid Post. Time about 4:30 a.m., after a very rough night in the trenches, during which we had many casualties. Among those who were killed outright was a very popular sergeant. In his breast pocket I found a Bible." Reading the Bible cannot save your life, he says, citing one soldier who was happy to get a copy because it might stop a bullet. He sees that the Bible is "a queer Book, as queer as life itself." Some of the stories are "bad" and even "blasphemous" if taken to be real truth. According to the stories, God "hardens Pharaoh's heart and then destroys him because his heart was hard"; a man tries to steady the Ark of the Covenant and is then struck dead; Elisha ensures that youngsters who laughed at his baldness are eaten by bears; Elijah brings down fire upon simple soldiers. "I don't believe in the truth of the six days' creation or the Flood and Noah's ark; . . . they are just splendid legends containing great truths." God reveals through human beings in all their ignorance and foolishness. "The Bible is not merely the history of God's self-revelation to man, it is the history of the making of man capable of receiving the revelation." God inspired the authors, yes, but he inspired them in their foolishness and stupidity, without making the foolishness and stupidity disappear. Across the pages of the Bible, we see the inspired struggle to write down stories filled with tragedy and somehow justify the killing of enemies who appeared to oppose God. Studdert Kennedy says, "The old testament is full of the pain of this problem which faces us today." And although the problem was argued at length in the book of Job, and resolution hinted at in Isaiah and Hosea, only in the reality of the suffering Christ did humans have the potential to understand the mystery of evil and suffering. "The final revelation of God in Christ Who suffered, died, and rose again to go on suffering in His Church, finally tears the Almighty God armed with pestilence and disease from His throne, and reveals the patient, suffering God of love Who endures an agony unutterable in the labour of creation, but endures on still for love's sake to the end." For Studdert-Kennedy the war has revealed this God to him: "the muddy, bloody hero of the trenches is showing us Who is the real King."[44]

Only in the light of the suffering God does prayer make sense, and here Studdert Kennedy could be surprisingly severe regarding the frightened,

FIG. 30 Geoffrey Studdert Kennedy, who preached a suffering God; a formal photo in clerical collar and military uniform. Photo: Lebrecht Music & Arts / Alamy Stock Photo.

frontline prayers of the soldiers. He reports the scene in "God and Prayer." "I wish that chap would chuck that praying. It turns me sick. I'd much rather he swore like the sergeant. It's disgusting, somehow. It isn't religion, it's cowardice. It isn't prayer, it's wind. I'd like to shut him up." At the end of his story, he repents of his anger and wants to offer the youngster a cigarette, but at that instant a shell buries them both, killing the poor young soldier. "The cup could not pass," he writes, evoking the words of Christ in the Garden of Gethsemane scene, which is central to his doctrine of the suffering God, and the highest form of prayer. For so many, "prayer is a kind of magic cheque upon the bank of Heaven, only needing the formal endorsement with Christ's name to make it good for anything." It does not work, he insists, because English, German, and Austrian prayer checks have gone unpaid in near infinite numbers. He prefers honest fatalism to selfish prayer.[45]

And indeed, Christ in the Garden of Gethsemane is the scene he evokes the most: "I always see it these days." He believes that Christ was praying against the horrors in his mind's eye, as he was submitting to God's will in order to get to the end: "Thy will be done." "That is the real prayer," he says, criticizing the simplifications of the New Testament narratives in the same mode as his take-down of Old Testament literalism. "They ruined it all for me as child; they told me that God's will was the Cross. God wished Christ to be crucified; He wished Judas to be a traitor, Pilate a coward, the priests to be fiends, and the crowd to be cruel and fickle-hearted." But this is nonsense, because "God cannot plan treachery and murder." At Gethsemane Christ's suffering and eminent death were not the will of God; everything should have gone better. Here, "Thy Will be done" is the recognition that God could not make life better, that Christ is part of the divine essence who could not make things better. Christ never promised deliverance from suffering and death, the shells rain down on the just and the unjust, the awfulness of human warfare "as inevitable as the cross." War is sin in a million ways, from human thoughts and deeds to deadly materiel—the shells themselves. Prayer can change nothing in physical life but can ensure that the real person is not destroyed. Victory will not mean so much marching into Berlin as marching into the New Jerusalem at the end of time.[46]

It was and is a challenge to match Studdert Kennedy's suffering God with the body of Christian tradition, although even in 1917 two other Anglican priests, one later a bishop, were pondering and publishing the suffering of God in a collection of essays, *The Church in the Furnace*. Clearly, Studdert Kennedy was not the only writer to probe the mystery of God's suffering, but the professional theologians never got it quite the same way as he did. His passion for theological meaning and his attempts to express it did not constitute a representation of the thought of earlier or contemporary writers. Stuart Bell writes, "Even a cursory glance at his work shows that the primary impetus to his writing and his primary pathway to his belief in divine possibility was socio-cultural rather than theological." He became impatient with on-paper orthodoxy when a fellow chaplain tried to make the case that he was reviving an early heresy. Studdert Kennedy shot back at his friend, "To hell with your metaphysics! I have to show God to 'Ole Bill in the trenches in a way which *he* can understand. I have to show him a God who can command his respect and win his love. And why, may I ask, should a doctrine which was considered a heresy in the fourth century necessarily be heresy still in the twentieth?" But his teaching was not a twentieth-century heresy, nor would it have been in any century. For these writers, as for Studdert Kennedy, the words of Christ, "He who has seen me has seen the Father" were the source of their certainty. In the view of Stuart Bell, "Studdert Kennedy was arguably the most original British theological thinker and writer to emerge during the Great War and its immediate aftermath. Looking at his work from a post-Holocaust perspective, it is very easy to conclude that he was the most influential advocate of divine passibility prior to 1939."⁴⁷

Franz Rosenzweig, Paul Tillich, Pierre Teilhard de Chardin, and Geoffrey Studdert Kennedy each created a formal theology fashioned out of a personal war experience and a unique religious formation. Rosenzweig argued his way to the uniqueness of Jewish witness and its fulfilling future in letters to his parents and colleagues, especially to Eugen Rosenstock, a convert to Christianity and close friend posted to the western front. The redemptive role of the people of Israel, Rosenzweig wrote, came to operate historically in relation to Christianity, which developed out of Judaism into a worldwide religion and will so bring the Judaism at its core to fruition at the end of time. By this remain-in-the-world living—in effect, existential experience—the human being attains wholeness. But philosophy undermines the experience of the individual facing death when it cheapens this religiously existential moment with the hazy notion that the human person thereby becomes one with the universe. In contrast to this, Judaism and Christianity move individuals to work together to share in God's creation, to guarantee revelation, and to achieve redemption. Tillich, the Lutheran pastor, preached traditional sermons as the thought-world that gave them life was vanishing, but he sought to valorize Christian faith and morals for the time when a God-concept (the subject of traditional God-talk) would be dead. Believers who cannot imagine or think "God" can still believe, he said. For the Jesuit Teilhard de Chardin, God was present in the war, in the quiet of prayer and on the killing fields, for even there the soldier encounters the God-reality. A mystic perceives that unity in the Absolute is the goal of the human person in the universe, and Teilhard the mystic portrayed Christ as the fulfillment of all the forces, evolutionary and evolution transcending, in the cosmos. Studdert Kennedy, the Anglican priest who totally engaged with the absurdity of the suffering his soldiers endured, told them that if God willed war, he would hate God. Only a God who suffers in the world's suffering, and in so doing renounces Almighty status, deserves worship.

Envoi

Quite a panorama it is, when we let our historical imagination travel across the fields of northern and central France, guided by the words of soldiers, their officers, and church people—at the front or imagining it themselves. I have tried to bring to the fore the varieties of religious experience of a war of nations, seen and felt as everything from absurd to glorious, with endless suffering as the background scenario for the God-talk and nation-talk of Europeans engulfed in the catastrophe. The trajectory of the narrative began with people at home making sense of and responding to the obligation to make war. It continued with the production of an *imaginaire*, a mental world of heavenly images, followed by the talk that gave substance to the realities of the *imaginaire*, and placed in relief the foundational religious experiences. We passed from inarticulate religion to a twentieth-century renewal of theology, from trembling teenagers in the trenches to young theologians aborning. In between lay the wartime faith and moral goals—or the loss of and disdain for both—of the hundreds of men and women arrayed here, as well as the millions of others caught up in the torment of World War I.

Our guiding lights have been William James and the existentialist psychologists introduced in the prologue, but it was the mid-twentieth-century psychologist Gordon Allport, decades after James and a few years before the existentialists, who focused on faith and morals as the essential elements of religious experience. In *The Individual and His Religion*, he defined faith as the "longing for a better world, for one's own perfection, for a completely satisfying relation to the universe" and defined morality as the ability to make choices in conformity with values that are genuinely one's own. Looking for faith and morality in this sense, Allport examined words or reports on actions that ranged from simple fulfillment of biological survival needs through to actions expressive of unique personalities; ideally, bodily sense and self-identity come together in a full self-image.[1] He concluded "there are as many types of religious experience as there are religiously inclined mortals upon the earth."[2] Even so, he prepared a profile of 290 veterans of World War II, who ran the gamut from the totally positive "If I had not had a personal religious philosophy when I entered combat I do not believe that I would have lasted at all" to the totally negative "War is the final proof that there is no God that religion is a failure," with all shades of light and darkness in between.[3] Are we entitled, then, to assume that twenty-five to thirty years earlier, armies of English, French, and German soldiers had similar experiences of religion and antireligion, and to assign our soldiers to these categories? In light of the preceding chapters, I can answer yes, and, without prejudice to the uniqueness of each soldier and church person, offer a final, brief faith-morality retrospect.

The earliest development of wartime faith and morality, expressed sometimes with joy and more often with anxiety, was based on the already-formed religious sentiment of the soldiers and their families. But everyday religion had to be retooled for heroism in wartime according to leading churchmen, who proposed a more graphic imagining of the heavenly rewards for this heroism. When these imaginings included a peak experience of visions, as they did in the first months of the war, they strengthened traditional faith. Wondrous survivals of shrines and statues excited the imagination and brought their own kind of consolation. Christmas nostalgia that first year was widely shared by soldiers of the opposing armies.

God-talk and nation-talk was the expression of faith that was tried by an atheism option inexorably taking shape in the presence of obscene slaughter. Increased faith and moral dedication grew out of the conviction that soldier death could be in imitation of the death of Christ. The mission to purge the world of the horrors of war by word and example became the specific vocation of soldier survivors. In the theology of the generals, leadership religiosity was an obligation and was formed at the interface of their devout faith and the destruction they had to perpetrate on others and the world around them.

Clergy were obligated to exemplary faith and morality, and its propagation. The German clergy professed that total political commitment to the nation must be grounded in a faith and morality that promotes kindness toward the occupied populations, divine worship free of nationalism, and control of militarism. The French clergy professed that self-sacrifice must be honed to include total submission to God and love of enemy in conjunction with a personal solution to the challenge of killing enemies for a greater good. The English clergy came to understand goodness as religion-free and natural. German and English rabbis held that the settings and services at the front were essential to the existence of Judaism there. Jews must assemble together where possible to guarantee that faith could become a reality in ways not possible to isolated individuals. French rabbis held that a moral obligation exists to defend the government and the freedom-guarantees of the French republic, to defend the heritage of the Revolution, and to promote the value of messianic hope. For the common soldier, the evils of war and the profiteering of individuals and the governments' refusal to negotiate justified their war weariness and severe moral judgments. War could be the setting for a mystical awareness of divinity and of community belonging, and interreligious respect could be learned from the war experience.

Soldier diaries recorded hopes and the temptations to give up on them. A belief in meaningful existence had to be balanced by the recognition of the absurdity of human life; a belief in value-motivated soldiering was balanced by belief in the uselessness of armed conflict; a belief in the justice and morality of the killing and capturing was balanced by doubts about this justice and morality. For German diary writers, the invasion of Belgium was the proof that one can kill somewhat indiscriminately to avoid being killed somewhat indiscriminately. For French diary writers, natural pessimism could be alleviated by devotional or rational religious acceptance of the war as the saddest of realities. A praise-filled interpretation of the home culture should be cultivated when possible. For English diary writers, meeting the challenge of suffering took precedence over the intellectual resolution of religious questions.

According to home-front preachers and writers, "chosen people" theologies could be distilled from the histories of the German, French, and English nations. For German writers, the four gospels were written ethnically, so each nation must bring its own genius to the promotion of the gospels, and German Christianity should be considered the equal of Greek and Roman Christianity. According to English writers, all must realize that a people of fundamental goodness and talent can become the victims of their own hubris and immoral choices; some believed that German evil had preexisted the war by centuries. And according to French writers, the past accomplishments as well as the recent apparitions and missionary efforts in Catholic France should be used for collective self-strengthening. For all, faith and moral action must encompass loyalty to the nation.

Franz Rosenzweig, Paul Tillich, Pierre Teilhard de Chardin, and Geoffrey Studdert Kennedy accomplished the apex transformation of the war experience into sublime God-talk for the twentieth and twenty-first centuries. The theologies of the Christian writers grow closer together as the years go on, because in each we can see elements of the other: Tillich was also a mystic and a pastor, Teilhard was also a theologian with a pastoral ministry, and Studdert Kennedy was a man of mystical prayer and a theological thinker.[4] All three converge on and unite with the Jewish philosopher Franz Rosenzweig, whose theology of creation-revelation-redemption was all-embracing, and the vision they offer us out of their World War I experience is of a future beyond wars and faith differences, where reconciliation will be the instrument of religious regeneration.

With continuing civil and international violence culminating in World War II and the Holocaust up through the poisonous wars of today as the setting, the positive achievement of the soldiers and the churches was the survival of heroism, confidence in heavenly aid, love of enemies, and willingness to accept the defects in human progress. But all this was accompanied by the survival of the worst elements of human nature, mutated into even greater destructiveness by World War I. My 11 November 2018 *Gottesdienst* (Worship Service) in the Berliner Dom celebrated the achievements, and they now belong to the history of Christianity and Judaism. As for the worst elements of human nature, they remain for us today the challenge they have always been.

ACKNOWLEDGMENTS

I have been touched and humbled by the generosity of colleagues who read multiple chapters of the manuscript. Anita May, Martha Hanna, Vicki Caron, Thomas Kselman, and Janet Marquardt opened up new vistas and showed me how to meet the challenges that go with such an all-encompassing narrative. Anita May was my first reader and pointed out the foundation value that the soldier theologians could bring to the whole story and the importance of reformulating the chapter conclusions accordingly, Martha Hanna pointed out the importance of evaluating letter and diary collections and suggested the bibliography vital to bringing this off. Vicki Caron helped me broaden the context and refine the interpretation of the varieties of European Judaism at play in the battlefront and home-front experiences. Tom Kselman pointed out the necessity of combining brief but in-depth vignettes within the wider range of quotes from the writings of soldiers and clergy. Jan Marquardt guided me line by line toward making optimal use of the images of the "Allies in Heaven," and urged me to clarify my rationale in presenting visual and psychological experiences of the soldiers and church people.

Days spent in historical archives provided their own special joys and challenges. These past three years, I have benefited from the kindness and energy of Henning Pahl, director of the Evangelisches Zentralarchiv in Berlin, and the staff of the Archiv des Erzbistums München und Freising in Munich. Some years earlier, as I was beginning my research on priests in World War I, Philippe Ploix and Vincent Thauziès, of the Archives historiques de l'Archevêché de Paris, introduced me to that remarkable *Livre d'Or* of the French priest combatants and to the related World War I files.

Twice, when Jay M. Winter was a keynote lecturer for our special History Department programs at Oklahoma State University, he encouraged the whole enterprise and reported the completion of Patrick J. Houlihan's study of Catholicism in Germany and Austria-Hungary during the war. If anyone deserves the title of paterfamilias in our family of World War I historians, it is certainly the selfless Jay Winter, who ensures that we all benefit from one another's work.

The editors at the Penn State University Press have tirelessly helped me to prepare a book for publication twice already. For this third book, Kathryn

Bourque Yahner, the acquisitions editor, guided my every step with patience and clarity, and ensured that I would have the best of readers. The affable and talented editorial staff, Jennifer S. Norton, Alex Ramos, and Maddie Caso watched over the production details, and my ultra-helpful copyeditor, Dana Henricks, examined every nook and cranny of the manuscript to ensure as much accuracy as possible. Here at Oklahoma State, our History Department administrative support specialists, Susan Oliver and Diana Fry, have generously and good-humoredly facilitated the production of Word documents and the image scanning. And Michael Larson, head of Cartography Services, adjusted recalcitrant images to publication-level quality. Jennifer Holt, my longtime and ever-patient *Sprachlehrerin*, helped me resolve translation challenges.

I must thank here the following presses for permission to quote from the books that provided some of my principal published sources: Penguin/Random House, Vallentine Mitchell, Galiani (Berlin), Éditions Agone, Kohlhammer Verlag, ABC-Clio (for Praeger), Pen & Sword Books, University of Pennsylvania Press, and Penn State University Press. For the illustrations, credit lines are given on the appropriate pages.

My daughter and son, Veronica Byrnes Bloomquist and Michael Byrnes, launched on their own careers now these many years, have always appreciated their dad's reading and writing habits, believing that such activity would help keep him young. Once again, it is my great pleasure to dedicate a book to them—and, this time, to their families.

NOTES

PROLOGUE

1. Histories of the development of the "just war" theory appeared in Vacant, Mangenot, and Amann, eds., *Dictionnaire de Théologie Catholique*, vol. 6 (Paris: Letouzey et Ané, 1920)—see the entry "Guerre" (eleven separate essays)—and Michael Buchberger, ed., *Lexikon für Theologie und Kirche*, vol. 6 (Freiburg: Herder, 1998)—see the entry "Krieg."

2. The limitations and possibilities are best summed up by William G. Rosenberg in his "Reading Soldiers' Moods: Russian Military Censorship and the Configuration of Feeling in World War I," *American Historical Review* 119 (2014): 738: "Some may still essentialize experiences as the rock-bottom foundation of 'historical reality' as if this reality were grounded in individual perceptions of what 'really' happened. What experience and its memory retrieve, however, we now widely understand as representations mediated by the concepts, practices and languages that gave them form." On these "concepts, practices, and languages," see Paul Ricoeur, *Memory, History, and Forgetting*, trans. Kathleen Blaney and David Pellauer (Chicago: University of Chicago Press, 2004), 234–80, who explains that the memories of those who want to preserve the traces of their own or others' activities are recorded, archived, and later represented by the historian, the formal reader of these texts.

3. William James left the study of medicine for a practical, evidence-based analysis of life and the human connection. But to do justice to his revered father's appreciation of the supernatural, he later followed up his *Principles of Psychology* (1890) with *The Will to Believe* (1897), such a will being—he believed—a basic tendency in human beings. Invited thereafter to prepare a long series of lectures on natural religion, he composed *The Varieties of Religious Experience: A Study in Human Nature* (1902). For modern editions of these texts, see Gerald E. Myers, ed., *Writings 1878–1899* [containing *Psychology: Briefer Course* and *The Will to Believe*] (New York: Library of America, 1992); Jaroslav Pelikan, ed., *The Varieties of Religious Experience* (New York: Library of America, 2009). On existentialist psychology and the influence of Martin Heidegger thereon, see Ludwig Binswanger's philosophical presentation, "The Existential Analysis School of Thought," in *Existence*, ed. Rollo May et al. (New York: Simon and Schuster, 1958), 193–213. For modern presentations of the theory and practice of existentialist psychology, see Emmy Van Deuzen, ed., *The Wiley World Handbook of Existential Therapy* (Hoboken, NJ: Wiley Blackwell, 2019), and Irving D. Yalom, *Existential Psychotherapy* (New York: Basic Books, 2020).

4. See Joseph F. Byrnes, *"Catholic and French Forever": Religious and National Identity in Modern France* (College Park, PA: Pennsylvania State University Press, 2004), appendix: "The 'Nation' Conundrum."

5. Gerd Krumeich says that the language of "God with Us" was often no more than reliance on the traditional culture of the nation. See his "'Gott mit uns?' Der Erste Weltkrieg als Religions Krieg," in *"Gott mit uns": Nation, Religion und Gewalt im 19. und frühen 20. Jahrhundert*, ed. Gerd Krumeich and Hartmut Lehmann (Göttingen: Vandenhoeck und Ruprecht, 2000), 273–81. John Horne sets "cultural" history of the war in a broader perspective that includes demographic and straight military history in "End of a Paradigm? The Cultural History of the Great War," *Past and Present* 242 (2019): 155–92.

6. Gottfried Korff recalls that the 1994 exhibition in Berlin, organized to commemorated the eightieth anniversary of the war by the Deutsches Historisches Museum, the Imperial War Museum, and the Barbican Art Gallery was entitled, following Kraus, "Last Days of Mankind." See Gottfried Korff, "Einleitung," in Krumeich and Lehmann, "*Gott mit uns*," 9–32.

7. Blaise Cendrars, *La Main Coupée* (Paris: Denoël, 1946), 136.
8. See Hanneke Takken, *Churches, Chaplains, and the Great War* (New York: Routledge, 2019), 10–14.
9. Xavier Boniface, *Histoire religieuse de la Grande Guerre* (Paris: Fayard, 2014), and Philip Jenkins, *The Great and Holy War: How World War I Became a Religious Crusade* (New York: Harper, 2014).

CHAPTER 1

1. For separate coverage of each of these themes, see Adrian Gregory, "Railway Stations: Gateways and Termini," and Emmanuel Cronier, "The Streets," in *Capital Cities at War*, ed. Jay Winter and Jean-Louis Robert, 2 vols. (New York: Cambridge University Press, 2007), 2:23–56 and 57–104, respectively. My principal guides have actually been other works by these same authors and editors. Soldiers are said to be "on," "at," or "behind" the front. "On" here signifies positioned on or very close to the front line; "at" is more generic and means everything other than "behind" the front, which suggests distance and absence of direct engagement. "Home front," of course is not a front at all, but indicates a range of wartime commitments by citizens of the belligerent nations.
2. There are two general explanations for this statistical decline in church going in England, France, and Germany, according to Hugh McLeod: (1) "the impact of Darwinism and of other new intellectual developments, such as biblical criticism," and (2) "the impact of industrialization and urbanization, and associated processes of 'modernisation.'" See Hugh McLeod, *Secularization in Western Europe, 1848–1914* (New York: St. Martin's Press, 2000), 179.
3. Ibid., 171–215.
4. See chapter 5.
5. Newspaper reports quoted in Jeffrey Verhey, *The Spirit of 1914: Militarism, Myth and Mobilization in Germany* (New York: Cambridge University Press, 2000), 58, 59, 60–61, 62–63, 63, 66.
6. Ibid., 62–63.
7. Ibid., 66, 68, 69, 71.

8. Antoine Delécraz, quoted in Bruno Cabanes, *Août 14: La France entre en Guerre* (Paris: Gallimard, 2014), 37–38.
9. *Le Figaro*, le 2 août 1914, 1.
10. Ibid.
11. *Le Figaro*, le 3 août 1914, 2.
12. Ibid.
13. Ibid.
14. *Le Figaro*, le 4 aout 1914, 2.
15. Cabanes, *Août 14*, 82n13.
16. Ibid., 83, for his masterful sorting out of the train station activities reported in *Le Figaro*, le 3 août 1914, 2. Yet to be published are the acts of the important colloquium "Gares en guerre (1914–1914), mairie du 10e arrondissement," 3–24 septembre 2014. https://www.sortiraparis.com/arts-culture/exposition/articles/75120-gares-en-guerre-l-evenement-a-la-gare-de-l-est.
17. Quoted in Cabanes, *Août 14*, 84.
18. Félix Klein, *Diary of a French Army Chaplain*, trans. M. Harriet and M. Capes, 4th ed. [printing] (London: Andrew Melrose, 1917), 17, 18.
19. Ibid., 14, 15.
20. Henri Desagneaux, *Journal de guerre, 14–18*, ed. Jean Desagneaux (Paris: Denoel, 1971), 12, 13, 15, 16, 17, 18.
21. Newspapers quoted in Adrian Gregory, *The Last Great War: British Society and the First World War* (New York: Cambridge University Press, 2008), 13, 14, 15, 16. In all narratives I privilege the words "England" and "English" over "Britain" and "British," unless a writer uses or a context requires the latter. When appropriate, I indicate that soldiers are from Scotland, Ireland, or Wales.
22. Ibid., 27.
23. The standard general introduction here is Adrian Gregory and Annette Becker, "Religious Sites and Practices," in Winter and Robert, *Capital Cities*, 2:383–427.
24. Kurt Maier, "Evangelische Kirche und Erster Weltkrieg," in *Der Erste Weltkrieg: Wirkung, Wahrnehmung, Analyse*, ed. Wolfgang Michalka (Munich: Piper, 1994), 697, 698, 703.
25. Heinz Hürten, "Die katholische Kirche im Ersten Weltkrieg," in Michalka, *Der Erste Weltkrieg*, 732.
26. Kurt Maier, "Evangelische Kirche," in Michalka, *Der Erste Weltkrieg*, 708, 710–13.
27. Evangelische Zentralarchiv (hereafter EZA) 7, Evangelischer Ober-Kirchenrat, Acta

2872 (Band I), pp. 103, 105, 156, 157. Kriegs-Korrespondenz des Evangelischen Preßverbandes für Deutschland—15 September 1914, Nr. 21.

28. EZA 7, Evangelische Ober-Kirchenrat, Acta 2873 (Band II), 10 December in this volume, where pages are not numbered.

29. "Furchtlos und treu, Rede (am Sonntag den 2 August am Bismarkdenkmal vor dem Reichstagsgebäude zu Berlin gehalten) über Offenbarung Johannis 2:10, von Hofprediger Lic. Doehring," in *Ein feste Burg*, ed. Bruno Doehring, 2 vols. (Berlin: Reimar Hobbing, 1914–15), 1:10, 11, 12, 13.

30. "Ist Gott für uns, wer mag wider uns sein? Predigt von Oberhofprediger D. Dryander, vor Eröffnung des Reichstages (am 4 August im Dom zu Berlin gehalten) über Römer 8, 31," in Doehring, *Ein feste Burg*, 15, 16, 17.

31. "Fürchte dich nicht, du wirst nicht sterben. Kriegspredigt (Am Kriegsbettag, Mittwoch den 5 August im Dom zu Berlin gehalten) über Richter 6, 23 von Hof-und Domprediger Ernst Vits," in Doehring, *Ein feste Burg*, 19, 20, 21, 22.

32. "Kriegstrauung. Traurede (Erhalten im Dom zu Berlin) aus den ersten Tagen der Mobilmachung von Hofprediger Geh. Konsistorialrat Krißinger," in Doehring, *Ein feste Burg*, 32.

33. Hans Jörg Nesner, *Das Erzbistum München und Freising zur Zeit des Erzbischoffs und Kardinals Franziskus von Bettinger (1909–1917)* (Erzabtei St. Ottilien: Eos Verlag, n.d.), 55.

34. Archiv des Erzbistums München und Freising (hereafter AEM), *Amtsblatt für die Erzdiözese München und Freising*, 1914, no. 21, 3 August.

35. See, "Michael Faulhaber in der Monarchie (1869–1918)" in *Kardinal Michael von Faulhaber, 1869–1952: Eine Ausstellung des Archivs des Erzbistums München und Freising, des Bayerischen Hauptstaats archivs und des Stadtarchivs München zum 50.Todestag*, exhibition catalog (Munich: Archiv des Erzbistums München und Freising, 2002), 109–64.

36. AEM, *Amtsblatt*, 1915, no. 5:41, 42, 43, 44.

37. AEM, *Amtsblatt*, 1915, no. 6:49, 57, 61.

38. Léon Amette, *Pendant la guerre: Lettres pastorales et allocutions (août 1914–février 1915)* (Paris: Bloud et Gay, 1915), 6, 16, 22–23. On the apostolate of Cardinal Amette during the war, see Philippe Levillain, "Itinéraire religieux et politique de Léon-Adolphe Amette, Cardinal Archevêque de Paris," in *La Politique de la Guerre: Pour comprendre le xxe siècle européen*, ed. Stéphane Audoin-Rouzeau et al. (Paris: Éditions Agnès Viénot, 2002), 450–74.

39. *Echo de Paris*, 8 août 1914, 1.

40. *Le Figaro*, 5 août 1914, 3.

41. Quoted in Jacques Fontana, *Les Catholiques français pendant la Grande Guerre* (Paris: Cerf, 1990), 29.

42. G. K. A. Bell, *Randall Davidson: Archbishop of Canterbury*, 3rd ed. (London: Oxford University Press, 1952), 736, 758, 759. During the war, Davidson worked to keep communication channels open between himself and German church leaders, dealt with organizational and theological disputes in England, and, finally, urged a "commonsense" (tolerant but not encouraging) approach to conscientious objection. See chapters 45–56.

43. Arthur Winnington-Ingram, *A Day of God: Being Five Addresses on the Subject of the Present War* (London: Wells, Gardner, Darton, 1914). See also Arthur Winnington-Ingram, *The Church in Time of War* (London: Wells, Gardner, Darton, 1915). Commentators have condemned and commended Winnington-Ingram's militarism. See Stuart Bell, "Malign or Maligned—Arthur Winnington-Ingram, Bishop of London in the First World War," *Journal for the History of Modern Theology / Zeitschrift für Neuere Theologiegeschichte* 201 (2013): 117–33.

44. Winnington-Ingram, *Day of God*, 2, 5, 6.

45. Ibid., 9, 12.

46. Ibid., 18, 19, 21, 26.

47. Ibid., 41, 42.

48. Ibid., 69–70, 75.

CHAPTER 2

1. Stéphen Coubé, *Nos alliés du ciel* (Paris: Lethielleux, 1915), v. See also Coubé's biography of Joan, *L'âme de Jeanne d'Arc* (Paris: Lethielleux, 1910). An exhibition in 2008 at Domrémy, the village where Joan of Arc was born, focused on the role attributed to her in World War I. See *Une sainte des tranchées: Jeanne d'Arc pendant la Grande Guerre, catalogue de l'exposition à Domrémy-la-pucelle du 1er juin au 30 septembre*

2008, catalogue exhibition (Domrémy: Conseil Général des Vosges, Site Départemental, 2008).

2. Quoted in David Clarke, *The Angel of Mons: Phantom Soldiers and Ghostly Guardians* (Chichester: John Wiley & Sons, 2004), 45, 54.

3. Ibid., 96–97.

4. Cited in ibid., 109.

5. Ibid., 235.

6. Terence Zuber, *The Mons Myth: A Reassessment of the Battle* (Gloucestershire: History Press, 2010), esp. 167, 257, 267.

7. *Le Courrier de Saint-Lô*, 8 Janaury 1917, and from a Bulletin de l'Abbé Venderbreken, Monastère Saint-François, 29380 Le Trevoux. I am grateful to Vincent Tanazacq, priest of the cathedral of Saint-Irénée in Paris, for these references.

8. *Missel du Miracle de la Marne* (Limoges: P. Mellottée, 1916); Annette Backer, *La Guerre et la Foi: De la mort à la foi, 1914–1930* (Paris: Armand Colin, 1994), 71.

9. See Stéphen Coubé, "préface," in *Missel*, 8n1.

10. Ibid., 12.

11. Ibid., 15, 16.

12. Diana Voigt, "Engel—allzeit bereit," in *Glaubenssache Krieg: Religiöse Motive auf Bildpostkarten des Ersten Weltkriegs*, ed. Heidrun Alzheimer (Bad Windsheim: Fränkisches Freilandmuseum, 2009), 134, 136.

13. Thomas Fliege, "'Mein Deutschland sei mein Engel Michael': Sankt Michael als nationalreligiöser Mythos," in *Alliierte im Himmel: Populare Religiosität und Kriegserfahrung*, ed. Gottfried Korff (Tübingen: Vereinigung für Volkskunde e.V., 2006), 192, 193–97.

14. Cited on p. 204 of Eva-Katharina Lang, "Das Kreuz von Saarburg-ein Wunder inmitten des Krieges?," in Alzheimer, *Glaubenssache Krieg*.

15. Ibid., 205, 207, 208.

16. Paul Fussell, *The Great War and Modern Memory* (New York: Oxford, 1975), 131–33.

17. See Raymond Jonas, *The Tragic Tale of Claire Ferchaud and the Great War* (Berkeley: University of California Press, 2005).

18. Claudia Schlager, *Kult und Krieg: Herz Jesu—Sacré-Cœur—Christus Rex im deutsch-französischen Vergleich, 1914–1925* (Tübingen: Tübinger Vereinigung für Volkskunde e.V., 2011), 226, 233, 296–306, 321–31.

19. Quoted in Becker, *Guerre et la Foi*, 60, 61, 68.

20. Ibid., 76, 77.

21. Inge Weid, "Mit Schutzpatronen in die Schlacht. Heilige auf Bildpostkarten des Ersten Weltkriegs," in Alzheimer, *Glaubenssache Krieg*, 151–57.

22. Terri Blom Crocker, *The Christmas Truce: Myth, Memory, and the First World War* (Lexington: University Press of Kentucky, 2015), 41. Still useful now as a complement to the Blom Crocker study is Michael Jürgs, *Der kleine Frieden im Großem Krieg: Westfront 1914, als Deutsche, Franzosen und Briten gemeinsam Weihnachten feierten* (Munich: C. Bertelsmann, 2003).

23. Sometimes soldier rank is available and sometimes (as here), brigade and division names. For a full list of brigades/divisions participating, see the list compiled by Dick Gilbreath, cartographer at the University of Kentucky, in Crocker, *Christmas Truce*, 66–67.

24. Ibid., 49, 50, 51, 52.

25. Ibid., 53, 54, 55, 82.

26. Ibid., 91, 94, 95, 96, 98.

27. Malcolm Brown, "The Christmas Truce 1914: The British Story," in *Meetings in No-Man's Land: Christmas 1914 and Fraternization in the Great War*, ed. Marc Ferro et al., trans. Helen McPhail (London: Constable & Robinson, 2007), 28–29.

28. Rémy Cazals, "Good Neighbors," in Ferro et al., *Meetings in No-Man's Land*, 122, 123.

CHAPTER 3

1. Gerald A. Jaeger, *Les poilus: Survivre à l'enfer des tranchées de 14–18* (Paris: l'Archipel, 2014), 138–39, 141, 154, 193–201 (in summary). In fact, a change from faith to atheism was the result. See Frédéric Gugelot, "La preuve de l'inéxistence de Dieu: Le premier des conflits mondiaux et l'abandon de la foi," in Audoin-Rouzeau et al., *Politique de la Guerre*.

2. Donald Hankey, *A Student in Arms* (New York: E. P. Dutton, 1917), anthologized in Marilyn Shevin-Coetzee and Frans Coetzee, *World War I and European Society: A Sourcebook* (Lexington, MA: D. C. Heath, 1995), 116, 117.

3. Ross Davies, *A Student in Arms: Donald Hankey and Edwardian Society at War* (Burlington, VT: Ashgate, 2013), 178.

4. Michael Snape, *God and the British Soldier: Religion and the British Army in the First and Second World Wars* (New York: Routledge, 2005), 23–25.
5. Charles Plater, ed., *Catholic Soldiers, by Sixty Chaplains and Many Others* (London: Longmans Green, 1919), 23, 25.
6. *Army and Religion*, quoted in Snape, *God and the English Soldier*, 32.
7. Ibid., 34–35.
8. Kurt Maier, "Evangelische Kirche und Erster Weltkrieg," in Michalka, *Der Erste Weltkrieg*, 717, 718, 719.
9. The 9 November 2018 issue of the *Times Literary Supplement*, which highlighted articles and books about World War I on the 100th anniversary of the end of the war, contains the invaluable essay by Bill Bell, "What Did Tommy Read? The Complex Mental Worlds of Soldiers on the Western Front," 10–11. The best introduction to the vast repertoire of soldier writers is Nicholas Beaupré, *Écrire en guerre, écrire la guerre: France, Allemagne 1914–1918* (Paris: CNRS Éditions, 2006).
10. Martha Hanna, "War Letters: Communication Between Front and Home Front," *International Encyclopedia of the First World War*, https://encyclopedia.1914-1918-online.net.
11. Martyn Lyons, "French Soldiers and Their Correspondence: Towards a History of Writing Practices in the First World War," *French History* 17 (2003): 87–88. Martha Hanna, "A Republic of Letters: the Epistolary Tradition in France During World War I," *American Historical Review* 108 (2003): 1138–61, and the more recent "War Letters."
12. See Gerd Krumeich, "Ego Documents as War Propaganda," in *Inside World War One? The First World War and Its Witnesses*, ed. Richard Bessel and Dorothee Wierling (New York: Oxford University Press, 2018), 241.
13. Jay Winter, "Forward: Philipp Witkop and the German Soldiers' Tale," in *German Students' War Letters*, ed. Philipp Witkop, trans. A. F. Wedd (Philadelphia: University of Pennsylvania Press, 2002), v–xxiv.
14. Witkop, *German Students*, 18, 20.
15. Ibid., 108, 109, 110.
16. Ibid., 73.
17. Ibid., 149,150,152.
18. Ibid., 200, 201.
19. Ibid., 32, 126–27, 195, 304–5, 280, 298, 330, 324.
20. *La dernière lettre écrite par des soldats français tombés au champ d'honneur 1914–1918*, original edition 1922 (Paris: Éditions Michel de Maule, 2014), 55, 56, 110.
21. Ibid., 75, 211, 86, 122, 136, 161, 211.
22. Ibid., 205, 207–8, 215.
23. Jay Winter, "Forward," in *War Letters of Fallen Englishmen*, ed. Laurence Housman (Philadelphia: University of Pennsylvania Press, 2002), v, xx, https://encyclopedia.1914-1918-online.net.
24. Housman, *War Letters of Fallen Englishmen*, 117, 118, 119–20, 123, 125.
25. Ibid., 67, 107, 167, 176, 276–77, 171.
26. Ibid., 200, 222, 177, 180.
27. Edward Madigan, *Faith Under Fire: Anglican Army Chaplains and the Great War* (New York: Palgrave Macmillan, 2011), 175.
28. Richard S. Fogarty, *Race and War in France: Colonial Subjects in the French Army, 1914–1918* (Baltimore: Johns Hopkins University Press, 2008), 175. I am grateful to Richard Fogarty for counsel on his topic and sources.
29. Ibid., 187.
30. Gilbert Meynier, "Algerians in the French Army, 1914–1918: From Military Integration to the Dawn of Algerian Patriotism," in *Combatants of Muslim Origin in European Armies in the Twentieth Century: Far from Jihad*, ed. Xavier Bougarel, Raphaëlle Branche, and Cloé Drieu (New York: Bloomsbury, 2017), 31.
31. See Fogarty, *Race and War in France*, 189–99.
32. David Omissi, intro. and ed., *Indian Voices of the Great War: Soldiers' Letters, 1914–1918* (New York: St. Martin's Press, 1999), 2–4, 13. I am grateful to David Omissi for counsel on his topics and sources.
33. Ibid., 39.
34. Ibid., 88.
35. David Omissi, "The Sikh Experience," in *The Indian Army in the First World War: New Perspectives*, ed. Alan Jeffreys (Helion: Solihull, 2018), 191, 193.
36. Jonathan H. Ebel, *Faith in the Fight: Religion and the American Soldier in the Great War* (Princeton: Princeton University Press, 2010), 2. I am grateful to Jonathan Ebel for counsel on his topics and sources.
37. Ibid., 65.

38. Ibid., 155.
39. Ibid., 145.
40. See ibid., 10–14. The data and quotation source is *For Liberty: American Jewish Experience in World War I*, exhibition organized by the National Museum of American Jewish History and the American Jewish Historical Society, Wylie Gallery, Kansas City, 29 June–11 November 2018.
41. On the Afro-American soldier experience of World War I, see Arthur Barbeau and Florette Henri, *Unknown Soldiers: Black American Troops in World War I* (Boston: DaCapo Press, 1974); and Chad Williams, *Torchbearers of Democracy: African American Soldiers in the World War I Era* (Chapel Hill: University of North Carolina Press, 2013). For racism after the war, see Richard Slotkin, *Lost Battalions: The Great War and the Crisis of American Nationality* (New York: Henry Holt, 2005); and Jennifer Anne Boittin, *Colonial Metropolis: The Urban Grounds of Anti-Imperialism and Feminism in Interwar Paris* (Lincoln: University of Nebraska Press, 2010), especially chapter 3, "A Black Colony."
42. Dieter Weiß, *Kronprinz Rupprecht von Bayern (1869–1955): Eine politische Biographie* (Regensburg: Friederich Pustet, 2007).
43. See Patrick de Gméline, *Le Général de Castelnau (1851–1944): Le soldat, l'homme, le chrétien* (St. Étienne: Charles Hérissey, 2014).
44. On Gwynne, see Snape, *God and the British Soldier*, 67–72.
45. Annika Mombauer, *Helmuth von Moltke and the Origins of the First World War* (Cambridge: Cambridge University Press, 2001), 51, quoting Moltke's *Erinnerungen* on 52, 53.
46. B. H. Liddell Hart, *Foch: The Man of Orléans* (Boston: Little, Brown), 118.
47. Ibid., 329, 409.
48. Snape, *God and the British Soldier*, 61, 62.
49. Ibid., 65–66.
50. G. S. Duncan, *Douglas Haig as I Knew Him* (London: George Allen and Unwin, 1966), 123, 124, 125.
51. Ibid., 127, 132. Cf. David Coulter, "Garrisoning the Nation's Soul: Calvinism, Douglas Haig and the Scottish Presbyterian Chaplaincy on the Western Front," in *The Clergy in Khaki: New Perspectives on the British Chaplaincy; The First World War*, ed. Michael Snape and Edward Madigan (New York: Routledge, 2013), 75–93; and Brian Bond and Nigel Cave, *Haig: A Reappraisal 70 Years On* (Barnsley, South Yorkshire: Leo Cooper, 1999), 240–60.
52. Snape, *God and the British Soldier*, 67.
53. Ibid., 68, 69, 70.

CHAPTER 4

1. See Anita Rasi May, *Patriot Priests: French Catholic Clergy and National Identity in World War I* (Norman: University of Oklahoma Press, 2018) for a full analysis of French priests on the front in World War I and a history of the development of legislation regarding chaplains and priest combatants. I have built my presentation here on my "Limits of Personal Reconciliation: Priests and *Instituteurs* in World War I," in *Catholic and French Forever: Religious and National Identity in Modern France* (University Park: Pennsylvania State University Press, 2005). English titles and labels for the Christian clergy vary somewhat, but I use "priest" to indicate Catholic clergy and the Anglican clergy who accept this label; "pastor" is appropriate for the Lutheran clergy in particular and other Protestant clergy on occasion; "minister" is the default label for Protestant clergy otherwise; "padre" ("father" in Spanish) appropriated by the English, was used widely of all clergy in World War I; "chaplain" applies to both Christian and Jewish clergy.
2. A few English chaplains took part, unofficially, in the actual fighting, and some German chaplains requested permission to do so and were refused. See Edward Madigan, *Faith Under Fire: Anglican Army Chaplains and the Great War* (New York: Palgrave Macmillan, 2014): 43–46; and Kurt Maier, "Evangelische Kirche und Erster Weltkrieg," in Michalka, *Der Erste Weltkrieg*, 716–17. And for a full presentation of German Catholic Chaplains on both fronts, and in comparison with the Austro-Hungarian Catholic chaplaincy, see Patrick J. Houlihan, "The Limits of Religious Authority: Military Chaplaincy and the Bounds of Clericalism," in *Catholicism and the Great War: Religion and Everyday Life in Germany and Austria-Hungary, 1914–1922* (New York: Cambridge University Press, 2015), 78–116.
3. "Euer Herz erschrecke nicht. Predigt über Johannes 14, 1," von Fischer,

Feld-Divisionspfarrer der 20. Division, Erhalten im Felde am 19 September für das braunschw. Husarens-Rgt Rr. 17) in Bruno Doehring, ed., *Ein feste Burg*, 2 vols. (Berlin: Reimar Hobbing, 1914–1915), 1:230–33.

4. EZA 7. Evangelischer Ober-Kirchenrat. Acta 2872 (Band I), 10 November 1914, pp. 241, 242, 246.

5. EZA 7. Evangelischer Ober-Kirchenrat 2873 (Band II), 4 December, 16 January. For this volume 2873, the pages are not marked; only dates.

6. EZA 7. Evangelischer Ober-Kirchenrat, 2875 (Band IV). July 1915–September 1915, pp. 99–116, 192. *Ein Laufender Feind hinter der Front* (Witten-Ruhr: Verlag Eckart, 1916).

7. Lisbeth Exner and Herbert Kapfer, eds., *Verborgene Chronik*, 2 vols. (Berlin: Galiani, 2014–16), 1:332, 334–35, 364–65. After the war, Eggebrecht served as pastor in Magdeburg and for thirty years before his retirement in 1957 was a church superintendent in Schleusingen/Thüringen. His handwritten diaries are preserved in the Deutsche Tagebucharchiv.

8. Exner and Kapfer, *Verborgene Chronik*, 2:16, 19, 36, 39, 55, 60, 66, 90, 122. Quotations from the Eggebrecht journal material entered before the war began are found in Hanneke Takken, *Churches, Chaplains, and the Great War* (New York: Routledge, 2019), xiii.

9. Exner and Kapfer, *Verborgene*, 2:205, 207, 209, 233–37, 236–37, 237–38.

10. Helmut Baier, ed., *Als evangelischer Feldgeistlicher im Ersten Weltkrieg: Wilhelm Stählins Tagebücher 1914–1917* (Stuttgart: W. Kohlhammer, 2016), 69–70, 76, 89, 103, 110–11. Born in Erlangen, Stählins was educated there and in Rostock and Berlin. After his training in theology, he was ordained an evangelical pastor, volunteering as a chaplain when the war began. He spent a third of the war years on the western front. In his ministry he was particularly engaged in liturgical renewal. Active in the Confessing (anti-Hitler) Church before World War II, he was made bishop of Oldenburg after the war.

11. Baier, ed., *Als evangelicher Feldgeistliche*, 16, 115, 126, 122, 152, 154, 165, 166.

12. Ibid., 169, 170–72, 187–88, 199, 195–96.

13. Ibid., 213, 220, 221, 242–43, 252, 257, 258.

14. The most tersely written, helpful introduction to an Evangelical Church theology and evangelical churchmen is "Mit Gott in dem Krieg," http://www.ekd.de/reformation-und-politik/politik/kirche_im_ersten_weltkrieg, but Günter Brakelman, *Protestantische Kriegstheologie, 1914–1918: Ein Handbuch mit Daten, Fakten und Literatur zum Ersten Weltkrieg* (Kamen: Hartmut Spenner, 2015) is 540 pages, covering every aspect of (mainly) German Protestant engagement with the war.

15. Martin Schian, *Gedanken im Lazarett*, 2 vols. (Berlin: Verlag des Evangelischen Bundes, 1914, 1916), 1:13, 2:128. EZA-RKB 1081 (for this and other rarely available texts in the following notes, the EZA call number is provided). At the same time A. D. Schreiber provided an explanation of chaplaincy arrangements and some statistics for the military prisons; see *Die Seelsorge an den Krigesgefangenene in Deutschland* (Leipzig: Verlag von Dörffling und Franke, 1916). EZA-F 15004.

16. Hans Lehmann, *Erinnerungen eines Feldpredigers*, 3 vols. (Berlin: Verlag des Evangelischen Bundes, 1916–1918), 1:1, 5, 21. EZA-RKB 1086. Fritz Philippi, in a collection of his sermons, covered the basic themes used by Christian preachers to justify the use of force, but with the (also) usual references to the ultimate need for universal love and peace. See his *An der Front: Feldpredigten* (Wiesbaden: Hofbuchhandlung Heinrich Staadt, 1916). EZA-2006/0575.

17. Heinrich Niemöller, *Sieben Bitten an das deutsch-evangelische Christenvolk in schwerer Kriegzeit* (Berlin: Verlag des Evangelischen Bundes, 1916), 3. EZA-RKB 1084. Heinrich Niemöller was the father of Martin Niemöller, U-boat commander in the war, and subsequently also a Lutheran pastor, who after initial support of Nazism and years of personal anti-Semitism, helped establish the Confessing Church against the government-controlled church. After World War II, he emphasized the guilt of the Christian churches in supporting Hitler. His prose-poem confession of personal guilt became world famous: "First they came for the socialists, and I did not speak out—because I was not a socialist. Then they came for the trade unionists, and I did not speak out—because I was not a trade unionist. Then they came for the Jews, and I did not speak out—because I was not Jew. Then they came

for me—and there was no one left to speak for me."

18. Heinrich Niemöller, *Friedenziele über die gesprochen werden darf und muss* (Berlin: Verlag des Evangelischen Bundes), 16. RZA–RKB 1085.

19. Gerd Krumeich, "Einführung," in *"Pro Fide et Patria!" Die Kriegstagebücher von Ludwig Berg 1914–1918: Katholischer Feldgeistlicher im Großen Hauptquartier Kaiser Wilhelms II*, ed. Frank Betker und Almust Kriele (Cologne: Böhlau Verlag, 1998), 22, 21.

20. Ibid., 27, 31–32.

21. Ibid., 33, 34, 35, 37, 40.

22. Hans-Josef Wollasch, ed., *Militärseelsorge im Ersten Weltkrieg: Das Kriegstagebuch des katholischen Feldgeistlichen Benedict Kreutz* (Mainz: Matthias-Grünewald-Verlag, 1987), xxx, 55, 71.

23. Jacques Fontana, *Les Catholiques français pendant la Grande Guerre* (Paris: Cerf, 1990), 271.

24. Brugerette has separate sections on combatants, stretcher-bearers, and medics [*infirmiers*]. Joseph Brugerette, *Sous le régime de la Séparation, la reconstitution catholique, 1908–1936*, vol. 3 of *Le Prêtre français et la société contemporaine* (Paris: Lethellieux, 1938), 349–427. On English and German clerical nationalism, see A. J. Hoover, *God, Germany, and Britain in the Great War: A Study in Clerical Nationalism* (New York: Praeger, 1989).

25. Henry Bordeaux, "Introduction," in *La Preuve du sang: Livre d'or du clergé et des congrégations, 1914–1922*, 2 vols. (Paris: Bonne Presse, 1925), 1:xxiv. Archives historiques de l'Archevêché de Paris (hereafter AHP). The Secrétariat de la documentation catholique assembled the information by sending questionnaires to the secretariats of bishops and religious congregations. Bordeaux was a lawyer and widely read novelist of the era.

26. Ibid., 1:xxiv, xxvi.

27. *Prêtre aux armées: Bulletin bimensuel des prêtres et des religieux mobilisés*, 1 May 1915, 84. AHP. For a discussion of canon law, see Fontana, *Catholiques français*, 277–80.

28. *Prêtre aux armées*, 1 July 1915, 169.

29. Ibid., 15 June 1917, 910.

30. Ibid., 15 August 1916, 583.

31. Ibid., 1 November 1916, 665.

32. Ibid., 15 November 1916, 687.

33. Ibid., 1 July 1918, 1304.

34. Daniel Moulinet, *Prêtres soldats dans la Grande Guerre: Les clercs bourbonnais sous les drapeaux* (Rennes: Presses universitaires de Rennes, 2014).

35. These books began as a private collection, the Bibliothèque et Musée de la Guerre. After World War I, this collection was transferred to the Nanterre campus of the University of Paris. See Daniel J. Sherman, "Objects of Memory: History and Narrative in French War Museums," *French Historical Studies* 19 (1995): 49–74.

36. A. Ménétrier, *Moine et soldat: Le R. P. Edouard de Massat, 1860–1915* (Toulouse: Voix franciscaines, 1918), 226, 332, 327–28, 335.

37. L. G., *L'Abbé Jean Audouin, clerc minoré, sergent au 135e d'infanterie* (Angers, 1917), 24.

38. P. L. Guinchard, *Un Jeune* (Paris: F. & J. Lecoq, 1918), 54, 58.

39. M. Grivelet, *Mémoires d'un curé: Fantassin, aviateur, résistant* (Is-sur-Tille: Robichon, 1970), 24–25, 28–29.

40. Mgr. Hector-Raphaël Quilliet, *Un Officier prêtre: L'Abbé Joseph-Eugène-Marie Arlet—Allocution prononcée en l'église de Saint-Michel-de-Lions* (Limoges: Dumont, 1918), 7, 5.

41. Chanoine Max Caron, *Un lys brisé* (Paris: René Haton, 1918), 152, 283, 180, 156–57.

42. Paul Vigue, *Le Sergent Pierre Babouard du 125e d'infanterie* (Paris: Beauchesne, 1917), 214.

43. *Vaillant Apôtre et vaillant capitaine: Le Père Pierre Durouchoux, prêtre de la Compagnie de Jésus, capitaine au 274e d'infanterie* (Toulouse: Apostolat de la presse, 1918), 25, 24. The Jesuits, because of the long years of seminary training, were more likely to have young men primed for apostolate and action, even as soldiers. See Marie-Claude Flageat, *Les Jésuites français dans la Grande Guerre: Témoins, victimes, héros, apôtres* (Paris: Cerf, 2008), chapter 2.

44. André de Font-Reaulx, SJ, *René de la Perraudière, novice de la Compagnie de Jésus, sergent d'infanterie française* (Toulouse: Apostolat de la presse, 1918), 85, 37, 43, 42, 44. A contrast to the social discomforts of de la Perraudière was the experience of André de la Barre de Carroy, a priest from an aristocratic family with generations in the military, who complained that his appointment as army chaplain isolated him from his men. André de la Barre de Carroy, *Une âme droite: André de la Barre de Carroy, aumônier militaire au 102e de ligne* (Paris: Action populaire, 1923), 115.

45. Lud. Loiseau, *Un bon prêtre et un bon Français: L'Abbé Georges Sevin, curé d'Yèvre-la-Ville* (Pithiviers: Imprimérie moderne, 1921), 112–13.
46. Albert Valensin, *Lucien Chabord: La vie mystique dans les tranchées* (Paris: Gabalda, 1918), 38, 37.
47. Ibid., 61.
48. Ibid., 47.
49. Ibid., 40.
50. Ibid., 74.
51. Jean Nourisson, *Lettres de Jean Nourisson, aspirant au 153e régiment d'infanterie* (Paris: Gabalda, 1919), 147, 151, 118.
52. Ibid., 120.
53. Alain Toulza, *La Grande Guerre des hommes de Dieu: Héros des tranchées entre persecutions et Union sacrée* (Paris: DRAC, 2014), 84.
54. Ibid., 86.
55. Chantal Paisant, *De l'exil aux tranchées 1901/1914–1915: Le témoignage des sœurs* (Paris: Karthala, 2014), 307.
56. Ibid., 309.
57. Ibid., 312.
58. Ibid., 312.
59. Alan Wilkinson, *The Church of England and the First World War*, 3rd ed. (Cambridge: Lutterworth Press, 2014), 70, 127. A full account of Bishop Gwynne's ministry during World War I is H. C. Jackson, *Pastor on the Nile: The Life and Letters of Llewellyn H. Gwynne* (London: SPCK, 1960), 144–72.
60. Edward Madigan, *Faith Under Fire: Anglican Army Chaplains and the Great War* (New York: Palgrave Macmillan, 2011), 94, 104, 105, 174.
61. Wilkinson, *Church of England*, 145.
62. Neville S. Talbot, *Thoughts on Religion at the Front* (London: Macmillan, 1919), 1, 8, 16, 17, 21, 24.
63. Ibid., 34, 41, 90.
64. P. B. Clayton, *Plain Tales from Flanders* (London: Longmans, Green, 1929), 44, 46; Wilkinson, *Church of England*, 146.
65. Ibid., 142, 143–44, 150, 140, 149.
66. Oswin Creighton, *Letters of Oswin Creighton, C.F. 1883–1918* (London: Longmans, Green, 1920), 126, 158, 159.
67. Ibid., 163, 164, 167, 170, 171, 178.
68. Ibid., 180–82, 190.
69. Ibid., 203, 209, 210, 222.
70. Ibid., 213.

71. Madigan, *Faith under Fire*, 193–94, 197. A. Herbert Gray, *As Tommy Sees Us: A Book for Church Folk* (London: Edward Arnold, 1919), 66. To set the Gray theology in context, see Sue Morgan, "'Iron Strength and Infinite Tenderness': Herbert Gray and the Making of Christian Masculinities at War and at Home, 1900–1940," in *Men, Masculinities and Religious Change in Twentieth-Century Britain*, ed. L. Delap and S. Morgan (London: Palgrave Macmillan, 2013), 119–45.

CHAPTER 5

1. See Werner Angress, "Prussia's Army and the Jewish Reserve Officer Controversy Before World War I," *Leo Baeck Institute Yearbook* 17 (1972): 19–42.
2. Maurice Barrès, *Les diverses familles spirituelles de la France* (Paris: Émile-Paul Frères, 1917), 1–2. For a fuller presentation of Barrès's change of heart, see Joseph F. Byrnes, *Catholic and French Forever: Religious and National Identity in Modern France* (University Park: Pennsylvania State University Press, 2005), 155–56.
3. See Derek J. Penslar, *Jews and the Military* (Princeton: Princeton University Press, 2015), 166–97, esp. 173.
4. Peter C. Appelbaum, *Loyalty Betrayed: Jewish Chaplains in the German Army During the First World War* (Portland, OR: Vallentine Mitchell, 2014); Philippe-E. Landau, *Les Juifs de France et la Grande Guerre: Un patriotisme républicain* (Paris: CNRS Éditions, 2008); Michael Adler, "Experiences of a Jewish Chaplain on the Western Front (1915–1918)," *Jewish Guardian* (1920): 33–58. Two collections of essays provide wide coverage of the varieties of Jewish experience of World War I: Marsha L. Rosenblit and Jonathan Karp, eds., *World War I and the Jews: Conflict and Transformation in Europe, the Middle East, and America* (New York: Berghahn Books, 2018), and Edward Madigan, ed., *The Jewish Experience of the First World War* (London: Palgrave Macmillan, 2018).
5. Appelbaum, *Jewish Chaplains*, 121, 123, 56.
6. Ibid., 26, 28, 31. The Salzberger texts are translated from *Aus meinem Kriegstagebuch: Von*

dem Feldgeistlichen bei der 5 Armee (Frankfurt: Sonderabdruck aus der Monatschrift *Liberales Judentum*, 1916).

7. Appelbaum, *Jewish Chaplains*, 37, 51.
8. Ibid., 54, 60, 65.
9. Ibid., 69, 73. For modern studies of Salzberger, see Albert H. Friedländer, ed., *Leben und Lehre: Georg Salzberger* (Frankfurt: Kramer Verlag, 1982).
10. Appelbaum, *Jewish Chaplains*, 88, 89, 90, 96, 119n51. The Salominski texts are translated from *Ein Jahr an der Somme* (Frankfurt: Trowitzsch, 1917).
11. Appelbaum, *Jewish Chaplains*, 148, 150–51.
12. Ibid., 156, 157, 159. The preservation of Baeck's heritage is central to the mission of the Leo Baeck Institutes in New York and London, which are more broadly set up for the study of Jewish history.
13. Ibid., 239, 241. The Alsatian birth and German loyalty of Emil Levy / Émile Lévy receive attention in Vicki Caron, *Between France and Germany: The Jews of Alsace-Lorraine, 1871–1918* (Stanford: Stanford University Press, 1988), 184–85.
14. Appelbaum, *Jewish Chaplains*, 256, 257, 258, 260. These rabbinical meditations are translated from *Sabbathgedanken für jüdische Soldaten* (Leipzig: Kaufmann, 1918). Full biographies as well as a wide variety of conferences and letters of all the rabbis can be found in Sabine Hank, Hermann Simon, and Uwe Hank, eds., *Feldrabbiner in den deutschen Streitkräften des Ersten Weltkrieges* (Berlin: Hentrich & Hentrich, 2013).
15. Philippe Landau, "'Patrie et religion': Juifs et Judaïsme dans la guerre totale," in *Foi, religion et sacré dans la Grande Guerre*, ed. Xavier Boniface and Xavier Cochet (Artois: Presses Université, 2014), 171. On Meiss's Alsatian birth and French loyalty, see Caron, *Between France and Germany*, 32.
16. Philippe Landau, *Les Juifs de France et la Grande Guerre: Un patriotisme républicain* (Paris: CNRS Éditions, 2008), 113.
17. Paul Netter, *Un grand rabbin dans la Grande Guerre: Abraham Bloch, mort pour la France, symbole de l'Union sacrée* (Triel-sur-Seine: Éditions italiques, 2013), 100–102. Netter is the great-grandson of Rabbi Bloch.

18. *Le grand rabbin Kaplan: Justice pour la foi juive. Dialogue avec Pierre Pierrard* (Paris: Cerf, 1995), 21, 22, 25, 32, 53.
19. Marc Saperstein, "British Jewish Preachers in Time of War (1800–1918)," *Journal of Modern Jewish Studies* 4 (2005): 260, 262.
20. Mark Saperstein, ed., *Jewish Preaching in Times of War, 1800–2001* (Portland, OR: Littman Library of Jewish Civilization, 2008), 315.
21. Michael Adler, "Experiences of a Jewish Chaplain on the Western Front (1915–1918)," *Jewish Guardian* (1920): 38.
22. Ibid., 39, 42, 49, 50.
23. Ibid., 51, 52, 54, 56, 57, 58. After the war, Adler collected the names and unit information of the approximately fifty thousand Jewish servicemen in World War I and published all this in the *British Jewry Book of Honour* (London: Caxton, 1922).
24. Herman Simon, ed., *Feldpostbriefe Jüdischer Soldaten, 1914–1918*, 2 vols. (Teetz: Hentrich & Hentrich, 2002), 1:19.
25. Ibid., 1:20, 21, 23–24. Pagination goes across the two volumes, so I'll not cite the volume number for the following references to the full sets of letters of the soldiers quoted: Cyapski, 152, 192; Marcus, 474–90; Jungmann, 339–50; Jastrow, 307–27; Cohn (Kon), 372–76; Levit, 407–50; Wisocki, 640–74; Wohlgemuth, 675–78.
26. Exner and Kapfer, *Verborgene Chronik*, 2:201–11, 213.
27. André Kahn, *Journal de guerre d'un juif patriote, 1914–1918* (Paris: Jean-Claude Simoën, 1978), 12–14.
28. Ibid., 37, 102.
29. Ibid., 208–9, 163, 280–81, 317.

CHAPTER 6

1. Literary expressions of the war experience are covered in the excellent works of Jerry Palmer and Leonard Smith and are not presented here. See Jerry Palmer, *Memories and Meanings of the Great War from Britain, France, and Germany* (New York: Palgrave, 2018); and Leonard V. Smith, *The Embattled Self: French Soldiers' Testimony of the Great War* (Ithaca: Cornell University Press, 2014), esp. 148–94.

2. Exner and Kapfer, *Verborgene Chronik*.
3. Ibid., 1:7. Jean Norton Cru, *Témoins: Essai d'analyse et de critique des souvenirs de combattants édités en français de 1915 à 1928* (1929; repr. Nancy: Presses Universitaires de Nancy, 1993); I reprint quotes here from the 2022 edition of *Témoins* (Marseilles: Éditions Agone, 2022) with their permission, but I refer to the pagination of the 1993 edition. For evaluations of the philosophical and political *partis pris* of Norton Cru, see Benjamin Gilles, "Mises en récits collectives de l'expérience combattante: Les premières anthologies de guerre en France et en Allemagne de 1914 à 1940," *Histoire @Politique*, no. 28, and Leonard V. Smith, "Jean Norton Cru, lecteur des livres de guerre," *Annales du Midi*, no. 232 (2000): 517–28. References for the Macdonald volumes are given below.
4. In John Horne and Alan Kramer, *German Atrocities, 1914: A History of Denial* (New Haven: Yale University Press, 2001), Horne and Kramer examine major incidents using data gathered by a French Commission and a Belgian Commission and supplementing this information with German sources. They sorted out these "incidents," in which ten or more civilians were killed, into the following categories, numbers, and percentages. Civilians killed—5,146; buildings destroyed—15,000 to 20,000; incidents related to combat—65 percent; panic by German troops involved—22 percent; civilians used by troops as human shields—25 percent; deportation of civilians. For summary and appendix 1, see pp. 74–78; for details including the German units responsible, see pp. 432–43.
5. Exner and Kapfer, *Verborgene Chronik*, 1:25, 26, 27, 28.
6. Ibid., 1:31, 32, 33, 35, 36, 43.
7. Ibid., 1:47, 60, 61, 65, 66, 69.
8. Ibid., 1:70, 81–88, 107, 109–10.
9. Ibid., 1:117, 124–25, 126–27, 135, 140, 141, 142.
10. Ibid., 1:165–66, 169, 217 and 238, 235, 259, 191, 270—in that order.
11. *Verborgene Chronik*, 2:45, 61, 201, 211, 245.
12. Ibid., 2:374, 416, 530–31, 554, 568, 658.
13. Stephan Kurt Westmann, *Surgeon with the Kaiser's Army*, ed. Michael Westman (South Yorkshire: Pen and Sword Books, 2014), 25, 28, 35.
14. Ibid., 42–43.
15. Ibid., 55–56.
16. Ibid., 80, 84.
17. Ibid., 123, 121.
18. Ibid., 137, 151.
19. Norton Cru, *Témoins*, 145, 146, 147, 151, 153. Anthologies of French soldier testimoneies appeared from 1914 on and so predated and followed after Jean Norton Cru. See the dossier compiled in Gilles, "Mises en récit collectives." An eminently useful list has been compiled by Philippe Lejeune, *Journeaux et carnets de guerre de 14–18, publiés dans les quinze dernières années (1997–2011)*, available online at http://www.autopacte.org. For a modern take on the career of Maurice Genevoix, see Annette Becker, "J'ai vu," in *"Comme on peut" en lisant, en photographant Ceux de 14 de Maurice Genevois* (Verona: GraphisEditors, 2017), 113–21.
20. Norton Cru, *Témoins*, 109, 110. "Masters of sacred and profane lyre" quote from my "The Limits of Personal Reconciliation: Priests and *Instituteurs* in World War I," in *Catholic and French Forever: Religious and National Identity in Modern France* (University Park: Pennsylvania State University Press, 2005), 174.
21. Norton Cru, *Témoins*, 117, 120, 121.
22. Ibid., 124. Here Norton Cru is so concerned to show the authenticity of the original carnet and the faults of the unfortunate publication worked out by Henry Bordeaux that his content coverage is unusually limited.
23. Ibid., 214, 215.
24. Ibid., 193.
25. Ibid., 249.
26. Ferdinand Belmont, *Lettres d'un officier des Chasseurs alpins (2 août 1914–28 décembre 1915* (Paris: Plon, 1916), 79–81, 83, 84, 161–62, 199.
27. Ibid., 269, 233, 274, 275, 280.
28. Lyn Macdonald, *1914–1918: Voices and Images of the Great War* (London: Michael Joseph, 1988) provides a list of the men she gives voice to, along with their military units, 339–41.

Lieutenant K. F. B. Tower—4th Battalion, Royal Fusiliers
Lieutenant E. H. T. Broadwood—1st Battalion, Norfolk Regiment
Corporal T. North—1st Battalion, Lincolnshire Regiment
Lieut. L. A. Strange—Royal Flying Corps
Lieut. H. S. S. Henderson—1st Battalion, West Yorkshire Regiment

Captain Maurice Mascall—Royal Garrison Artillery
Gunner Herbert Smith—5th Battery, Royal Field Artillery
Captain Bryden McKinnel—10th Battalion, King's Liverpool Regiment
Trooper Sydney Chaplin—1st North Hamptonshire Yeomanry
S. V. Britten—13th Battalion, Royal Highlanders of Canada
Sergeant Bill Hay—9th Battalion
2nd Lieut. Ewart Richardson—4th Battalion, Yorkshire Regiment
Sergeant W. F. Low—10th Battalion, Durham Light Infantery
Private Harry Fellowes—12th Battalion, Northumberland Fusiliers
Private Carson Stewart—7th Battalion, Cameron Highlanders
Mjr. H. F. Bidder—Royal Sussex Regiment
Corporal W. H. Shaw—9th Battalion, Royal Welsh Fusiliers
Sergeant J. E. Yates—6th Battalion, West Yorkshire Regiment
Corporal Harold Diffey—5th Battalion, Royal Welsh Fusiliers
Private W. Hay—9th Battalion, Royal Scots
Gunner Frank Spencer—C Battalion, 152nd Brigade, Royal Field Artillery
Private Charles Cole—1st Battalion Coldstream Guards
Private H. Baverstock—1st Canterbury Battalion, New Zealand Division
Major H. F. Bidder—Royal Sussex Regiment
CSM W. J. Coggins—1st/4th Battalion, Oxfordshire and Buckinghamshire Light Infantry
Corporal H. Holbrook—4th Battalion, Royal Fusiliers
Private J. Bowles—2nd/16th Battalion, Westminster Rifles
Private Reg Lawrence—3rd South African Infantry Battalion, South African Brigade
Rifleman Ralph Langley—16th Battalion, Church Lads Brigade, Royal Rifle Corps
Captain J. M. McQueen—Sanitation Officer, 15th Highland Divisio
Major Cowan—Royal Engineers
Lieut. H. L. Birks—4th Battalion, Tank Corps
Rifleman V. Shawyer—13th Battalion, the Rifle Brigade

2nd Lieut. C. D. Horridge—1st/5th Battalion, Lancashire Fusiliers
Sergeant E. Davidson—Royal Engineers
Captain C. M. Slack—1st/4th Battalion, East Yorkshire Regiment, 150th Brigade, 50th Division
Gunner George Worsley—276th Brigade, Royal Field Artillery
Observer Bernard Oliver—No. 23 Balloon Section, Royal Flying Corps
Sergeant Harry Bartlett—293rd Brigade, Royal Field Artillery
Private Adrian Hart—New Zealand Engineers

29. Macdonald, *1914–1918*, 17–19.
30. Ibid., 32–33, 34, 36–37.
31. Ibid., 43, 44–45, 47, 48.
32. Ibid., 79–80, 80–83, 84. For a list of other soldiers who contributed to Macdonald's chronicling here, see Lyn Macdonald, *1914* (New York: Athenium, 1988), 433–35.
33. Macdonald, *1914–1918*, 90, 91, 93. For further testimonies from W. F. Low, see Lyn Macdonald, *1915: The Death of Innocence* (New York: Henry Holt, 1993), 419–20, 425–27.
34. Macdonald, *1914–1918*, 106. For further testimony from Harry Fellowes, see Macdonald, *1915*, 73, 479, 495, 515, 535–37, 552–53.
35. Macdonald, *1914–1918*, 155, 156, 157, 160, 161, 164, 166, 167, 169. For further testimonies from W. H. Shaw, W. Hay, Frank Spencer, and Charles Cole, see the pages listed under their names in the index of Lyn Macdonald, *Somme* (London: Michael Joseph: 1983).
36. Macdonald, *1914–1918*, 178, 180, 181, 196.
37. Ibid., 200, 203.
38. Ibid., 232, 238, 239, 241, 247, 255. For further testimonies from H. L. Birks and C. D. Horridge, see Lyn Macdonald, *Passchendaele* (London: Michael Joseph, 1978), 186, 162–65.
39. Macdonald, *1914–1918*, 272, 273, 276–77, 300–301, 302, 291. In Lyn Macdonald, *To the Last Man: Spring 1918* (New York: Carroll & Graf, 1998), see a listing for E. Davidson on p. 366.
40. Arthur Graeme West, *Diary of a Dead Officer: Being the Posthumous Papers of Arthur Graeme West*, ed. Cyril Joad, intro. Nigel James (n.p.: Greenhill Books, 2007), part 1, A Fine Day. The West diary arranged and edited by Joad seems unremittingly negative. According to Dominic Hibberd, the diary thus "tends to underestimate West's happiness and spiritual

courage." Neither Hibberd nor other critics of the West diary criticize the Joad selection of West's antireligious statements. See Janet S. K. Watson, *Fighting Different Wars: Experience, Memory, and the First World War in Britain* (New York: Cambridge University Press, 2004), 310.
41. West, *Diary of a Dead Officer*, Part II, The Others.
42. Ibid., part 2, Ethical Creed.
43. Ibid., part 3, Beginning of New Views.
44. Ibid., part 3, On Change.
45. Ibid., part 4, Points of View.
46. Ibid., part 4, In the Trenches.
47. Ibid., part 4, Utterances of a German Prince.

CHAPTER 7

1. Alfred Baudrillart, ed., *La guerre allemande et le catholicisme* (Paris: Bloud et Gay, 1915); Georg Pfeilschifter, ed., *Deutsche Kultur, Katholizismus, und Weltkrieg: Eine Abwehr des Buches La Guerre allemande et le catholicisme* (Freiburg-im-Breisgau: Herdersche Verlagshandlung, 1916).
2. Arlie J. Hoover, *God, Germany, and Britain in the Great War: A Study in Clerical Nationalism* (New York: Praeger, 1989).
3. "Christian Scholars of Europe and America: A Reply from Oxford to the German Address to Evangelical Christians" (Includes a translation of the "Address") (London: Oxford University Press, 1914), 23.
4. Ibid., 15.
5. Hoover, *God, Germany, and Britain*, 51–52, 53, 54.
6. Adolph von Harnack, *Aus der Friedens- und Kriegsarbeit* (Giessen: Alfred Töpelmann, 1916), 293, 295.
7. Ibid.
8. Ibid.
9. Hoover, *God, Germany, and Britain*, 57, 62, 60–61. Troeltsch's essays on German and English culture, "Die Metaphysische und religiöse Geist der Deutschen Kultur" and "Über Eigentumlischkeiten der angelsachsischen Zivilisation" appeared in Ernst Troeltsch, *Deutscher Geist in WestEuropa: Gesammelte kulturphilosophische Aufsätze und Reden*, ed. Hans Baron (Berlin: Mohr, 1925).
10. Hoover, *God, Germany, and Britain*, 74–75, 76–77, 114. In contrast to the maximalists, the tradition of peace seeking, and even pacifism, continued across the war according to Karlheinz Lipp, *Berliner Friedenspfarrer und der Erste Weltkrieg: Ein Lesebuch* (Freiburg: Centaurus, 2013).
11. Reinhold Seeberg, *Geschichte, Krieg, und Seele: Reden und Aufsätze aus den Tagen des Weltkrieges* (Leipzig: Quelle & Mezer, 1916), 32, 34, 35, 247.
12. Hoover, *God, Germany, and Britain*, 87–90.
13. Ibid., 98, 92, 92–94, 86. Otto Dibelius was pastoring in Berlin during World War I, but he is best known today as a leader of the Confessing Church, set up in opposition to the German evangelical church leaders who promoted union of the church with the Hitler state.
14. William Sanday, *The Meaning of the War for Germany and Great Britain: An Attempt at Synthesis* (Oxford: Clarendon Press, 1915), 19, 110–11, 97–99, 107, 118, 123.
15. Hoover, *God, Germany, and Britain*, 30, 43, 23. In their criticisms of Germany, English theologians had many subtle differences, according to Charles E. Barley, "The British Protestant Theologians in the First World War, Germanophobia Unleashed," *Harvard Theological Review* 77 (1984): 195–221.
16. Hoover, *God, Germany, and Britain*, 40, 41, 26, 27, 29.
17. Austin Harrison, *The Kaiser's War* (London: George Allen & Unwin, 1914), 19, 42–43, 225, 231, 235.
18. Hoover, *God, Germany, and Britain*, 27, 29, 30, 23, 43. Hoover uses the "first blind man" symbol—leading the others to destruction—to describe Germany's "greater guilt," 44–47.
19. Ibid., 69, 73. The James Russell Lowell lines are from his poem, "The Present Crisis," which in his day was slavery.
20. Baudrillart, *Guerre allemande et le catholicisme*, vii.
21. Ibid., 11–12.
22. Ibid., 49, 50, 52, 57. To follow up on French missionary efforts and examine the involvement of French missionaries in World War I, specifically the members of the Société des Missions Étrangères, see Paul Christophe, *Des missionnaires plongés dans la Grand Guerre, 1914–1918: Lettres des missions étrangères de Paris* (Paris: Cerf, 2012).
23. Baudrillart, *Guerre allemande et le catholicisme*, 77, 79.

24. Ibid., 191, 192.
25. Ibid., 195, 197, 202.
26. Ibid., 205, 206, 211–12.
27. Ibid., 214. Baudrillart's notebooks from this period, as well as related later essays, were published concomitantly. See notes 32 and 39 below.
28. Baudrillart, *Guerre allemande et le catholicisme*, 239.
29. Ibid., 244, 245, 246, 248, 251. A biography of Turinaz was published long after the war. René Hoggard, *Monsigneur Turinaz, évêque de Nancy et de Toul: Quarante-cinq ans d'épiscopat* (Nancy: Librairie Vugner, 1938).
30. Baudrillart, *Guerre allemande et le catholicisme*, 256, 259, 260, 261.
31. Ibid., 263, 265. The wartime writings of Lobbedey were published the year of his death in 1916 and have been reissued recently. See Émile-Louis Cornil Lobbedey, *La guerre en Artois: Paroles épiscopales: Documents, récits* (Paris: Pierre Téqui, 1916).
32. Baudrillart, *Guerre allemande et le catholicisme*, 271, 272, 273, 275. During the war F. A. M. A. Mignet published *Confiance, prière, espoir: Lettres sur La Guerre* (Paris: Bloud et Gay, 1915).
33. Baudrillart, *Guerre allemande et le catholicisme*, 276, 277. Gibier, cited for his theological acumen by Stéphen Coubé is his "Introduction" to *Le Missel du Miracle de la Marne* (see chapter 2 above), published after the war in *Les temps nouveaux, 1914–1918: Paroles de la Guerre* (Paris: Téqui, 1919).
34. Although working out of the German text, I have used the American translation that appeared shortly after the German original: Georg Pfeilschifter, ed., *German Culture, Catholicism and the World War: A Defense Against the Book "La guerre allemande et le catholicisme"* (St. Paul, MI: Wanderer, 1916), 13–27, 161–208. Mausbach was a Catholic priest and scholar, who published moral and dogmatic theological works beginning decades before the war and ending shortly before his death in 1931. Some writings were translated into English. See his *Catholic Moral Teaching and Its Antagonists*, reprinted in 2018 by the St. Athanasius Press.
35. Sauer held the chair of patrology and Christian archaeology at the University of Freiburg. See C. Arnold, "Joseph Sauer—A German Modernist in Wartime," in *Roman Catholic Modernists Confront the Great War*, ed. C. G. T. Talar and L. F. Barmann (New York: Palgrave, 2015).
36. Pfeilschifter, *German Culture*, 238–44.
37. Ibid., 245, 254. Pfeilschifter was a church historian and professor at the University of Freiburg-im-Breisgau. Apart from his scholarly writings, he published during the war three volumes of soldier letters, *Feldpostbriefe katholischer Soldaten* (Freiburg: Herder, 1918).
38. Pfeilschifter, *German Culture*, 399, 418.
39. Pacelli was appointed papal nuncio to Bavaria 23 April 1917 (a nunciature for all of Germany was not in place at that time) and was consecrated a bishop 113 May 1917. See Paul Christophe, ed., *Les carnets du Cardinal Alfred Baudrillart (1 août 1914–31 décembre 1918)* (Paris: Cerf, 1992), 560.
40. Alfred Baudrillart, *La France, les catholiques et la guerre* (Paris: Bloud & Gay, 1917), 23–24, 65.
41. Kardinal Michael von Faulhaber, 1869–1952. Some chronological parallels here: Faulhaber was appointed archbishop of Munich-Freising in 1917 and was made a cardinal four years later. Baudrillart was consecrated a bishop in 1921 and made a cardinal in 1935.
42. Ibid., 148–49.
43. Ibid., 150, 153–55.
44. Michael von Faulhaber, *Das Schwert des Geistes: Feldpredigten im Weltkrieg* (Freiburg-im-Breisgau: Herder, 1918), 2.
45. Ibid., 233–35.
46. Ibid., 245.
47. Ibid., 289, 293.
48. Ibid., 366, 367. The full study of Faulhaber's war theology is Johann Klier, *Von der Kriegspredigt zum Friedensappell: Erzbischoff Michael von Faulhaber und der erste Weltkrieg: Ein Beitrag zur Geschichte der deutschen katholischen Militarseelsorge* (Munich: Neue Schriftenreihe des Staatsarchivs München, 1991).

CHAPTER 8

1. Many other Jewish intellectuals discussed the war and the culture of war. See Ulrich Sieg, *Jüdische Intellektuelle im Ersten Weltkrieg: Kriegserfahrungen, weltanschauliche Debatten und kulturelle Neuentwürfe* (Berlin: Akademie Verlag,

2001). Rosenstock married in 1914 and after the war, in 1925, combined his and his wife's family names to Rosenstock-Huessy.

2. Robert Wohl, in *The Generation of 1914* (Cambridge: Harvard University Press, 1979), highlights the writings of Henry de Montherlant in France, Karl Mannheim in Germany, and Siegfried Sassoon in England; Stephen Schloesser, in *Jazz Age Catholicism: Mystic Modernism in Postwar Paris, 1919–1933* (Toronto: University of Toronto Press, 2005), studies the experience and writings of Jacques Maritain. See especially Schloesser's chapter 2, "Trauma and Memorial: Repatriating the Repressed."

3. Nahum N. Glatzer, *Franz Rosenzweig: His Life and Thought* (New York: Schocken Books, 1961), 38, 44, 48. In fact, Rosenzweig's hopes for a flourishing Mittel-Europa and his belief in Hegelianism seem to mirror German idealism. I thank Vicki Caron for bringing this to my attention.

4. Eugen Rosenstock-Huessy, ed., *Judaism Despite Christianity* (New York: Schocken Books, 1971), 98–99, 112, 113, 114, 115. Rosenzweig's approval of, and debt to, Judah Halevi is reported in Samuel Hugo Bergman, *Faith and Reason: Modern Jewish Thought* (New York: Schocken Books, 1961), 69; note especially the full exposition of the seed growing into a tree that then engenders new seeds.

5. Rosenstock-Huessy, *Judaism Despite Christianity*, 131, 133, 138, 160.

6. Glatzer, *Rosenzweig, His Life and Thought*, xxii–xxiii. Franz Rosenzweig, *The Star of Redemption*, trans. Barbara E. Galli (Madison: University of Wisconsin Press, 2005), 9, 10, 31.

7. Ibid., 31.
8. Ibid., 185, 214–20.
9. Ibid., 230, 231, 259.
10. Glatzer, *Rosenzweig*, 283.
11. Rosenzweig, *Star*, 438, 439, 447.
12. Wilhelm and Marion Pauck, *Paul Tillich: His Life and Thought* (New York: Harper & Row, 1976), 41, 43, 45, 47.
13. Ibid., 48.
14. Matthew Lon Weaver, "Thrown to the Boundary: Tillich's World War I Chaplaincy Sermons," *Bulletin of the North American Paul Tillich Society* 32, no. 2 (Spring 2006): 21–27. In the same issue, see David H. Nikkel, "The Mystical Formation of Paul Tillich," 15–21.

Weaver's book-length study of Tillich's war theology is *Religious Internationalism: The Ethics of War and Peace in the Thought of Paul Tillich* (Macon, GA: Mercer University Press, 2010).

15. Paul Tillich, *Früher Predigten (1909–1918)*, ed. Erdmann Sturm (Berlin: Walter de Gruyter, 1994), #119 (1916), 509. Hereafter FP.
16. FP #77 (1915), 382.
17. FP #95 (1916), 434.
18. FP #135 (1917), 562.
19. FP #98 (1916), 443.
20. Pauck and Pauck, *Paul Tillich*, 49, 51, 53–54.
21. Paul Tillich, *Briefwechsel und Streitschriften: Theologische, philosophische und politische Stellungnahmen und Gespräche*, ed. Renato Albricht and René Tautmann (Frankfurt: Evangelisches Verlagswerk, 1971), 98–104.
22. Pauck and Pauck, *Paul Tillich*, 55.
23. *Écrits du temps de la guerre (1916–1919)* (Paris: Bernard Grasset, 1965; *Génèse d'une pensée: Lettres 1914–1919* (Paris: Bernard Grasset, 1961); *Journal*, vol. 1 (26 Août 1915–4 janvier 1919) (Paris: Fayard, 1975). See the studies by Claude Cuénot, *Teilhard de Chardin* (Paris: Seuil, 1962); Edith de la Héronnière, *Teilhard de Chardin: Une mystique de la traversée* (Paris: Albin Michel, 2003); Ursula King, *Spirit of Fire: The Life and Vision of Pierre Teilhard de Chardin*, rev. ed. (Maryknoll, NY: Orbis Books, 2015); Kathleen Duffy, *Teilhard's Mysticism: Seeing the Inner Face of Evolution* (Maryknoll, NY: Orbis Books, 2014).
24. For a discussion of mysticism useful for the historian, see Bernard McGinn, *The Foundations of Mysticism, Origins to the Fifth Century* (New York: Crossroad, 1995), esp. 3–8 and 265–343.
25. Teilhard, *Écrits*, 16.
26. Teilhard, *Journal*, 68. Boldface capitals and underlining are in the original.
27. Teilhard, *Écrits*, 33, 38, 41, 46, 49, 60.
28. Teilhard, *Génèse*, 173.
29. Teilhard, *Écrits*, 96, 105.
30. Teilhard, *Génèse*, 254.
31. Teilhard, *Journal*, 204, 207.
32. Teilhard, *Écrits*, 139, 140, 141, 160, 162, 164, 165.
33. Teilhard, *Génèse*, 264.
34. Teilhard, *Écrits*, 182, 183.
35. Teilhard, *Journal*, 222. Boldface capitals and underlining are in the original.
36. Teilhard, *Génèse*, 308.

37. Teilhard, *Écrits*, 237, 241, 248.
38. Teilhard, *Génèse*, 371 (for Cuénot datum, 371n2).
39. Teilhard, *Écrits*, 276.
40. Quoted in Alan Wilkinson, *The Church of England and the First World War* (London: SPCK, 1978), 137–38. A collection of essays on Studdert Kennedy still serves as a useful source for his formation and ministry, *G. A. Studdert Kennedy by His Friends* (London: Hodder & Stoughton, 1929), but the essential biography covering not only the war years but the entire career is Linda Parker, *A Seeker After Truths: The Life and Times of G. A. Studdert Kennedy ("Woodbine Willie") 1883–1929* (West Midlands: Helion, 2017). No one appreciated Studdert Kennedy more than the head chaplain of the English forces, Bishop L. H. Gwynne. Gwynne on Studdert Kennedy is quoted in Jackson, *Pastor on the Nile*, 156–57.
41. G. A. Studdert Kennedy, *The Hardest Part* (London: Hodder & Stoughton, 1918), 11.
42. Ibid., 19–20.
43. Ibid., "God in History," 32, 33, 36, 37, 40, 41–42, 47.
44. Ibid., "God in the Bible," 51, 54, 55, 61–62, 67, 71, 73.
45. Ibid., "God and Prayer," 101, 119, 102–3.
46. Ibid., 107, 108, 109, 114.
47. Stuart Bell, "The Theology of 'Woodbine Willie' in Context," in *Clergy in Khaki: New Perspectives on British Army Chaplaincy in the First World War*, ed. Michael Snape and Edward Madigan (Aldershot: Ashgate, 2013), 105, 106, 110.

ENVOI

1. Gordon Allport, *The Individual and His Religion: A Psychological Interpretation* (New York: Macmillan, 1950), 149, 101–2. On the steps in the development of the individual, see Allport, *Becoming: Basic Considerations for a Psychology of Personality* (New Haven: Yale University Press, 1955), 41–56. I still stand by my "Suggestions on Writing the History of Psychological Data," *History and Theory* 16 (1977): 297–305, and my *Psychology of Religion* (New York: Free Press, 1989), chap. 9, "General Theories and Unique Lives." The thesis here is that the historian should study a variety of psychological concepts and terms for appropriateness and clarity. Use of a term out of a classical theory, e.g., "defense," does not, however, imply acceptance of the whole framework, e.g., Freudian psychoanalysis.
2. Allport, *Individual*, 30. The statistics on soldier reports were clear, if unsurprising: 55 percent said that the war made them neither more nor less religious; 26 percent, that it made them more religious; 19 percent, that it made them less religious. Allport concludes that the war created slightly more antireligious attitudes than the percentage found at comparable age levels of nonsoldiers, but those who valued religion valued it more because of the war.
3. Ibid., 52–53, 54.
4. A propos of Tillich's "mysticism," see the work of Sanghoon Baek, "'Baptized Mysticism': An Exploration of Paul Tillich's Theology of Mysticism and Its Spiritual Theological Implications" (PhD thesis, Knox College and the University of Toronto, 2014). Although Tillich entitled a major series of lectures *Dogmatik* right after the war, he later labeled his work *Systematische Theologie*. See Werner Schüssler, "Metaphysik und Theologie: Zu Paul Tillichs 'Umwendung' der Metaphysik in der 'Dogmatik von 1925,'" *Zeitschrift für Katholische Theologie* 117 (1995): 192–202.

FURTHER READING

Here readers will find (1) texts that are the setting for the book as a whole and for individual chapters, (2) classical collections of letters and diaries, both older and more recent, and (3) primary sources that merit more extended readings. Some of these references are found in the endnotes, where I cite the editions used in my research. When appropriate, more recent editions or English translations now available are listed below. I offer a constantly updated bibliography on my website, where new publications, as well as translations of already cited sources, will be found at https://www.josephfbyrnes.com/further-reading.

GENERAL READING

The main resource is the online *International Encyclopedia of the First World War*, covering the themes of Pre-war, Violence, Power, Media, Home Front, and Post-war in 1,368 articles, 164 of them on the subject of religion: https://encyclopedia.1914-1918-online.net.

Among the many excellent general studies of the war, the fullest and most balanced is Jörn Leonhardt, *Pandora's Box: A History of the First World War*, trans. Patrick Camiller (Cambridge: Belknap/Harvard University Press, 2018). The translator nodded at least once, somehow making General von Moltke the younger the grandson of General von Moltke the elder, instead of his nephew—this given correctly in the original German edition and virtually everywhere else.

Indispensable also is John Horne, ed., *A Companion to World War I* (Oxford: Wiley-Blackwell, 2012). Encyclopedic in form, the individual articles, with their bibliographies, are by experts in the field.

Virtually all of the works authored or edited by Jan Winter are essential. To begin with, see the *Cambridge History of the First World War*, which he edited in three volumes (Cambridge University Press, 2016).

And Nicolao Merkur, *La guerra di Dio. Religione e nazionalismo nella Grande Guerra* (Rome: Carocci, 2015) would be the classic text on the topic of God-talk and nation-talk if it were better known! One hopes for a second edition and even more for an English translation in the near future.

The major book on conscientious objectors, war resisters, and pacifists is Adam Hochschild, *To End All Wars: A Study of Loyalty and Rebellion, 1914–1918* (New York: Houghton, Mifflin, Harcourt, 2011).

CHAPTER 1

"Railway Stations: Gateways and Termini" and "The Streets," by Adrian Gregory and Emmanuelle Cronier respectively, chapters 2 and 3 of *Capital Cities at War*, vol. 2, Jay Winter and Jean-Louis Robert, eds. (New York: Cambridge University Press, 2007) provide excellent coverage for each of these themes.

For German newspaper reports in greater detail, Jeffrey Verhey, *The Spirit of 1914: Militarism, Myth and Mobilization in Germany* (New York: Cambridge University Press, 2000). And for British newspaper reports in greater detail, Adrian Gregory, *The Last Great War: British Society and the First World War* (New York: Cambridge University Press, 2008).

Bruno Cabanes, *August 1914: France, the Great War, and a Month That Changed the World* (New Haven: Yale University Press, 2016) is a detailed look at the first days of the war in Paris.

Reports on the earliest days of the war in Paris are from the diaries of Félix Klein and Henri Desagneaux. Félix Klein, *Diary of a French Army Chaplain*, trans. Harriet M. Capes, 4th ed. [printing] (London: Andrew Melrose, 1917), and Henri Desagneaux, *Journal de guerre, 14–18*, ed. Jean Desagneaux (Paris: Denoel, 1971).

Articles on religion in *Der Erste Weltkrieg: Wirkung, Wahrnehmung, Analyse*, ed. Wolfgang Michalka (Munich: Piper, 1994) are basic for Protestant and Catholic engagement in the war.

Also, for official German Protestant and Catholic church engagement with the war, the collection of sermons edited by Bruno Doehring, *Ein feste Burg*, 2 vols. (Berlin: Reimar Hobbing, 1914–15).

A stunning presentation of the writings and accomplishments of Bishop, eventually Cardinal, Michael von Faulhaber can be appreciated even by those readers who would not otherwise attempt a German text. It is *Kardinal Michael von Faulhaber, 1869–1952: Eine Ausstellung des Archivs des Erzbistums München und Freising, des Bayerischen Hauptstaatsarhivs und des Stadtarchivs München zum 50. Todestag. München, 6. Juni bis 28. Juli 2002* (Munich: Archiv des Erzbistums München und Freising, 2002).

The basic writings of the Archbishop of Paris, Cardinal Amette, Léon Amette, *Pendant la guerre: Lettres pastorales et allocutions (août 1914–février 1915)* (Paris: Bloud et Gay, 1915).]

Two principal collections of the sermons and writings of the Bishop of London, Arthur Winnington-Ingram, are *A Day of God: Being Five Addresses on the Subject of the Present War*. (London: Wells, Gardner, Darton, 1914) and *The Church in Time of War* (London: Wells, Gardner, Darton, 1915).

CHAPTER 2

The sober theological interpretation of the "Miracle of the Marne" as presented in Stéphen Coubé's "Introduction" to the *Missel du Miracle de la Marne* has a sober secular parallel in the David Clarke, *The Angel of Mons: Phantom Soldiers and Ghostly Guardians* (Chichester: John Wiley & Sons, 2004), as well as in the Terence Zuber, *The Mons Myth: A Reassessment of the Battle* (Gloucestershire: History Press, 2010).

War religion was portrayed in an enormous and enormously important collection of picture postcards, which is presented in Heidrun Alzheimer, ed., *Glaubenssache Krieg: Religiöse Motive auf Bildpostkarten des Ersten Weltkriegs* (Bad Windesheim: Fränkisches Freilandmuseum, 2009). I hope to negotiate a special arrangement with the Fränkisches Freilandmuseum, to make this material more readily available.

On English soldier experience of and production of literature, including religion talk, Paul Fussell, *The Great War and Modern Memory* (New York: Oxford, 2000) is a classic, and has generated extensive commentary and criticism since its first publication in 1975.

The Christmas truce of 1914 engendered false hope back then and ever since. Two books deserve a full reading: Terri Blom Crocker, *The Christmas Truce: Myth, Memory, and the First World War* (Lexington: University Press of Kentucky, 2015), and Marc Ferro, Malcolm Brown, Rémy Cazals, and Olaf Mueller, eds., *Meetings in No Man's Land: Christmas 1914 and Fraternization in the Great War*, trans. Helen McPhail (London: Constable & Robinson, 2007).

The model study of soldier faith and the church in France is Annette Becker, *War and Faith: The Religious Imagination in France, 1914–1930*, trans. Helen McPhail (Bloomsbury Academic, 1998), but Jacques Fontana, *Les catholiques français pendant la Grande Guerre* is still eminently useful. For German Catholic—as well as Austro-Hungarian—soldier faith, see Patrick J. Houlihan, *Catholicism and the Great War: Religion and Everyday Life in Germany and Austria-Hungary, 1914–1922* (New York: Cambridge University Press, 2015), 117–52, chapter 5: "Faith in the Trenches: Catholic Battlefield Piety During the Great War."

For war devotions in Germany, both Protestant and Catholic, check Gottfried Korff, ed., *Alliierte im Himmel: Populare Religiosität und Kriegserfahrung* (Tübingen: Vereinigung für Volkskunde e. V., 2006), and the most exhaustive study in any language of Sacred Heart devotion across the war is Claudia Schlager, *Kult und Krieg: Herz Jesu—Sacré-Cœur—Christus Rex im deutsch-französischen Vergleich, 1914–1925* (Tübingen: Vereinigung für Volkskunde e. V., 2011).

The preeminent cultural history of the war is Ernest Piper, *Kulturgeschichte des Ersten Weltkriegs* (Berlin: Propyhläen, 2013).

CHAPTER 3

On the range of God-talk, the English soldier and former divinity student Donald Hankey is a key figure, engagingly presented in Ross Davies, *A Student in Arms: Donald Hankey and Edwardian Society at War* (Burlington, VT: Ashgate: 2013). But on the possibility and especially the near impossibility of God-talk, Gerard A. Jaeger, *Les poilus: Survivre à l'enfer des tranchées de 14–18* (Paris: l'Archipel, 2014).

Michael Snape, *God and the British Soldier: Religion and the British Army in the First and Second World Wars* (New York: Routledge, 2005) is most helpful for England, and, for Germany, Wolfgang Michalka, ed., *Der Erste Weltkrieg: Wirkung, Wahrnehmung, Analyse* (Munich: Piper, 1994).

For texts of soldier letters, the three classic collections are Philip Witkop, ed., and A. F. Wedd, trans., *German Students' War Letters* (Philadelphia: University of Pennsylvania Press, 2002), *La dernière lettre écrite par des soldats français tombés au champ d'honneur 1914–1918*, a recent edition of which appeared in 2014 (Paris: Éditions Michel de Maule), and Laurence Housman, ed., *War Letters of Fallen Englishmen* (Philadelphia: University of Pennsylvania Press, 2002). Readers would do well to first check Martha Hanna, "War Letters: Communication Between Front and Home Front," *International Encyclopedia of the First World War*, https://encyclopedia.1914-1918 -online.net.

Indispensable for the study of colonial forces fighting in the French and English armies are Richard A. Fogarty, *Race and War in France: Colonial Subjects in the French Army, 1914–1918* (Baltimore: Johns Hopkins Press, 2008) and David Omissi, intro. and ed., *Indian Voices in the Great War: Soldiers' Letters, 1914–1918* (New York: St. Martin's Press, 1999). For a religious history of the American soldiers in France, see Jonathan H. Ebel, *Faith in the Fight: Religion and the American Soldier in the Great War* (Princeton: Princeton University Press. 2010).

The most useful studies of the generals and their religious proclivities are Annika Mombauer, *Helmuth von Moltke and the Origins of the First World War* (Cambridge: Cambridge University Press, 2001), B. H. Liddell Hart, *Foch: The Man of Orléans* (Boston: Little, Brown, 1931), and Brian Bond and Nigel Cave, eds., *Haig: A Reappraisal 70 Years On* (Barsley, South Yorkshire: Leo Cooper, 1999). Haig's favorite chaplain, G. S. Duncan, later published *Douglas Haig as I Knew Him* (London: George Allen and Unwin, 1966)

Haig, in fact, is used as a beginning point for the one recent study of the agnostic Catholic general, the Bavarian prince Rupprecht, by Jonathan Boff, *Haig's Enemy: Crown Prince Rupprecht and Germany's War on the Western Front* (New York: Oxford University Press, 2018)—although the religion aspect is covered only in Dieter Weiß, *Kronprinz Rupprecht von Bayern (1869–1955): Eine politische Biographie* (Regensburg: Friedrich Pustet, 2007).

CHAPTER 4

Hanneke Takken, *Churches, Chaplains, and the Great War* (New York: Routledge, 2019) is the all-encompassing study.

The experiences and ministries of the German chaplains are collected in Lisbeth Exner and Herbert Kapfer, eds., *Verborgene Chronik 1914* and *Verborgene Chronik, 1915–1918* (Berlin: Galiani, 2014–16), and in Helmut Baier, ed., *Als evangelischer Feldgeistlicher im Ersten Weltkrieg: Wilhelm Stählins Tagebücher 1914–1917* (Stuttgart: W. Kohlhammer, 2016). For the Catholic chaplains, the fullest published records are Frank Betker and Almut Kriele, eds., Gerd Krumeich, intro., *"Pro Fide et Patria!" Die Kriegstagebücher von Ludwig Berg 1914–1918: Katholischer Feldgeistlicher im Großen Hauptquartier Kaiser Wilhelms II* (Cologne: Böhlau Verlag, 1998), and Hans-Josef Wollasch, ed., *Militärseelsorge im Ersten Weltkrieg: Das Kriegstagebuch des katholischen Feldgeistlichen Benedict Kreutz* (Mainz: Matthias-Grünewald-Verlag, 1987).

For both representative testimony and perceptive analysis of the importance of the French priests who were drafted into actual combat as well as appointed as chaplains, see Anita Rasi May, *Patriot Priests: French Catholic Clergy and National Identity in World War I* (Norman: University of Oklahoma Press, 2018). Although limited to the priests of one region of France, the most insightful presentation of the priests' spiritual and psychological involvement in the war is Daniel Moulinet, *Prêtres soldats dans la Grande Guerre: Les clercs bourbonnais sous les drapeaux* (Rennes: Presses universitaires de Rennes, 2014). The earlier work by Jacques Fontana, *Les Catholiques français pendant la Grande Guerre* (Paris: Cerf, 1990), covers both the priests on the front lines and the churches back home.

The essential study of Church of England chaplains is Edward Madigan, *Faith Under Fire: Anglican Army Chaplains and the Great War* (New York: Palgrave Macmillan, 2011), and the study that combines chaplain and home-church history is Alan Wilkinson, *The Church of England and the First World War*, 3rd ed. (Cambridge: Lutterworth Press, 2014).

(1920): 33–58. This century-old journal article can be found on the internet.

For the letters of German Jewish soldiers, an invaluable two-volume work is Herman Simon, ed., *Feldpostbriefe Jüdischer Soldaten, 1914–1918* (Teetz: Hentrich & Hentrich, 2002). I fear it is likely that these letters, set in a brilliantly edited presentation, will remain untranslated in the near future.

A French Jewish witness that is outstanding in its combination of patriotism and honesty regarding the nation, and outstanding in its combination of agnosticism and respect for Jewish tradition, is André Kahn, *Journal de guerre d'un juif patriote, 1914–1918* (Paris: Jean-Claude Simoën, 1978).

CHAPTER 5

The remarkable collection of the diaries and sermons of rabbis in World War I that must serve as a model for all such presentations—whether of rabbis or clergy of any faith—is Peter C. Appelbaum, *Loyalty Betrayed: Jewish Chaplains in the German Army During the First World War* (Portland, OR: Vallentine Mitchell, 2014).

With its chapter on Jewish soldiers in World War I, Derek J. Penslar, *Jews and the Military* (Princeton: Princeton University Press, 2005) is a helpful, inclusive history.

Philippe E. Landau is the scholar whose histories of Judaism in France, at home and at the front, are primary here. His major book is *Les Juifs de France et la Grande Guerre: Un patriotisme républicain* (Paris: CNRS Éditions, 2008), but he presents a brief cross-section of his work in "Patrie et religion: Juifs et Judaïsme dans la guerre totale," in *Foi, religion et sacré dans la Grande Guerre*, ed. Xavier Boniface and Xavier Cochet (Artois: Presses Université, 2014).

For the preaching of English and other rabbis across two hundred years, including World War I, Marc Saperstein, ed. and intro., *Jewish Preaching in Times of War, 1800–2001* (Portland, OR: Littman Library of Jewish Civilization, 2008). For English rabbi chaplain Michael Adler, whose efforts supported, if not overshadowed, those of his peers, see his, "Experiences of a Jewish Chaplain on the Western Front (1915–1918)," *Jewish Guardian*

CHAPTER 6

The gold standard for an individual soldier diary, in this case French, has recently been published in an English translation: Edward M. Strauss, trans., *Poilu: The World War One Notebooks of Corporal Louis Barthas, Barrelmaker, 1914–1918* (New Haven: Yale University Press, 2014). Although Barthas has his own political and social agenda, the personal, moral, and physical resiliency of the man, not pious but assuming the goodness of his family Christianity, comes through at every turn. An anthology of other diaries that gives readers a cross section of soldier-diary concerns and themes is Marilyn Shevin-Coetzee and Frans Coetzee, eds., *Commitment and Sacrifice: Personal Diaries from the Great War* (New York: Oxford University Press, 2015).

The gold standard for collected diaries is Lisbeth Exner and Herbert Kapfer, eds., *Verborgene Chronik*, 2 vols. (Berlin: Galiani, 2014–2016).

And for the French diaries, the classic collection is Jean Norton Cru, *Témoins: Essai d'analyse et de critique des souvenirs de combattants édités en français de 1915 à 1928* (1929; repr. Nancy: Presses Universitaires de Nancy, 1993). Now readers have the advantage of a new edition with an introduction by Philippe Olivera (Marseilles: Éditions Agone, 2022).

Extremely valuable collections of British soldier experiences have been published by Lyn Macdonald. See her basic *1914–1918, Voices and*

Images of the Great War (London: Michael Joseph, 1988). For further testimonies, see her individual volumes: *They Called it Passchendaele* (1978), *Somme* (1983), *1914* (1988), *1915* (1993), *To the Last Man: Spring 1918* (1998).

The individual diaries singled out for presentation in chapter 6 are all worth a full reading. The Englishman: Arthur Graeme West, *Diary of a Dead Officer: Being the Posthumous Papers of Arthur Graeme West*, ed. Cyril Joad, intro. Nigel James (n.p.: Greenhill Books, 2007). The German: Stephan Kurt Westmann, *Surgeon with the Kaiser's Army*, ed. Michael Westman (South Yorkshire: Pen-and-Sword Books, 2014). The Frenchman: Ferdinand Belmont, *Lettres d'un officier des Chasseurs alpins (2 août 1914–28 décembre 1915)* (Paris: Plon, 1916).

CHAPTER 7

Arlie J. Hoover, *God, Germany, and Britain in the Great War: A Study in Clerical Nationalism* (New York: Praeger, 1989) covers the Protestant war of theological and philosophical words on the German and English home fronts. Some of the German clergy who took a stand against the war are presented in Karlheinz Lipp, *Berliner Friedenpfarrer und der Erste Weltkrieg: Ein Lesebuch* (Freiburg: Centauras, 2013).

For the French and German Catholic mutual recriminations, the sources are Alfred Baudrillart, ed., *La guerre allemande et le catholicisme* (Paris: Bloud & Gay, 1915), and George Pfeilschifter, ed., *Deutsche Kultur, Katholizismus, und Weltkrieg: Eine Abwehr des Buches La Guerre allemande et le catholicisme* (Freiburg-im-Breisgau: Herdersche Verlagshandlung, 1916). German Americans published a translation of this book, also in 1916, to try to present the German point of view to the then neutral Americans: Georg Pfeilschifter, ed., *German Culture, Catholicism and the World War: A Defense Against the Book "La guerre allemande et le catholicisme"* (St. Paul, MI: Wanderer, 1916). Reprint available.

The writings of Alfred Baudrillart were edited thirty years ago by Paul Christophe in *Les carnets du Cardinal Alfred Baudrillart (1 août 1914–31 décembre 1918)* (Paris: Cerf, 1992). But see also Baudrillart's own later war writings, *La France, les catholiques et la guerre* (Paris: Bloud & Gay, 1917).

There is no translation, or even a modern edition, of Faulhaber's preaching at the war front, *Das Schwert des Geistes: Feldpredigten im Weltkrieg* (Freiburg-im-Breisgau: Herder, 1918). Worth repeating here, however, is the above reference to *Kardinal Michael von Faulhaber, 1869–1952: Eine Ausstellung des Archivs des Erzbistums München und Freising*.

CHAPTER 8

The outstanding Jewish philosophical/theological accomplishment of a combatant (on the southern front, but in close relationship to the western front) is Franz Rosenzweig's *The Star of Redemption*, trans. Barbara E. Galli (Madison: University of Wisconsin Press, 2005). Before working on this text, readers will find it helpful to look at the war-era sections of Nahum N. Glatzer, *Franz Rosenzweig: His Life and Thought* (New York: Schocken Books, 1961).

There is a rich bibliography of Tillich studies, but for World War I purposes, readers should start with the thus-far definitive biography, Wilhelm and Marion Pauck, *Paul Tillich: His Life and Thought* (New York: Harper & Row, 1976), and then see the studies of Matthew Lon Weaver, *Religious Internationalism: The Ethics of War and Peace in the Theology of Paul Tillich* (Macon, GA: Mercer University Press, 2010). Frederick J. Parrella and Raymond F. Bulman, eds., *Religion in the New Millennium: Theology in the Spirit of Paul Tillich* (Macon, GA: Mercer University Press, 2001) is a study of Tillich's continuing influence.

Obviously, the two volumes of Teilhard de Chardin's war writings deserve the fullest possible attention: *Writings in Time of War*, trans. René Hague (New York: Harper, 1967); and *The Making of a Mind: Letters from a Soldier Priest, 1914–1918*, trans. René Hague (New York: Harper, 1965). Claude Cuénot, *Teilhard de Chardin: A Biographical Study*, trans. Vincent Colimore (New York: Helicon, 1965), has been a mainstay for decades, but the best work to read in relation to chapter 8 is Ursula King,

Spirit of Fire: The Life and Vision of Pierre Teilhard de Chardin, rev. ed. (Maryknoll, NY: Orbis Books, 2015).

For a full presentation of the life and ministry of Geoffrey Studdert Kennedy, readers must turn to the carefully researched and eminently readable Linda Parker, *A Seeker After Truths: The Life and Times of G. A. Studdert Kennedy ("Woodbine Willie") 1883–1929* (West Midlands: Helion, 2017). Studdert Kennedy's own wartime sermons and essays are collected in *The Hardest Part* (London: Hodder & Stoughton, 1918), and the old volume of appreciations written by his contemporaries, *G. A. Studdert Kennedy by His Friends* (London: Hodder & Stoughton, 1929), is a primary source. But on the theological accomplishments, the essay by Stuart Bell, "The Theology of 'Woodbine Willie' in Context," in *Clergy in Khaki: New Perspectives on British Army Chaplaincy in the First World War*, ed. Michael Snape and Edward Madigan (Aldershot: Ashgate, 2013), 95–110, is indispensable.

INDEX

Page references in *italics* indicate an illustration.

Adler, Michael
   burial services, 130, 131
   photograph of, *129*
   prayer book of, 129–30, 136
   services in theaters, 130, 131
   war experience of, 117, 128–29
Advent Sunday celebration, 144
Agincourt, Battle of, 28, 36
Aisne river
   German retreat to, 37, 43, 45, 144, 156
Alacoque, Marguerite-Marie, 50
Allport, Gordon
   The Individual and His Religion, 214–15
All Saints' Day, 154
Amette, Léon
   praise of the French troops, 20, 26, 31
   sermons and publications of, 3, 25, 26, 178
Amiot, abbé of Angers, 97
amulets, 64, 65
Angels of Mons, 35, 36, 80
Anglican church. *See* Church of England
Anglicanism, 10, 64, 76, 80, 107, 174
Anglo-Jewish elite, 116
Ankenbrand, Alfons, 67
Appelbaum, Peter C.
   Loyalty Betrayed, 117
Arlet, Joseph, 100
Army and Religion report, 64
Arndt, Ernst, 23
Arras, Battle of, 145, 161
Ascension celebration, 91, 151
atheism, 84, 135, 166, 200, 215
Audouin, Jean, 99–100

Babouard, Pierre, 101
Baeck, Leo
   on cultural mission of German people, 124
   hospital service of, 133
   photograph of, *118*
   preservation of heritage of, 229n12
   reports of, 122
   sermons of, 123

Baerwald, Leo, 118, 124
Ballard, Frank, 176
Barbara, Saint
   imagery of, 53–54
Barre de Carroy, André de la, 227n44
Barrès, Maurice, 116
Barry, Frank, 106, 109, 115
Bartlett, Harry, 231n28
Basilica of Notre-Dame de Brebières at Albert, 48, *49*, 50
Bates, Arthur, 57
Baudrillart, Alfred
   ecclesiastical career of, 167, 233n41
   on French cause, 191
   La guerre allemande et le catholicisme, 167, 177, 187
   letters of, 181
   religious polemics of, 180, 187, 191
Baverstock, H., 231n28
Becker, Annette, 38, 51, 52
Becker, Georg, 139, 141
Belgian priests, 141, 164
Belgium
   Catholicism, 134
   destruction of, 93
   English defense of, 176
   formation of state of, 185
   German invasion of, 21, 152, 169, 170, 175, 176, 216
   war atrocities in, 140–41, 185
Bell, Stuart, 212
Belmont, Ferdinand, 138, 154, *155*, 165
Benson, Robert Hugh, 203
Berg, Ludwig, 95–96, 114
Berlin
   churches of, 10
   war enthusiasm in, 12–13, 21, 31
Berliner Dom
   crowds in front of, *12*
   warship service in, 22, 217
Bernhardi, Friedrich von
   Germany and the Next War, 174

Bethmann-Hollweg, Theobald von, 21, 170
Bettinger, Franziskus von
 death of, 24
 publications of, 3, 24, 25
 service for the troops, 24–25, 31
 support of German advances, 20
 visit to Saarebourg, 47
Bidder, H. F., 159, 231n28
Bindrum, Josef, 145
Bing, Bernard, 133, 136, 145
Birks, H. L., 161, 231n28
Bismarck, Otto von, 173, 179
Black, Frank, 55
Blanckenhorn, Gertrud, 139, 140
Bloch, Abraham
 character of, 126, 128
 commemoration of, 127
 ecclesiastical career of, 117, 126
 legendary death of, 125, 126–27, 136
 painting of, 125
Blumenfeld, Franz, 66
Blunden, Edmund, 50
Boittin, Jennifer, 76
Bordeaux, Henry, 97
Boughton, Ernest, 71–72
Bowles, J., 72, 160, 231n28
British Expeditionary Force, 34, 106, 128
Britten, S. V., 231n28
Broadwood, E. H. T., 156, 230n28
Brooke, Rupert, 28
Brown, Malcolm
 "The Christmas Truce 1914: the English Story," 57
Brugerette, Joseph, 97
Bryan, H. D., 55
Buckingham Palace
 crowd gathering at, 19
Bülow, Karl von, 34, 37, 39
burials, 55–56, 90–91, 106–7, 118, 130, 131
Byng, Julian, 76, 82

Cabanes, Bruno, 16
Calvinism
 re-awakening of, 64
Campbell, Edward, 106, 115
Campbell, Phyllis, 36
Carlyle, Thomas, 76
Carver, Christian, 71
Castelnau, Noël de, 47
Catholicism. *See* French Catholicism; German Catholics

Cazin, Paul, 150, 151
Cendrars, Blaise, 3
Chabord, Lucien, 102, 115
 memento card for, *103*
Chamberlain, Houston Stewart, 76
chaplains, 7–8, 62, 87
 See also English chaplains; German chaplains; Jewish chaplains
Chaplin, Sydney, 157, 231n28
Charles Martel, ruler of Francia, 30
Charteris, John, 36, 80
Chater, Alfred, 55
Christian iconography, 39, 40, 44, 48, 50, 51
Christmas truce, 54–60
 carol singing, 57–58
 fraternizing troops, 54, 56, 57, 58
 gift exchanges, 56
 holiday celebrations, 54–55, 57–58, 60, 92, 134–35
 joint burials, 55–56
 newspaper coverage of, 56–57
Chrysologus (Jesuit publication), 51
church going
 decline of, 10–11, 221n2
Church Lads Brigade, 161
Church of England
 Catholicism and, 179
 clergy, 225n1
 devotion to the Virgin Mary, 52
 liturgies, 85
 Orthodox Russia and, 29, 187, 191
 on sins of Germany, 173–77
Clarke, David, 35, 36
Clayton, Philip, 107, 115
 Plain Tales from Flanders, 108
Clemenceau, Georges, 99, 131
clergy
 categories of, 225n1
 diaries of, 5
 education of, 86
 preaching of, 22–23
 war experience of, 5
 See also English chaplains; French clergy; German chaplains; Jewish chaplains
Cochet, Annick, 65
Coggins, W. J., 160, 231n28
Cohn, Josef, 132
Cole, Charles, 160, 231n28, 231n35
Cook, Theodore A.
 Kaiser, Krupp, and Culture, 175
Coubé, Stéphen, 34, 38, 39, 184

Creighton, Oswin
 photograph of, *111*
 reflections on war, 112–13
 religious beliefs of, 110, 111–12, 115
Crocker, Terri Blom, 54
Cuénot, Claude, 207
Cyapski, Herbert, 132

Davidson, E., 162, 231n28
Davidson, Randall, 26, 222n42
Dawson, Joseph
 Christ and the Sword, 175
Deauville, Maurice, 150
Delécraz, Antoine, 13, 14
Delvert, Charles, 150, 152
Desagneaux, Henri, 18, 19
Deutsche Kultur, Katholizismus, und Weltkrieg (German Culture, Catholicism, and World War), 167, 177, 184, 187
Deutsche Tagebuch Archiv, 137
Dewdney, George, 108
diaries
 of clergy, 5
 as primary sources, 75
 of soldiers, 131, 133–34, 137–38, 150, 165, 216
 See also English diaries; French diaries; German diaries
Dibelius, Otto, 173, 232n13
Diffey, Harold, 159, 231n28
diffusive Christianity, 63–64
Doehring, Bruno, 22, 31
Douai, Siege of, 145
Doudney, Charles, 113
Dreyfus affair, 116
Dryander, Ernst, 22–23
Dubail, Auguste, 47
Duncan, George S., 80, 81, 82
Durouchoux, Pierre, 101, 115
Duwez (Deauville), Maurice, 152

Easter celebration, 146
Ebel, Jonathan, 75
Écrits du temps de la guerre (Writings in Time of War) (Teilhard), 201
Eggebrecht, Siegfried
 burial service of, 91
 commitment to the German cause, 114
 diary of, 90, 139, 144
 education of, 90
 field hospital service of, 90–91
 on German defeat, 146
 postwar career of, 226n7

Engall, John, 71
English chaplains, 106–15
 burial services of, 106–7, 108
 communion services of, 106, 108
 frontline experience of, 107, 113
 lay soldiers and, 109–10
 loss of faith, 111, 112
 preaching for pastoral care, 5, 115
 reflections on war, 112–13
 on sins of Germany, 173–77
 understanding of goodness, 216
English diaries, 156–66
 on Battle of Passchendaele, 161–63
 on Battle of Somme, 159–61
 on care for the wounded, 157
 collections of, 138, 156
 deliberations on religion, 163–64
 on French civilian behavior, 165–66
 on horrors of war, 157–58, 160, 161–62, 164, 165
 reflections on death and normal life, 157
 on suffering, 216
 testimonies of new arrivals, 158–59
English imperialism, 169, 172, 176
English Jews, 128, 135
English Protestants
 religious debates, 190–91
English rabbis, 128–31
 burial services of, 130, 131
 front line experience of, 130
 influence of, 128
 Passover service, 129
 photo of, *129*
 prayers of, 129–30, 136
 Yom Kippur service of, 130
Evangelical Church, 20, 21, 89–90
Exner, Lisbeth, 137, 138

faith
 definition of, 214
fatalism, 64, 84
Faulhaber, Michael von
 chaplaincy of, 92
 criticism of French clergy, 186
 Deutsche Kultur, Katholizismus, und Weltkrieg, 177
 ecclesiastical career of, 233n41
 Kaiser's telegram to, 189–90
 military service of, 188
 pastoral letter of, 96
 photograph of, *188*
 on role of religion in German public life, 186

INDEX   245

sermons of, 189, 191, 192
visits to the front, 24, 187–88
Feist, Sigmund, 132
Fellowes, Harry, 158–59, 231n28
Ferchaud, Claire, 51
Fliege, Thomas, 46
Foch, Ferdinand
    collection of letters of, 68
    as commanding officer, 37, 39
    deaths in family of, 78
    education of, 77
    religious views of, 4, 76, 77–79
Fogarty, Richard S., 73
Forrest, Archie, 108
Fort Vaux, 133
France
    countryside of, 15
    German invasion of, 21, 142, 143, 144
    mobilization decrees, 15, 18
    patriotism, 30–31
    secular ideology, 103–4
    separation of church and state, 10–11, 87, 97
    war enthusiasm in, 13–19
France, les Catholiques et la guerre, La (French Catholics and the War), 187
Frank, Gottlieb, 146
French, John, 130
French Catholicism
    influence of, 104, 178–79, 180–81, 182, 184, 186
    patriotism and, 39, 95
French clergy
    care for the dying soldiers, 105–6
    combat experience of, 100–101, 102
    concern about vocation, 99–100
    devotional practices of, 98–99
    German perception of, 142
    hagiographies of, 99
    letters of, 98
    missionaries, 179
    mobilization of, 97
    moral reflections of, 101, 102, 115
    pastoral letters of, 26, 181–84
    patriotism of, 101, 102, 104
    photographs of, 79
    polemics with German Catholics, 167, 177–87, 191
    priestly services of, 97, 98
    religious nationalism of, 99, 114
    secular ideology and, 103–4
    sermons of, 216
    service for the wounded, 135
    spirituality of, 98, 101, 114

war experience of, 87, 97–98
women, 104–5
French diaries, 150–56
    authors of, 150
    on battle of Verdun, 153
    defence of Catholicism, 155
    on horrors of war, 150–51, 165
    on loss of Christian morality, 165
    on pity for the soldiers, 153–54
    publication of, 138
    reflections on death, 153
    religious reflections, 151–52, 154, 165, 216
    on respect for comrades, 155–56
French Jews, 116, 135
French rabbis, 125–28
    average age of, 125
    fraternity of, 127–28
    front line experience of, 126–27
    moral obligation of, 216
    number of, 125
    use of Yiddish, 125
    writings of, 125–26
French Revolution, 50
French soldiers
    heroism of, 191
    letters of, 65
    Muslims, 73
    religious formation of, 180–81
Fussell, Paul, 48, 50

Gabrielle, Sister, 115
Galbreath, Robert
    Spiritual Science, 77
Gallipoli front, 110
Gare Montparnasse, 15, 16
Gehrke, Otto, 139, 141, 142, 143
generals
    religious identity of, 76–86
Génèse d'une pensée (Genesis of His Thinking) (Teilhard), 201
Geneviève, Saint
    veneration of the relics of, 38, 43, 59
Genevoix, Maurice, 65, 150–51
George, Saint, 33, 36, 53
German Atrocities: 1914: A History of Denial (Horne and Kramer), 139
German bishops
    Christmas pastoral letters of, 51
    religious polemics of, 167, 177
German Catholics
    French clerical polemics with, 167, 177–87, 191

246 INDEX

German chaplains, 88–96
  burial service, 90, 91
  commitment to the German cause, 114
  delivery of "dead" or "fallen" notices, 89
  diaries of, 90, 96
  distribution of pamphlets to the troops, 89–90
  field hospital service of, 90–91, 92, 93–94
  memoirs of, 94–95
  number of, 95
  pastoral service of, 114
  photograph of, 89
  propagation of commitment to the nation, 215–16
  reflection on Sabbath service, 94
  spiritual service of, 88–89, 95
  on U-boat, 93
German diaries
  authors of, 139, 145
  on Battle of the Marne, 143
  on Catholic service, 145–46
  on destruction of French cities and villages, 142, 143
  on Easter celebration, 146
  on enemy piety, 141
  on horrors of war, 140–42, 143, 164–65
  on invasion of Belgium, 139–41, 164, 216
  on invasion of France, 142, 143, 144
  on medical field stations, 144
  on merciless killings, 147–48
  on promotion of the gospels, 216
  publications of, 137
  reflection on German defeat, 146
  reflections on religion, 139, 142, 144, 145–46, 165
  on treatment of civilians, 147
German rabbis
  burial services of, 118
  fatalism of, 121
  field hospitals service, 122
  New Year sermons of, 123
  Passover celebration, 120
  photograph of, *118*
  prayers of, 118, 124
  Sabbath services, 119, 123
  service to the dying and wounded, 118, 119
  writings of, 117, 122, 124
German soldiers
  compassion of, 71, 121–22
  criticism of, 21
  interaction with civilians, 147, 164
  letters of, 66–68
  sacrifice of, 122
  war experiences, 6
German Students' War Letters, 70
Germany
  anti-Semitism, 116
  Christian faith in, 168, 172–73, 174, 175, 179, 184, 190
  folk nationalism, 190
  idea of superiority of, 172, 174
  "immorality" of, 175–76
  imperialism of, 168
  Jews in, 135
  militarism of, 176
  popular reaction on declaration of war, 11, 13
  public support for the army, 185
  theology of nationalism, 172–73
  Turkish alliance with, 185
Gibbs, Philip, 50
Gibier, Charles, 38, 184
Gieselmann, August, 145
Girard, Joseph, 38
Glatzer, Nahum, 196, 197
God-talk, 2, 31, 62, 84, 135, 190, 214, 215, 217
Goens, D. G., 173
"*Gott Mit Uns*" ("God is with us") saying, 47, 148, 161, 220n5
Gough, Hubert, 76, 82
Gray, Arthur, 113
Grenfell, Julian, 70
Grey, Edward, 173
Grivelet, Maurice, 100
Groppe, Karl, 139, 142
Groser, John, 108
guardian angels, 37, 46, 59
  See also Angels of Mons
guerre allemande et le catholicisme, La
  (The German War and Catholicism)
  (Baudrillart)
  address to the Germans, 181
  cover of, *177*
  criticism of, 187
  description of heroic actions, 181
  introductory notice, 178
  main themes of, 177–78
  pastoral letters, 181–83
  publication of, 167
Gwynne, Llewellyn Henry, 76, 82, 106

Haas, Johannes, 68
Haig, Douglas, 56, 131
  comments on Sunday sermons, 81
  personal chaplain of, 80

photograph of, 83
religious faith of, 4, 76, 80–81, 82–84
Spiritualism of, 80
Hankey, Donald, 62–63, 63, 84
Hanna, Martha, 66
Hannay, James, 113
Harden, Elmer, 75
Hardy, Theodore Bayley, 208
Harfleur Reinforcement Camp, 128
Harnack, Adolph von
  criticism of, 175
  on England's betrayal of Anglo-Saxon heritage, 190
  letter to English theologians, 169–70
  on moral value of war, 170–71
  photograph of, 171
Harrison, Austin, 176, 190
  The Kaiser's War, 175
Hart, Adrian, 231n28
Hart, Basil Liddell, 82
Hart, Liddell, 78
Hartmann, Felix von, 96
Hastings, Melville, 70
Hausen, Max von, 39
Hay, Bill (sergeant), 158, 231n28
Hay, W. (private), 159, 231n28, 231n35
heavenly allies, 33, 45, 58
Heine, Heinrich, 175
hell-talk, 72, 84
Henderson, H. S. S., 157, 230n28
Hermalle-sous-Huy, Belgium, 141
Hindenburg, Paul von, 47, 76, 85, 96
Hirsch, Emmanuel, 200
Holbrook, H., 231n28
Hoover, Arlie
  God, Germany, and Britain in the Great War, 167
Horne, Henry, 76, 83
Horne, John, 139
Horridge, C. D., 162, 231n28
Horsley, S. S., 50
hospitals
  conditions in, 104–5, 148–49
  pastoral service in, 90–94, 122, 133, 143, 189
Housman, Laurence, 70
Hubert, Saint, 53

imaginaire
  production of, 33, 47, 50, 61, 84, 214
Islam in the French army, 73
Italiener, Bruno
  patriotic sermon of, 117–18

Jacks, Lawrence P., 174
Jaeger, Gerard, 61
James, William, 2, 214, 220n3
Jastrow, Benno, 132
Jellicoe, John, 29
Jesuits, 51, 77, 115, 201–2, 227n43
Jewish chaplains
  call for Jewish solidarity, 5
  pastoral services, 87–88, 133
  war experience, 116–17
  See also English rabbis; French rabbis; German rabbis
Jewish mysticism, 7
Jewish soldiers
  in the American army, 75
  diaries of, 133–34
  national loyalties, 5, 85
  number of, 75
  patriotism of, 132
  preservation of identity, 116
  religious values of, 133
  testimonies of, 136
  view of God, 134
Joan of Arc
  canonization of, 52
  in World War I, role of, 33–34, 38, 39, 40, 59, 222n1
Joffre, Joseph, 37, 39
Joseph, Morris, 128
Joseph, Saint, 53
Judaism
  in France, 125–26, 129, 133
  in Germany, 5
  militarism and, 123
  universal role of, 194–97, 213, 216
Jungmann, Siegbert, 132

Kähler, Martin, 201
Kahn, André, 133, 134, 135, 136
Kahn, Julius, 75
Kaiser, Paul, 47
Kapfer, Herbert, 137, 138
Kaplan, Jacob, 127, 136
Kell, Herman, 145
Kettle, Thomas, 71
Kettler, Marie, 139, 144
Kilmer, Joyce, 75
Kitchener, Herbert, 96
Klein, Félix, 17, 18
Klein, Maria, 200
Kluck, Alexander von, 37, 39
Köhler, Karl, 171

Kollmannsberger, Josef, 145
Korb, Samuel, 125
Korff, Gottfried, 220n6
Kramer, Alan, 139
Kraus, Karl
    The Last Days of Mankind, 3, 9
Krebs, Jacob, 139, 143, 144
Kreutz, Bernhard, 95, 96, 114
Krissinger (court preacher), 23–24
Krumeich, Gerd, 66, 95
Kulturkampf, 178, 179, 184, 191

Landau, Philippe, 117, 126
Langley, Ralph, 161, 231n28
Lanrezac, Charles, 37
Lavergue, Marie-Bernard, 100–101
Lawrence, Reg, 161, 231n28
Layard, Peter, 71
Le Cateau, Battle of, 34, 36, 37
Lehmann, Hans, 93, 94
Lehmann, Walter, 172
Lemercier, Eugène, 58
letters of soldiers
    Christmas messages in, 68
    on divine providence, 69
    ethical and devotional reflections in, 4, 66, 67–69, 71, 72, 85
    on German cause, 67
    hell-talk in, 72
    publications of, 66, 68, 70
    on reception of communion, 68–69, 71
    search for spirituality, 70
    statistics of, 65
    on suffering and death, 54, 69, 72
    theme of sacrifice in, 84–85
Levit, Karl, 132
Lévy, Alfred, 127, 129, 136
Levy, Emil, 118, 123
Lévy-Dhurmer, Lucien, 125, 127
Lewald, Reinhard, 145, 146
Lewin, Reinhold, 118, 124, 136
Liber, Maurice, 125
Liège, Battle of, 21, *140*
Lloyd-Burch, D., 55
Lloyd George, David, 131
Lobbedey, Émile-Louis, 182–83
London
    churches of, 10
    war enthusiasm in, 19–20, 31
Loos, Battle of, 130, 147, 156, 158–59
Louvain library
    shelling of, 6, 185

Louveigné, Belgium, 140, 141
Low, W. F., 158, 231n28
Lowell, James Russell, 176
Lubbock, Eric, 72
Ludendorff, Erich, 133
Ludovicus, Brother, 148
Ludwig III, King of Bavaria, 12
Lyne, C. E., 72

Macdonald, Lyn, 138, 156, 158, 165
Machen, Arthur, 36
Madigan, Edward
    Faith Under Fire, 72
Mairet, Louis Jean-Émile, 150, 153
Mangin, Charles, 153
Marcus, Julius, 132
Marne, Battle of
    artistic depictions of, 44, 45
    dramatization of, 38–39
    German postcards, 45–46
    reports of miracles, 4, 34, 37–38, 59
    soldiers' accounts of, 69, 143
Mascall, Maurice, 157, 231n28
Massat, Edouard de, 99
Mausbach, Joseph, 184–85, 186, 233n34
Maze, Paul, 49
McKinnel, Bryden, 157, 231n28
McQueen, J. M., 231n28
Meier, Kurt, 21
Mellottée, P., 38
Mercier, Désiré, 181, 185
Meynier, Gilbert, 73
Michael, the archangel
    function of, 47
    images of, 46
    "nail figure" of, 59
    popularity of, 33
    statues of, 47
Mignot, Eudoxe-Irénée, 183–84, 185
Mirabail, abbé of the Collège de Saint-Caprais, 97
miracle stories, 4, 33, 34–47, 59
Missel du Miracle de la Marne
    adoration of the Blessed Sacrament, 42
    contact scene, 42
    engravings, 39, 40
    French infantry march, 40
    illustrations, 39, *41*, 59
    image of Joan of Arc, 40
    image of Sacré Coeur Basilica, 45
    image of Saint Peter's Basilica in Rome, 45
    image of three days of special prayers, 43

images of Christ, 39, 40, 44
march of officers, 40
Mass in the trenches, 44–45
military tombs, 45
mobilization theme, 40, 42
portrayal of soldiers before and after a battle, 44
preface to, 184
publication of, 38
scene of retreat across the countryside, 42
scene of the enemy within sight of Paris, 42
mobilization decrees, 18
Moltke, Helmuth von, 39, 76, 77, 85
Mombauer, Annika, 76
Mommsen, Theodore, 76
Mons, Battle of, 4, 34–36, 37, 81
Morel-Journel, Henry, 150, 152, 153
Moritz, Saint, 53
Moulinet, Daniel, 98

"nail figures," 47, 59
nationalism, 2
nation-talk, 2, 31, 84, 190, 214, 215
Neuve Chapelle, Battle of, 92
Niemöller, Heinrich, 93, 94, 226n17
Niemöller, Martin, 93, 226n17
Nietzsche, Friedrich, 174, 191
Nivelle offensive, 161
North, T., 157, 230n28
Norton Cru, Jean, 138, 150, 152, 165
Notre Dame Cathedral in Paris
  bombing of, 25
Nourisson, Jean, 104, 115

Old Testament
  German interpretation of, 183
Oliver, Bernard, 163, 231n28
Oman, John, 175
Omar Khayyam, 64
Omissi, David, 73, 74
Orthodox Russia
  ecumenical dialogue with, 191

Pacelli, Eugenio, 187, 233n39
Paris
  departure of troops from, 16, 17, 18–19
  war enthusiasm in, 10, 13–15
Passchendaele, Battle of, 72, 84, 161–63, 165
Pau, Paul, 47
Pauck, Marion, 198, 200
Pauck, Wilhelm, 198, 200
Péguy, Charles, 52

Pelham-Burn, Arthur, 55
Pentecost celebration, 145–46
Penzlar, Derek, 117
Perraudière, René de la, 101, 115
Peterson, Kurt, 67
Pfeilschifter, Georg, 177, 185, 187, 233n37
  Deutsche Kultur, Katholizismus, und Weltkrieg, 167
Pic, Eugène, 58
Piccadilly Circus
  war enthusiasm on, 20, 31
Pilz, Richard, 139, 142, 144
Plater, Charles
  Catholic Soldiers report, 64
Plowman, Max
  A Subaltern on the Somme, 50
Plumer, Herbert, 76, 82, 85, 106
Poincaré, Raymond, 51
poison gas, 26–27, 108
postcards
  crucifix on, 48
  of death of a hero, 45, 46
  depiction of angels on, 46
  image of the Virgin Mary, 48
  scene after the battle, 47–48
  titles of, 48
Pott, August, 168
prayer books, 4, 38, 130, 136
Prêtre aux armées (Priest in the Armies), 97–98
Prodigal Son, Parable of, 112, 113, 115
prostitution, 149
Protestant German-English debate, 167, 168

Quillet, Hector Raphaël, 38

Rapoport, John, 72
Realpolitik, 174
Rebondins, Sister, 105, 115
Reims Cathedral
  bombardment of, 6, 44, 105, 168, 175, 185, 191
religion
  in public life, 186
  war and, 1, 3, 7, 31–32, 112–13, 215
religious experience of war, 2, 61, 64, 214, 215
religious objects, 4, 59, 74, 84
religious polemics, 167, 168–77, 180, 184–87, 190–91
Richards, Frank, 48
Richardson, Ewart, 158, 160, 231n28
"rôle catholique de la France dans le monde, Le" ("The Catholic Role of France in the World"), 178

rosaries, 4, 64
Rosenstock, Eugen, 193, 194, 234n1
Rosenzweig, Franz
    background of, 194
    on Christianity, 194–96
    on horrors of war, 196
    on Judaism and Jewish identity, 194–96, 213
    letter to Rosenstock, 194
    philosophical ideas of, 194, 234n3
    photograph of, *195*
    on Redemption, 197, 213
    on Revelation, 196, 213
    The Star of Redemption, 194, 196–97
    theology of, 2, 7, 193, 196–97, 213, 217
Rosnet, Gabrielle, 104, *105*
Rupprecht, Crown Prince of Bavaria, 76

Saarebourg, France
    crucifixion monument in, 47, 48
Sacré Coeur Basilica in Montmartre, 45
Sacred Heart
    belief in patronage of, 59
    images of, 52, 153
    propagation of, 51
    scapular medal, 51
    symbol of, 50–51
Saint-Brieuc station, 15
Saint Martin's Day celebration, 144
Saint Paul's Cathedral in London, 27, 28
Saint-Péreuse, Sister, 105, 106, 115
Saint Peter's Basilica in Rome, 45
Saint-Quentin cathedral, 121
Salomonski, Martin, 121, 122, 135
Salonika military camps, 102
Salzberger, Georg
    fatalism of, 121
    in field hospitals, 119
    front line experience of, 121
    Passover celebration, 120
    photograph of, *118*
    prayers of, 118–19, 120
    Sabbath services of, 119
    service to the wounded, 119–20
    war diaries of, 118
Sanday, William, 173–74, *174*, 190
    Meaning of the War for Germany and Great Britain, 173
Sarrail, Maurice, 78
Sauer, Joseph, 185, 186
Scheel, Otto, 46
Schian, Martin, 93–94

Schlieffen, Alfred von, 76
Schmidt, Ferdinand J., 169
Schmidt, Max, 139, 143, 144
Schubert, Hans von, 172
Seeberg, Reinhold, 169, 171, 172, 190
Sevin, Georges, 102
Sevin, Hector, 98
Shaw, W. H., 159, 231n28, 231n35
Shawyer, V., 162, 231n28
Sikh religious artefacts, 74
Slack, C. M., 162, 231n28
Slotkin, Richard, 76
Smith, Arthur, 64
Smith, Herbert, 157, 231n28
Smith, John Taylor, 106
Smith-Dorrien, Horace, 56
Snape, Michael, 80
Society for the Propagation of the Faith, 179
soldiers
    African American, 75–76, 85
    Algerian, 73–74
    battle experiences, 61–62
    death of Christ and death of, 101
    departure for the front, 16, 18–19, 20
    diaries of, 131, 216
    everyday life of, 5–6
    exchanges of gifts, 55
    Indian, 74, 85
    joint burials, 55
    morale of, 19
    Muslim, 85
    religious experiences of, 1–2, 4, 7–8, 59–60, 62–63, 73–74, 75, 85, 235n2
    sacrifice for the fatherland, 66
    spiritual loneliness of, 67
    See also letters of soldiers
Somme, Battle of
    casualties of, 108–9
    comparison to Passchendaele, 162
    descriptions of, 159–61
    horrors of, 62, 80, 130, 160
    soldiers' experience of, 33, 145, 149, 156, 158
Spencer, Frank, 160, 231n28, 231n35
Spencer, Wilbert, 55
Spiritualism, 77, 80
Squire, E. H., 55
Stählin, Wilhelm
    on church matters, 92, 93
    diary of, 90, 91–92
    education of, 226n10
    field hospital service of, 92

on hatred of Germany, 93
pastoral service of, 114, 226n10
Star of Redemption, The (Rosenzweig), 194, 196–97
Steiner, Rudolf, 77
Stewart, Carson, 159, 231n28
Strange, L. A., 157, 230n28
Straub, Willy, 139, 141–42, 143
Studdert Kennedy, Geoffrey
  background and education of, 207–8
  on Bible, 210
  chaplaincy of, 208
  on Christ in the Garden of Gethsemane, 211–12
  essays of, 209, 210, 211, 212
  on mystery of God's suffering, 208, 210–11, 212, 213
  nickname of, 208
  pastoral services of, 208
  photograph of, *211*
  religious interpretations of war, 7
  theology of, 2, 193, 208–10, 212, 213, 217
Subedar, Garhwali, 74
synagogues, 1, 87, 120, 121, 123, 128–29

Talbot, Neville
  chapel at house of, *109*
  on ideal Christian soldier, 108
  pastoral services of, 115
  Thoughts on Religion at the Front, 107
Teilhard de Chardin, Pierre
  background and education of, 201–2
  on battle of Verdun, 204
  on Dante's passion to reality, 204
  Écrits du temps de la guerre (Writings in Time of War), 201
  Génèse d'une pensée (Genesis of His Thinking), 201
  on God's presence in war, 213
  on the Great Monad, 206–7
  on horrors of war, 202–3
  idea of cosmic life of, 202–3
  "*La nostalgie du front*" ("Nostalgia for the Front"), 205–6
  letters of, 201, 202–3, 207
  photograph of, *206*
  sermons of, 213
  theology of, 2, 7, 193, 202, 204–5, 206, 213
  on union of God and matter, 203–4, 205
  vision of the universe, 207
  war experience of, 205–6

Teillard-Chambon, Marguerite, 201
Tennant, Edward, 71
theology
  of a "chosen people," 191–92
  of creation, revelation, and redemption, 2, 7, 193, 196–97, 213, 217
  dogmatic, 193
  mystical, 2, 193, 202, 204–5, 206
  of nationalism, 172–73
  of providence, 80
  twentieth-century renewal of, 214
  war and, 6–7
Thérèse of Lisieux, Saint
  canonization of, 52
  tale of salvation of, 52–53
Tillich, Paul
  background and education of, 197
  chaplaincy of, 198
  on faith without God, 200–201
  letters of, 200
  pastoral work of, 217
  on path of Christian devotion, 199–200
  religious interpretations of war, 7
  sermons of, 199, 200
  theology of, 2, 193, 213
  war experience of, 198, 200, 201
Top, Gaston, 150, 153–54
Touchet, Stanislas, 79
Tower, K. F. B., 156, 230n28
train stations
  departure of troops from, 15–17, 18–19
Treitschke, Heinrich von, 174
Troeltsch, Ernst, 170
Turinaz, Charles-François, 182, 185

Verdun, Battle of, 33, 91, 120, 153, 204
Verhey, Jeffrey, 11
Vieil-Armand, Battle of, 127
Vimy Ridge, Battle of, 136
Virgin Mary
  belief in patronage of, 59
  images of, 51–52
  prayers to, 52, 99
  statues of, 48–49, *49*, 49–50
visions, 33–36, 64, 215
Vits, Ernst, 23

Walker, John Michael Stanhope, 108
Walzer, Richard, 139
War Letters of Fallen Englishmen, 70
wartime faith and morality, 66, 214, 215

Waterloo, Battle of, 30
Weaver, Mathew Lon, 199
Weber, Peter, 139, 144
Weigand, Barbara, 51
Weisser, Herbert, 67
Werner, Martin, 145
West, Arthur Graeme
    deliberations on religion, 6, 163–64, 166, 232n40
    Diary of a Dead Officer, 138, 231n40
Westmann, Stephan
    air force posting of, 149–50
    demobilization of, 150
    description of hospitals, 148–49
    diary of, 138, 146, 150
    education of, 146
    photograph of, 147
    reflections on war, 148
    on regulation of prostitution, 149
    on treatment of civilians, 147
    views on religion, 6, 164, 165
    wound of, 148
Wilamowitz-Moellendorff, Ulrich von, 173
Wilhelm II, Kaiser of Germany
    appeal to the masses, 13, 30
    prayer ordered by, 21
    public appearance of, 11–12, 30
    sacralization of, 22
Winnington-Ingram, Arthur
    photograph of, 29
    promotion of war, 3, 27–28
    reference to Judgment Day, 30
    sermons of, 28–30, 190
    on suffering of Christ, 31
    support of English cause, 20
    on use of poison gas, 26–27
    visit to the Navy, 29
Winter, Denis, 82
Winter, Jay, 66
Wise, Stephen S., 75
Witkop, Philipp, 66, 70
Wohlgemuth, Paul, 133
World War I
    atrocities of, 140–41
    beginning of, 169
    casualties, 33, 54, 230n4
    church blessings and send-offs, 20–21
    commemoration of, 220n6
    historiography of, 7, 224n9
    immorality of, 175
    truces, 54–56
    as war of extermination, 182
Worsley, George, 162, 231n28
Wundt, Wilhelm, 173

Yates, J. E., 159, 231n28
Yom Kippur celebration, 119, 120, 122, 130, 132, 136
Ypres, Battles of, 81, 92, 156, 158, 205
    See also Passchendaele, Battle of

Zuber, Terence, 37

www.ingramcontent.com/pod-product-compliance
Lightning Source LLC
Chambersburg PA
CBHW022045290426
44109CB00014B/995